# MANAGING PRODUCT SUCCESS

## Cool, Good, And Great Products

EDISON TSE
Stanford University

innovativeink
PUBLISHING

Cover image © Shutterstock.com

www.innovativeinkpublishing.com
*Send all inquiries to:*
4050 Westmark Drive
Dubuque, IA  52004-1840

Published in the United States of America

# Contents

*Preface  v*
*Books on Product Management  xiii*

Chapter 1: Cool, Good, and Great Products  1

Chapter 2: New Product Idea  21

Chapter 3: Turn Idea into Solution  37

Chapter 4: Lean Startups  55

Chapter 5: Data Analytics, Metrics, and Models  79

Chapter 6: Cool to Good  103

Chapter 7: One to N Product Expansion  127

Chapter 8: Good to Great  151

Chapter 9: Never Too Late!  173

References  193

# Preface

Product management is the role and function within a company that is responsible for a product's overall success. A product manager is the person that leads the product team to create and fulfill the goals for a given product – thus the product manager is responsible for the success or failure of the product. But what constitutes the success of a product? The Altair 8800 was the first personal computer introduced in 1975. It created a lot of excitement and sold more units than expected in its first year. But the Altair never gained a position in the personal computer market and disappeared after a few years. Would you consider this a success? The Apple II broke open the personal computer market and grew Apple Computer from $770,000 in 1977 to $118 million in 1980. The Apple II dominated the personal computer market until IBM launched the IBM PC in 1980 and took the lead quickly. The Apple II and its next generation Apple III were practically non-existent in the personal computer market by the middle of 1980s. Would you consider the Apple II a success?

Most people in the computer industry would consider the Apple II a product success, but many might not consider the Altair 8800 a product success. I would consider both products to be successful, though on different levels. The Altair 8800 inspired Steve Wozniak to develop the Apple I, which was similar but an improvement over the Altair 8800. Steve Wozniak and Steve Jobs later evolved the Apple I to the Apple II which marked the beginning of the personal computer market. The Altair 8800 was a product success because it identified an entry segment for a new product category and was successfully developed in such a way that it attracted some customers in the entry segment. It failed to expand and capture a strong position in the market, but its success laid the foundation for the creation of the personal computer.

I shall distinguish two levels of product success: a **cool product** and a **good product**. A cool product receives consumer excitement when first introduced into the market, but fails to sustain its market position afterwards. A good product is one that can maintain a strong market position for an extended period of time. The life of the product, the market share it captures, and the profit during its lifecycle determine how good the product is. An **excellent product** is one that is profitable and dominates the market for a long time.

There is yet another level of product success that I refer to as a great product. A **great product** is one that is "taken for granted by" others to create new businesses based on it – it is a source of innovation and a foundation in creating new marketplaces. A cool product introduces an exciting new possibility that doesn't quite have a market yet, but others may be able to create a version of it to build a good product. A good product contributes to the company's growth. A great product not only contributes to its company's growth, it also contributes to the growth of the economy.

The Altair 8800 was a cool product, and the Apple II was a good product that evolved from the Altair 8800. The Gillette razorblade has dominated the safe shaving market since 1917, and with good profit margins throughout the period. It is an excellent product. Many new businesses in the sharing economy (like Uber, Lyft, Airbnb) and online delivery services (like DoorDash, Uber Eats) "took for granted" that most consumers have smartphones and built their businesses on top of the iPhone and Android phones. These new businesses contributed to the growth of the economy. Thus, the iPhone and Android OS are both great products.

## Product Manager's Role in Product Evolution

Every product that we know has evolved over time. Product evolution starts with turning a product idea into a product accepted by a large enough group of people. I refer to this as 0-1 product innovation. Then the product evolves in terms of features, functionalities, quality, offerings, technology improvement, etc. over time to better serve its purpose and customer needs and expand its market share. I refer to this as 1-N product expansion. Product success in 0-1 product innovation is turning a cool product into a good product. Product success in 1-N product expansion is improving market competitiveness, maintaining profitability, and prolonging the product lifecycle that continuously makes a good product better or evolves the product from good to great. The product manager's main job is to lead a cross functional team to manage product success in product evolution.

The Macintosh had a very interesting product evolution history. It started off as a cool product, and with many twists and turns, evolved into a good product, and then into a great product. Throughout history, different product managers played an important role in determining its product success at different levels.

The Macintosh was introduced in 1984 with an exciting graphical user interface. It had the most exciting ad campaign associated with its product launch at the time which contributed to its strong initial sales. But the sales fell off sharply after a few months and continued to drop. Steve Jobs, the product manager for the Macintosh, was eventually forced out of Apple in 1985.

John Scully took over Steve Jobs' responsibility and turned the Macintosh profitable by creating the desktop publishing market (which it was the best in). By 1990, the Macintosh captured 8% of worldwide personal computer market share. However, Scully failed to expand the Macintosh into the mainstream personal computer market and it continued to lose market share as the competition intensified. Scully resigned in 1993.

The Macintosh continued its downward trend and Apple was having financial difficulties. When Steve Jobs returned to Apple to take charge of the Macintosh in 1997, it was down to 3% market share and it was getting smaller. Steve evolved the Macintosh into the "iMac" with a unique design that offered a cutting-edge, tightly integrated user experience. This brought Apple back to profitability, but the iMac market share was still declining (albeit at a slower rate).

In 2001, the iMac's market share was around 2.4%. This was the year that Jobs successfully introduced the iPod; marking a turning point for Apple. Right around that time, an inflection point appeared in the hand phone industry where the hand phone was slowly evolving into a smartphone where a powerful and sophisticated OS was required. Steve leveraged this opportunity and combined the iPod's handheld device concept with a smaller version of the iMac to create the iPhone – totally disrupting the smartphone market. By opening the iPhone to mobile app developers, the iPhone evolved from a good product into a great product wherein now almost everyone owns a smartphone.

We see that in this evolution, Steve Jobs successfully introduced the Macintosh as a cool product but failed to bring it from cool to good – this was done by John Scully. But Scully performed poorly during the Macintosh's 1-N product expansion. It was Jobs that turned the situation around by evolving the Macintosh into the iMac. Jobs then successfully introduced the iPod as a cool product and also successfully turned it into a good product. Jobs combined the iPod's and iMac's 1-N product expansion paths to come up with the iPhone. Under Job's leadership, the iPhone evolved from a good product into a great product. Steve Jobs and John Scully played important roles in different stages of the Macintosh's evolution from a cool product to a good product and then to a great product.

## This Book

There are many good books on product management. Building a product that people love is the main topic in most of these books. They were written by founders or product managers that have lived through the experiences of building successful products. They organized their tacit knowledge from the product building process to provide guidance for others to build good products. This book is not like those. This book is based on a course that I developed at Stanford University on product management. The role of the product manager is dynamically changing over time because of fast technological advancement and other exogenous events. It is also different across different industries, different sizes of companies, and different regions. However, the theoretical foundations of product success are constant and applicable across all industries, all sizes of a company, and all regions.

To become a successful product manager, one needs to learn three things: 1) the theoretical foundations of product success, 2) the ability to learn on the job to acquire tacit knowledge and 3) how to apply theories to the specific context to increase the chance of product success in different stages of product evolution. The course at Stanford that I am still teaching is composed of two tracks: the theoretical track and the industry track. The theoretical track is composed of weekly lectures on the theoretical foundation of product success at every stage of production evolution: 0-1 product innovation and 1-N production expansion. This book is based on the lectures in this track. The industry track is composed of weekly lectures and workshops by product managers and industry professionals on market research and negotiation. The product managers share their practical experiences in applying theory and how to develop tacit knowledge in managing product success.

The theoretical foundations of product success consists of two major themes. The first theme is that product management can be viewed as managing risks in every stage of product evolution to achieve product success. There are two types of risk that product managers need to deal with: unknown and known. In 0-1 product innovation, the risk arises from the complete unknown (whether there is even a market, who would be the competitors, etc.) and is unquantifiable because it is a onetime event and cannot be quantified by statistics. In 1-N product expansion, the risk comes from competition that can be modeled and quantified by statistics and conventional expected cost-benefit tradeoffs. But during the 1-N expansion, inflection points could occur that would introduce unquantifiable risk that the product manager must deal with.

The second theme is that people do not buy a product but instead buy the value proposition that the product promises to deliver. In other words, the product is a means and the value proposition is the end. However, for the customers to have the value proposition a product intends to deliver, a proper supporting holder structure must be in place. For example, for a car to deliver the value proposition of "a vehicle to provide safe transportation", it would require proper road infrastructure, a refilling network, traffic regulations, driving schools etc. that provide the holder structure to realize the intended value.

A new value proposition is accepted in a marketplace when there are enough people on the demand side buying into the value proposition and enough economic agents on the supply side that can derive benefit in providing the holder to support the value proposition. The demand side and supply side constitute the ecosystem of a product. Product success in 0-1 product innovation hinges on adapting a process that would mitigate the unquantifiable risk to create and shape a sustainable new ecosystem where all the members within the ecosystem can derive net benefit. Therefore in 0-1, the competition is not in product attributes but in building stronger ecosystems to support the value proposition. In 1-N, where the established holder structure is in place and is taken for granted, product category plays the key role in delivering the value proposition. Therefore, in 1-N, the competition is driving to improve product category attributes to improve the value proposition and to create differentiation through design and special features. During the 1-N expansion, inflection points could occur that would require the product manager to switch to 0-1 product innovation to deal with the new situation.

I've mentioned the two phases of product innovation: the 0-1 innovation and 1-N expansion. The 0-1 product innovation that turns a cool product into a good product is a journey with many twists and turns. This journey starts with a new value proposition idea that would create value in society. The next step is to validate the idea and then turn this idea into a product that many people would accept. In this process, the product manager needs to mitigate unquantifiable risk and develop a strong ecosystem that would support the value proposition.

The 1-N expansion is a different kind of journey consisting of two phases. The first phase focuses on improving product attributes to strengthen its position. The second phase focuses on leveraging the strong product position to turn a good product into a great product. Not all products can turn from good to great. Some just become excellent products.

The book leads the readers through these two journeys, detailing how to manage unquantifiable risk and how to build strong economic systems in the product evolution. Extensive case studies are used to illustrate how the theory can explain some of the surprising results in historical events. Both positive and negative examples are used to help readers to understand the theoretical foundations of product success. Case examples include products with the same value proposition but in different eras, products with the same value proposition but in different countries, 0-1 product innovation by startups and large companies, and products in different industries. These examples are used to illustrate that the theoretical foundations of product success are constant and applicable to all industries, all sizes of a company, and all regions.

Chapter 1 distinguishes and defines different levels of product success: cool products, good products, and great products. The chapter also uses a grabber-holder dynamics framework to describe what would made a product cool, good, and great. Chapter 2 suggests approaches to come up with a potentially good product idea quickly. The main theme is to start with a value proposition instead of a product idea. Chapter 3 introduces design thinking as an interactive process to understand the user, challenge assumptions, redefine the problem, and identify strategies and solutions that might not be apparent with our initial understanding. The chapter also discusses how design thinking can be used as a framework to manage unquantifiable risk in product management. Chapters 4 to 6 cover the 0-1 product innovation. The main theme is to manage unquantifiable risk. The approach is to spend as little as possible to learn as much as possible, and iterate to discover the right solution before developing a plan to implement it. I call this the iterative discovery and implementation cycle process. This process should be applied in the 0-1 journey whenever the company faces a new situation. In 0-1 competition, the focus is to apply the iterative discovery and implementation cycle to build a strong ecosystem to support the value proposition. Chapters 7 and 8 cover 1-N expansion. Chapter 7 covers product improvements to strengthen market position and Chapter 8 covers moving from a good product to a great product. A successful product indicates that many people have accepted its value proposition. A latecomer entering the market has no value proposition risk – the major risk it faces is the market competition risk. If the latecomer can manage this risk properly, then it is never too late to enter a market. Chapter 9 discusses the proper mindset that a product manager needs to have to develop a strategy that would have a good chance to enter a matured market successfully.

## Teaching in Product Management

This book is used as a textbook in my Stanford University course "Introduction to Product Management". At the end of each chapter, I have listed a set of discussion topics. These discussion topics guide the students to apply the theories from each chapter to practical situations. Study teams are formed where students read the chapter and engage in discussions on these topics before coming to class. During the class, students are asked to give their views and opinions. Stanford has a quarter system, and each quarter has a period of ten weeks. There are two lectures each week. For the first lecture of the week, I cover one chapter and the other lecture is delivered by an invited guest lecturer (often a product manager in the industry) who discusses the practical side of that week's material. The course also requires students to form teams to work on a project. In the period of ten weeks, each team is to come up with its product idea and turn the idea into a new 0-1 product innovation that has a market or come up with a 1-N product expansion of an existing product that would strengthen its market position. Through the project, the students gain hands-on experience of applying what they have learned from class to the real world. In the 10th week, each team presents its product with actual market validation. In the 9th week, we organize a workshop on interviews for product manager positions.

The course is offered to Stanford graduate and undergraduate (mostly junior and senior) students. Off campus non-Stanford students can also enroll in the class through SCPD (Stanford Center for Professional Development). SCPD students are engineers, data analysts, and other working professionals that are interested in pursuing product management or founding a startup. There are also product managers that enroll as SCPD students. Many of them do not have formal product management training and they picked up their skills while on the job. They want to learn the theoretical foundation of product success that will prepare them to face new situations in this fast changing world.

# Acknowledgement

I want to acknowledge the Department of Management Science & Engineering at Stanford University which provided the atmosphere and resources for me to complete this book. In particular, I would like to thank Professor Nicholas Bambos and Professor Margaret Brandeau for encouraging me to takeover teaching a course on product management in the Department. Many of the discussion topics at the end of each chapter were developed jointly with my teaching assistants. I want to thank my teaching assistants - Raul Overdijk Girbal, Krish Chelikavada, Greg Soh, Justin Gai-Leun Lui, and Corey Gaetano Baker - who have read the evolving drafts and helped to make improvements throughout. The final version of the book is improved by the insightful comments of several practicing program managers - Aditya Challapally, Leslie Barry, Laura Marino, and Sandeep Ayyar.

I also want to thank my wife Mimie for her encouragement and endurance. Finally, I want to thank the students who, by their active participation in the classroom and creative work on their product development projects, provided useful feedback that shaped the final version of this manuscript.

# Books on Product Management

There are lots of excellent books about product management. I compiled a list here that covers many of the practical side in product management, and is complementary to the theoretical foundation in product success that I address in this book. The book subtitle summarizes pretty much the topic that the book is focused on.

1. David Allen, Getting Things Done: The Art of Stress-free Productivity, Penguin Books, Revised ed. Edition, March 17, 2015
2. Josh Annon and Carlos Gonzalez de Villaumbrosia, The Product Book: How to Become a Great Product Manager, Product School, 1st edition, April 30,2017
3. Richard Banfield, Martin Eriksson and Nate Walkingshaw, Product Leadership: How Top Managers Launch Awesome Products and Build Successful Teams, O'Reilly Media; 1st edition, June 13, 2017
4. Marty Cagan, Inspired: How to Create Tech Products Customers Love, Wiley; 2nd edition, December 4, 2017
5. Marty Cagan and Chris Jones, Empowered: Ordinary People, Extraordinary Products, Wiley; 1st edition, December 3, 2020
6. Clayton Christensen, The Innovator's Dilemma: When New Technologies Cause Great Firms to Fail, Harvard Business Review Press; Reprint edition, January 5, 2016
7. Clayton Christensen and Michael Raynor, The Innovator's Solution: Creating and Sus-

taining Successful Growth, Harvard Business Review Press, Illustrated edition, November 19, 2013

8. Jim Dethmer and Diana Chapman, The 15 Commitments of Conscious Leadership: A New Paradigm for Sustainable Success, Dethmer, Chapman & Klemp, January 10, 2015

9. David DeWolf and Jessica Hall, The Product Mindset: Succeed in the Digital Economy by Changing Your Organization Thinks, Lioncrest Publishing, November 5, 2019

10. Nir Eyal, Hooked: How to Build Habit-Forming Products, Portfolio; Illustrated edition, November 4, 2014, Business Books, Platinum Edition, January 1, 2014

11. Roger Fisher and William Ury, Getting to Yes: Negotiating Agreement without Giving in, Penguin Publishing Group; 3rd Revised ed. Edition, May 3, 2011

12. Chip Heath and Dan Heath, Made to Stick: Why Some Ideas Survive and Others Die, Random House; 1st edition, January 2, 2007

13. Ben Horowitz, The Hard Thing About Hard Things: Building a Business When There Are No Easy Answers, Harper Business, March 4, 2014

14. Ben Horowitz, What You Do Is Who You Are: How to Create Your Business Culture, Harper Business, October 29, 2019

15. Walter Isaacson, Steve Jobs, Simon & Schuster; 1st edition, October 24, 2011

16. Bernadette Jiwa, Meaningful: The Story Ideas that Fly, Perceptive Press, October 2015

17. Daniel Kahneman, Thinking, Fast and Slow, Farrar, Straus and Giroux; 1st edition, April 2, 2013

18. Jake Knapp, Sprint: How to Solve Big Problems and Test New Ideas in Just Five Days, Simon & Schuster; illustrated edition, March 8, 2016

19. Matt LeMay, Product Management in Practice: A Practical, Tactical Guide for Your First Day and Every Day After, O'Reilly Media; 2nd edition, June 21, 2022

20. Steven Levy, In the Plex: How Google Thinks, Works, and Shapes Our Lives, Simon & Schuster; American First edition, April 12, 2011

21. Gayle McDowell, Cracking the PM Interview: How to Land a Product Manager Job in Technology, CareerCup; 1st edition, December 2, 2013

22. Brian Merchant, The One Device: The Secret History of the iPhone, Back Bay paperback edition, May 2018

23. Geoffrey Moore, Crossing the Chasm: Marketing and Selling Disruptive Products to Mainstream Customers, Harper Business; 3rd edition, January 28, 2014

24. Dan Olsen, The Lean Product Playbook: How to Innovate with Minimum Viable Products and Rapid Customer Feedback, Wiley; 1st edition, June 2, 2015

25. Al Ries and Jack Trout, Positioning: The Battle for Your Mind, McGraw Hill; 1st edition, January 3, 2001

26. Eric Ries, <u>The Lean Start: How Today's Entrepreneurs Use Continuous Innovation to Create Radically Successful Business</u>, Currency; 1<sup>st</sup> edition, September 13, 2011

27. Peter Thiel and Black Master, <u>Zero to One: Notes on Startups, or How to Build the Future</u>, Currency; 1<sup>st</sup> edition, September 16, 2014

28. Teresa Torres, <u>Continuous Discovery Habits: Discover Products that Create Customer Value and Business Value</u>, Product Talks LLC, April 14, 2021

29. Ximera Vengoechea, <u>Listen Like You Mean It: Reclaiming the Lost Art of True Connection</u>, Portfolio, March 30, 2021

30. Julie Zhuo, <u>The Making of a Manager: What to Do When Everyone Looks to You</u>, Portfolio; Illustrated edition, March 19, 2019

# 1

# Cool, Good, and Great Products

New products are the lifeblood of a company. Successful company produces new products that will shape the way people work or live in the future. One way we create the future is through product innovation, by introducing new products that will improve our way of working and living moving forward. In his book, "Zero to One: Notes on Startup, or How to Build the Future", Peter Thiel addresses the paradigm of thinking in creating the future. Every time we create something from nothing, we go from zero to one (0-1). Bringing a new product category into the market is a 0-1 creative product development process. Building on what we already know to expand into the future is from one to N (1-N). Evolving an existing product by introducing new variants or improvement of an existing category is a 1-N creative product development process. Whether it is 0-1 or 1-N, introducing an innovative new product is expansive, risky and full of surprises. The main characteristic of 0-1 product innovation is that the creation is a one-time event, path dependent and the result is unpredictable and sometimes beyond our imagination.

There are many cases in the past where a "cool" product that had an initial smashing success lost its clamor in a short period of time. Here are a few:

- The first personal computer, Altair 8800, was introduced by MITS in 1975. When it was introduced, it created a lot of excitement among young electronic enthusiasts and software hackers. The Altair was widely recognized among personal computer community as the spark that ignited the microcomputer revolution. But Altair 8800 and its extension never gain a position in the early personal computer market. MITS was acquired by Pertec Computer Corporation in 1977 because it faced financial difficulty.

- In early 1980's, all personal computer had a text base user interface and the IBM PC was dominating the market. Steve Jobs introduced the Macintosh, a revolutionary new personal computer with a graphical base user interface (GUI). The objective was to disrupt the IBM PC's market position. The Macintosh's GUI got a lot of early attention that led to strong sales after its initial launch in January 22, 1984, but its sales declined rapidly in the second half of 1984. The IBM PC was still going strong while the Macintosh's sales slump.
- Pebble Smartwatch made a splash in the smartwatch market in 2012. Pebble shipped 300,000 units by December 2013 and 1 million by December 31, 2014. However, on December 7, 2016 Pebble Technology filed for insolvency, and much of the company's assets and employees was acquired by Fitbit.

Many people believe that in product innovation, first mover advantage is very important – history tells us otherwise. The Altair 8800 was the first mover in trying to create a new product category called the personal computer, but it was the Apple II in 1976 that first established a strong position in the personal computer market (two years after Altair 8800 was introduced). Five years later in 1981, IBM entered the market by introducing IBM PC. This was a 1-N new product that completely changed the personal computer industry. The Macintosh was the first mover in Graphical OS, but the follower Windows became the dominant player. Pebble was the first mover in smartwatch, but the Apple Watch was the successful follower. However, not all first movers lost out to the follower. Notable examples include Amazon's online shopping platform and Cisco's routers.

When you are planning for a new product, your most threatening competitor may not be known to you. If you are not successful, no one will care. If you are successful, many competitors will enter the industry. One of them will become your most threatening competitor. It may be a new startup (like Apple Computer the case of Altair 8800) or an established company in a related industry (like IBM in the case of Apple II). Sometimes your greatest threat does not come from within the industry but instead from some exogenous event that is out of your control. For example, Covid-19 posts the greatest threat to Uber, Lyft, Airbnb, and any product in the offline entertainment and hospitality industries.

After you have successfully introduced a new product, you may think that releasing a new generation of improved products in a short cycle would maintain your market position. But history tells us that you cannot count on the one-time success. Competitor would out win you from a totally different angle. Motorola's cell phone dominated the hand phone market in the 90's. In late 90's it started to lose market share to Nokia, and by 2005, Motorola's cell phone division were stagnant and losing money. In 2006, Motorola staged a comeback by introducing the Motorola Rarz with a unique clamshell design and a thin profile. It was successfully positioned as an exclusive fashion phone. The success of the Rarz made the division profitable again. In the following four years, 130 million units were sold making the Rarz the best-selling clamshell hand phone in the world. Motorola continued to roll out new generation of Rarz with better design but the thin profile clamshell design lost its appeal to feature-rich touchscreen design and lost market share in the late 2000's.

Behind every product there is someone that leads the product team to combine technology and design to solve real customer problems in a way that meets the needs of the business. This can be the product manager, a startup CEO, or someone within the organization who steps up because they can fulfill those needs. A product manager is responsible for long-term development and health of a product, and he/she is measured on the success of the product, not the output of the design work. A successful product manager can move up the ladder to become the CEO of a company or the founder of a new startup. A successful start-up could be acquired by a more established company and the CEO of the acquired startup could become a product manager of the established company.

The main responsibility of a product manager is to do proper risk management that balances the risks and benefits of 0-1 product creation and 1-N expansion. While some of the risks that the product manager faces in 1-N product expansion are statistically quantifiable, many risks that they may face in 0-1 product creation are unquantifiable: the outcome is unique and cannot be quantified by statistics. Product teams, marketing teams, sales teams, and customers play very important role to determine the outcome of taking on those risks – this is why a successful product manager needs to have a proper mind-set and core skills in managing unquantifiable and quantifiable risks.

## 0-1 Product Development

There are two risks that a 0-1 product development can face. One is that the invented product has no market. The other is that the product successfully creates a market but cannot sustain its market position. There are two levels of product success in 0-1 development. One is a cool product and the other good product. A cool product is one that grabs a lot of attention and excitement but it fails to achieve profit to sustain its position in the market place. There are two possibilities: either the product is like a meteoroid that has a short bright moment and disappears in the industry quickly, or the excitement in the product attracts more investment to continue market development. In other words, a cool product is exciting and loved by many, but it is not self-sustainable financially. A good product may or may not have a smashing success in its initial launch, but it steadily builds a strong market position in an extended period of time to recover cost of investment in product development. A cool product is considered successful because even though it doesn't quite have a market yet, but its excitement provides inspiration for others to create a version of it to build a good product.

To mitigate the risk of a product having no market, a product manager needs to find out whether a new product category would be accepted by a certain market segment and what is the least amount of effort to build it before starting the product development process. To mitigate the risk of not sustaining a product market position, the product manager needs to understand the basic principle of what constitute a cool product, what constitute a good product, and how to evolve a cool product to a good product.

0-1 product development is a process that requires innovation thinking. Innovation thinking is a mind-set, a collection of thoughts and beliefs that shape the habit of finding new ways to achieve an ideal. The starting point of an innovative mind-set is to think about how to create new value to the society. A value proposition is a promise of value to be delivered, communicated, and acknowledged. It is also a belief of how value will be delivered, experienced and acquired. A Value proposition can be viewed as a vision promoted by a country, a region, an industry, an organization, or product – but product managers care about product.

The value proposition of a product describes how the product can be used to deliver value by solving a specific problem. Those people who believe that solving the specific problem will bring them benefit will buy-in the value proposition; those do not will not buy-in and they may even reject and oppose the value proposition. The group of people that buy-in the value proposition are the **demand side**. But what is the supply side? As an example, to realize the benefit of a gasoline car as a vehicle to provide convenient, safe and comfortable transportation, we need to have paved roads, a gas station network, traffic rule, garages, fast food chain, and many other products/services that are not related but are complementary to the car's value proposition. These products and services represent the **supply side**.

In general, in addition to the product, we need the supporting infrastructures to effectively facilitate communication, finance, production, and distribution; government policy and regulation that would restrict, encourage or ensure fair transactions; as well as the technology that provides new possibility and complementary products/services for the customer to experience the value that value proposition intended to provide. The collection of product, supporting infrastructures, policy and regulation, technology and complementary products and services that can deliver the intended value of the value proposition is referred as the **holder** for the value proposition. The attributes of the product, status of the supporting infrastructure, the specific government policies and regulation, the status of technology and attribute values and prices of complementary products/services at a particular time constitute the **holder structure** for the value proposition at that time. It is the holder structure that determines the benefit level a product can deliver with a given cost. The product has a strong holder means the benefit/cost ratio is high. The supply side of the value proposition is the collection of government, economic agents, and organizations and the supply chain for the products and complementary products that provide the holder.

The collection of supply side members and demand side members constitute the **ecosystem system** supporting the product's value proposition, or simply ecosystem of the product. (See diagram below)

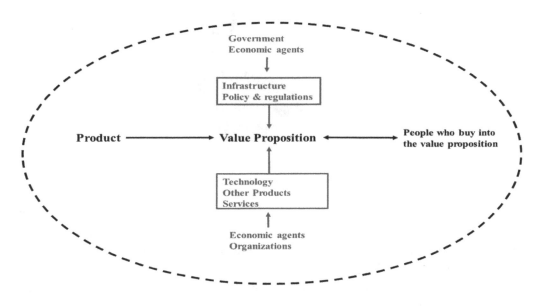

**Ecosystem Supporting the Product**

0-1 product introduction ends with the launch of a product that deliver a new value proposition that the world has not experienced before. Because of this, there is little idea of what the demand side would be. Product creators may believe that many people would buy into their value proposition, but they may find out otherwise. The reason may be that the people do not believe the new value proposition would offer a better solution to their problem, or that they are so used to the old way of solving the problem that they do not want to learn new, even though it may be better. Some may even oppose and persuade others not to use it. The other reason may be that the holder is incomplete or weak in that some complementary products are missing or too expansive, some infrastructures is lacking, or the needed technology is not ready – resulting in benefit level the holder can derive is being too low to attract customers. So it is not clear whether there will be a market for the new product. Zero to one product development should start with a new value proposition, and through a process of exploration and validation, create and shape a sustainable ecosystem where all members in the ecosystem can derive net benefit.

Lao-tzu, one of the most influential philosophers in China during the period 770 to 476 BC, advocated that the creation of "something from nothing" is the synergistic interaction of two polarities, **Yin** and **Yang**. This interaction is referred as **Yin-Yang** dynamics. This dynamics can be symbolized by a diagram below.

**The Yin and Yang Symbol**

The Yin is usually referred to something that is soft, shady, cold, abstract and passive; and the Yang is usually referred to something that is hard, sunny, warm, real and active. Nothing is completely Yin or Yang. Each contains some aspect of the other and thus they are interdependent. Yin and Yang are not static, and they change over in time. The dynamic interaction is that excess Yin will stimulate Yang and vice versa. In the Yin and Yang Symbol, the white portion represents the Yin and the black portion represents the Yang. The swirl represents the dynamic interaction of the Yin and the Yang, that when one increases the other decreases. The little circle in each portion represents that each contains some aspect of the other. The Yin and Yang are two halves that form the wholeness. When something is whole, it is static and no not change. If the whole is split into two unequal halves, it upset the equilibrium of the wholeness. This triggers the Yin-Yang dynamics to find a new equilibrium. Therefore the Yin-Yang are the starting point of creation of something from nothing.

In the 0-1 new product development context, the two extreme polarities are rationality and emotion. Rationality is the Yin and emotion is the Yang. When a new product with new value proposition is introduced, consumers do not initially know what benefit they can derive from the product. It is emotion rather than rationality that would drive customer to buy a new product. A *"Grabber"* is any excitement that can grab people's interest. The grabber for a product is the excitement generated by projecting how the fulfilling the value proposition can solve people's pain problem, provide people a better life, or improve peoples' efficiency. Product launch and promotional materials that appeal to people's emotion rather than rationality are a grabber for a product. The grabber will grab people to buy the product and incentivize economic agents in the supply side to provide a holder structure. But whether the people who have bought and used the product actually realize the anticipated benefit level depends on the holder structure for the value proposition. If the holder is strong, there is a market for the product where both supple side and demand side can derive net benefit. If the holder is weak, company can improve its product based on market feedback and provide incentive to attract more economic agents to provider a stronger holder. If the dynamic interaction of the grabber and the holder can lead to the development of a sustainable ecosystem where all agents can derive net benefit, then the product is a good product. If not, then it is a cool product. The grabber-holder dynamics are illustrated in a diagram below. The dash arrow indicates the dynamics of holder development, from weak to strong, to bring a cool product to a good product.

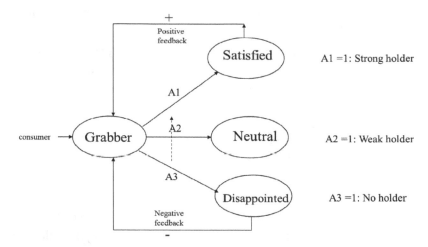

$$A1+A2+A3 =1$$

**Simple Diagram of Grabber-Holder Dynamics**

The grabber-holder dynamics framework can be used as a guide for 0-1 product development that turn a cool idea into a good product. See diagram below.

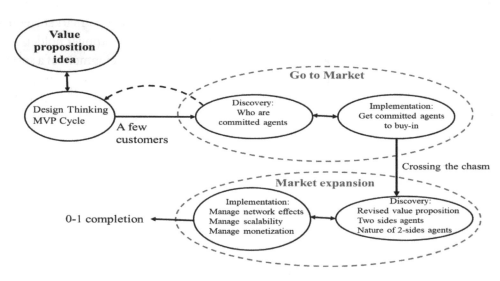

**0-1 Journey: Managing Unquantifiable Risk**

In the 0-1 journey, the product manager needs to overcome many unquantifiable risks. Product is a means to deliver a value proposition. The 0-1 journey starts with an idea for new value proposition. The next step is to turn this idea into a product that people would accept. The first major risk is whether there are people who will buy-in the value proposition. To manage this unquantifiable risk, there is a design thinking Minimum Viable Product (MVP) iterative cycle to get a product that is accepted by a few forward-looking customers. The next risk level to overcome is to get enough people buying into the value proposition.

There are two groups of customers and economic agents. The **committed agents** are forward-looking, emotional, and willing to try something new before seeing actual benefit. The **opportunistic agents** are pragmatic, rational, and only try something new after someone has actually derived benefit. To get started, focus on the first group within a narrowly targeted market segment. The targeted segment are people similar to the few buy-in customers captured in the **MVP** iterative cycle. The "Go to market" phase consists of discovering the committed agents in the targeted segment, and then developing an implementation plan to get these committed agents to buy-in. When the product is getting some traction, new companies would enter the market with products offering same or similar value proposition. These companies would help to get more people to buy-in the new value position and help with attracting committed agents to support the value proposition. These initial companies are more like partners than competitors. When more and more people buy-in the value proposition, the market structure would change. Those that were partners before become competitors, and large established companies with strong financial backing may try to offer a similar value proposition or promote a more competitive value proposition. Facing this structural change in the market, the product manager needs to adjust their market expansion strategy by employing another discovery and implementation process to develop a strong ecosystem in the value proposition competition. The journey from the "go to market" phase to "market expansion phase" requires a change in mind-set from targeting committed agents to targeting opportunistic agents. This is like crossing a chasm.

The next few chapters will go through the journey step by step – giving details on how to manage the unquantifiable risks to turn an idea into a cool product, and evolve a cool product into a good product.

# Examples of Transition from Cool to Good Product

Micro Instrumentation and Telemetry System (MITS) was founded in 1969 by a group of engineers that had experience working in the Air Force weapon laboratory. Their objective was to exploit their knowledge in electronics to produce small kits like radio transmitters and instruments for model rocket hobbyists. The business model had a modest success and in 1970, MITS got into the calculator kit business. Its first calculator product, MITS 816, used chipset and was featured on November 1971 cover of Popular Electronics. MITS was successful in the calculator kit business and its products were mainly sold through electronics magazines like Popular Electronics and Radio Electronics where many new electronics projects that appeal to electronics hobbyists were featured. In 1974, the newly appointed editor of Popular Electronics wanted to feature some new microprocessor related projects. At that time MITS was working on an Intel 8080 based microprocessor computer project. Popular Electronics persuaded MITS to feature this project in its January 1975 issue. To grab people's attention, the editors of Popular Electronics selected the name "Altair", the brightest star in the constellation of Aquila and the twelfth brightest star in the night sky. Altair was also a destination that USS Enterprise would go to in the popular TV series Star Trek. Most electronics hobbyists were Star Trek fans, and the name "Altair 8800" would certainly grab their attention and imagination. Interest grew quickly after it was featured on the cover of the January 1975 issue and it was sold by mail order through advertisements in other electronics hobbyist magazines like Radio Electronics. In the marketing materials, MITS stated: "Building your own computer won't be a piece of cake, but we'll make it rewarding experience". This reflects that the mindsets of MITS's executives were about creating value for electronics hobbyists. The basic Altair 8800 included the CPU, front panel control, front panel lights and switches, power supply and expander board enclosed in an aluminum case. It provided connection to memory cards, static memory cards, parallel and serial I/O cards, keyboard, display monitor, audio tape, and floppy disc drive which MITS sold as options. People could also purchase these components from other electronic component suppliers.

Before the Altair 8800 was released, MITS optimistically estimated that it would sell 800 computers in the first year. When it was feature in the January issue of *Popular Electronics*, MITS was flooded with inquiries and orders. In February MITS received 1,000 orders for the Altair 8800. The quoted delivery time was 60 days but it ended up being a few months. MITS delivered 2,500 Altair 8800s by the end of May, and over 5,000 by August 1975. In every account, its initial launch was a great success. The initial success of the Altair 8800 in the electronic hobbyists market attracted many young electronics and software enthusiasts to develop add-on options for the basic Altair 8800. For example, Bill Gates left Harvard before finishing his degree and co-founded Microsoft with his friend Paul Allen to develop Altair BASIC for the Altair8800 which was released in July 1975.

The hobbyists market is very small and can quickly become saturated if other kits suppliers enter the market. In the first half of 1975, MITS faced no competitor, and MITS sold a lot more Altair 8800 than its optimistic expectation. This news invited many other electronic engineers and electronic companies entered the market and supplied similar products in late 1975. In spite of its initial success, Altair8800 could not capture large enough customer base to reach profitability to invest more in its development in order to sustain in the hobbyist market. Apple Computer was founded in 1975 with the release of its first product (the Apple I) which was similar but an improvement over the Altair 8800. Its CPU was based on the MOS Technology 6502 instead of Intel 8080.

Apple Computer packaged the Apple I with a monitor, key board, dynamic and static memory cards, parallel and serial I/O cards, and floppy disk drive into a foam-molded plastic case and released it as a new product, Apple II, in 1976. It included integer BASIC in ROM in its initial offering and the 1978 version of Apple OS which enabled third party software developers to develop applications for Apple II. Steve Wozniak was the lead technical designer for both the Apple I and Apple II, and Steve Jobs oversaw the design and development of the case. The case design concealed the internal cards, boards and wire connection. Steve Jobs had a unique mindset – he believed that the value proposition of the personal computer is to help people to process and manage information. He extensively pushed for a case design visually appealing to people outside of electronics hobbyists and made Apple II look more like an 'appliance computer'. People could buy the system off the retail shelf, taken it home, plugged in and start using.

The Apple II had an open architecture design that enabled third party developers to design a variety of devices that could increase the value proposition of the Apple II to more people. Initially, the Apple II sold very successfully to hobbyists and computer enthusiasts; which triggered software developers to develop software for it. This resulted in 16,000 applications for the Apple II. Sales expanded exponentially into the business and professional market when the spreadsheet program VisiCalc by VisiCorp was launched for the Apple II in mid-1979. Many regarded VisiCalc as the "killer app" in the early computer industry. With this, Apple II created the new product category of the "personal computer" within the computer industry. From 1977 to 1980, Apple Computer grew from a valuation of $775,000 to $118 million. This triggered a new revolution in personal computing that disrupted the computer industry. Apple II successfully turned a cool product, initiated by the Altair 8800, to a good product, by developing a sustainable ecosystem supporting its value proposition. The success of the Apple II triggered a new revolution in personal computing that disrupted the computer industry. The Apple II maintained the market leadership position until 1981 when IBM introduced its IBM PC that took over.

IBM introduced the IBM PC in 1981 which was similar but an improvement over the Apple II given its faster speed. With IBM's strong position in the computer industry, the new release attracted a lot of third-party hardware and software developers to develop peripherals and application software for the IBM PC. Very quickly, the IBM PC became a dominant player in the personal computer industry. Apple Computer was losing market share quickly, and its next generation product, the Apple III, was not gaining market acceptance. Steve Jobs led a team to develop the Macintosh with the objective of developing a new standard in personal computer; with the goal of regaining market share from IBM. At that time all personal computers had a text base user interface, instead the Macintosh had a graphical user interface (GUI). While the IBM PC and Apple II had open architectures, the Macintosh had a closed architecture. The Macintosh was introduced through a US$1.5 million television commercial advertisement, "1984". It was aired during Super Bowl XVIII on January 22, two days before Macintosh's official release. "1984" used an unnamed heroine to represent the coming of the Macintosh as a means of saving humanity from "Big Brother" (IBM). "1984" was considered one of the most successful advertisement in the industry and it also contributed to the strong sales of Macintosh after its initial launch. However, the GUI required a lot more computing power to support and as a result the Macintosh's processing speed was too slow. Also not many third party software developers had the skill to develop programs under GUI and thus very few applications were available. These two deficiencies coupled with the high price led to a rapid sales decline in the second half of 1984. The IBM PC was still going strong in the market place, and by 1985 it became the dominant market leader while Macintosh's sales slumped. Steve Jobs was under tremendous pressure and decided to resign.

After Steve Jobs left, the Macintosh continued to struggle. Even though it received a lot of praises from its fans, its sales were still sluggish. In 1985, John Scully took over the product lead for the Macintosh. Scully was the president of Pepsi Cola before he was recruited by Steve Jobs to join Apple Computer. Scully had no technology background but was recognized as an expert in marketing. Scully bundled the Macintosh with Apple's laser printer, Mac-specific software like MacPublisher and PageMaker. These applications facilitated users to design, preview, and print page layouts with text and graphics and created the desktop publishing market. With improved processing power and more graphic related software applications, the Macintosh turned profitable by establishing a strong position in the emerging desktop publishing market. John Scully successfully evolved Macintosh from a cool product to a good product by strengthening the holder.

# 1-N Product Expansion

Many consider 1-N product development to be less risky and the risk can be quantified – there is already a market for the product, and cost/benefit analysis can be produced through market research to determine an optimal product lines portfolio and improvement road map to capture market share and garner long term profit. However, 1-N also has unquantifiable risk even though its nature is different from that for 0-1. In 0-1, the main unquantifiable risk come from two sources:

1. Most people do not buy into the proposed value proposition. Those who buy-in is not big enough to support a sustainable market.
2. The holder structure is not strong enough to support a sustainable market.

But in 1-N, there are enough people who buy into the value proposition and the holder structure is strong enough to sustain the market, so the unquantifiable risk in 0-1 does not exist in 1-N. The different unquantifiable risk in 1-N comes from unknown competitors that may enter the market when an inflection point occurs.

When a new product category was accepted by the market, everyone can analyze the product attributes that provide value to customers in different segments. Some may feel that they can enter the market and capture some of the market share by offering similar but better products. Competition among players offering similar but better products can be analyzed and optimal 1-N expansion can be developed using probabilistic cost/benefit model. This is quantifiable uncertainty. Engaging in such 1-N product competition would result in linear expansion: the growth is proportional to the effort put in. Moreover, it is probable that the growth/cost ratio will diminish over time, ultimately leading to stagnation.

What is unquantifiable is that a totally unknown competitor enter the market from a completely different angle and introduce a new product that is totally different and disrupt the existing market. Moreover, no one in the industry can anticipate when it would happen.

Take the hand phone market as example. Motorola, Nokia and Samsung were competing in the marketplace through better design, more functionality, and better quality for more than 30 years via 1-N linear expansion. It was Apple that introduced iPhone with a completely different concept that disrupted the hand phone market. Apple was in the personal computer industry, not the hand phone industry. Before Apple revealed its intention to enter the hand phone market, not many would think that Apple would be a player in the hand phone market.

There are two types of 1-N product expansion – linear and exponential expansion. Expansion by extending product lines and improving product attributes is called **1-N linear expansion** because the growth is linearly dependent on the investment made. If the product can maintain a certain market share position, it is a **competitive product**. In such expansion, the value proposition remain the same (or may be slightly changed) and therefore the holder remains stable and its strength increases. 1-N linear expansion takes a good product to a better product and then to an excellent product. A measure of goodness is the length of the product life cycle and its profitability. For example, Gillette razor-blade is an excellent product (or an exceptional product) because it dominated the razor-blade market for more than 100 years and had good profit margin.

But there is second type of expansion. Instead of linear expansion, **1-N exponential expansion** occurs by leveraging the holder structure and customer base as a platform, extending the product through adding new attributes to help others to do 0-1 product innovation based on the product, creating network effects among innovators to achieve positive feedback growth. This expansion does not focus at improving the product's value proposition, but focus on actively helping others to succeed in providing new value propositions based on the product. Using others' efforts, the product can achieve an exponential instead of a linear growth, creating a **great product**.

A competitive product improves its benefit/price ratio to gain market share while a great product offers opportunities for others to be innovative to transcend its original value proposition. A competitive product strengthen the holder of its ecosystem to support the product, a great product build positive feedback effects between its own ecosystem and new ecosystems build by other entrepreneurs which not only strengthens the holder for the product and also transcends the product's initial value proposition.

Apple released the iPhone in 2007 which included some third party games and applications. In 2008, Apple released SDK that third party can download freely to develop application.

Apple developer program was set up to help third party application developers to be successful through Apple. Subscribers to the program received technical support from Apple, application programs developed were tested by Apple and if they passed the quality standards then they were distributed through the App Store. With iPhone's large customer base, this offered opportunities for entrepreneurs to create new 0-1 apps innovation hosted on the iPhone. With mobile infrastructure upgraded to 4G, many new businesses in mobile social networking, sharing economy sprang out based on the iPhone. The iPhone created a new product category within the smartphone, and its value proposition transcended its original value proposition: "a smart device to enhance communication anywhere and anytime". The iPhone is a great product.

Google's main product is a search engine with the value proposition of offering cost effective advertising services to companies. Google is not in the search engine business but in the advertising business. Its 1-N linear expansion is to improve the search engine and offer many free applications to end user like Google map, Google Translate, Gmail, and many others to strengthen its holder. Then Google expanded its product line by creating Android, an OS for smartphone, and offer it for free to all smartphone manufactures. This offered opportunities for many electronics based companies and entrepreneurs to enter the smartphone market to compete with Apple's iPhone. Google also offered SDK and support programs for developing apps in the Android platform. Through the effort of smartphone manufactures and apps developers, Google's customer base grows exponentially which solidified its advertising business. Google's product lines, including search engine, various applications and the Android that promote the same value proposition – and it is a great product. WeChat, Windows, and China's bullet train network system are examples of great product.

The 1-N journey is shown in the flow diagram given below. It consists of two phases. The first phase is 1-N linear market expansion that focuses on improving product attributes to strengthen its product position. The second phase is to leverage on the strong product position and pivot the product into a platform that expands the product's ecosystem and provide opportunities for others to do 0-1 innovation and develop new ecosystems on top of the product's system.

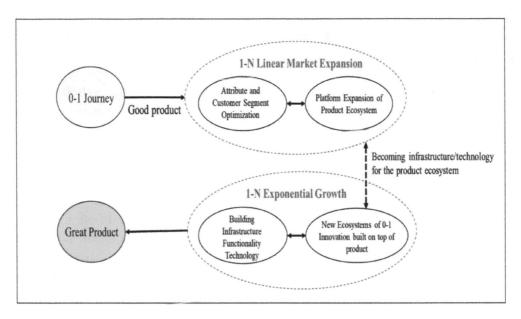

**1-N Journey: Linear Expansion and Exponential Growth**

# Product Manager Core Competencies

A product manager is responsible for leading a cross functional team through the highly uncertain 0-1 journey and the highly competitive 1-N journey, but they do not have direct authority over the team members. The core competencies of a product manager are the abilities to develop a strong product vision, develop a strong team with the same passion to fulfill the vision, provide North Star to guide direction, mobilize team to contribute creatively to fulfill the vision, lead the team to overcome risks in 0-1 product creation, and strengthen a product's position in 1-N linear and exponential expansion.

The biggest risk in 0-1 product innovation is developing a product that has a very small market or no market. This is an unquantifiable risk. Very often, this comes about when the product team falls in love with product too much and loses sight of the fact that this may not be what people need or the holder is incomplete or too weak. Many people advocate that product manager should be passionate about the product, but this may also increase the risk of being too passionate about the product and resistant to change when the market tells otherwise. Product managers should first determine what would be a meaningful new value proposition to provide new value to the society and be passionate about the value proposition, but not the product. Build a cross functional team that is passionate about the value proposition, provide guidance and mobilize the team to design a product that would realize this value proposition. The risks the product manager faces in the 0-1 product innovation process are mostly unquantifiable, and thus the product manager needs to have the competency in managing interaction of extreme polarities.

- **Vision Driven and Fact Driven:** Facing unquantifiable uncertainty, the product manager cannot mobilize the team via rationality, but must via emotion. Give a team an exciting vision that can guide and energize the team to move synergistically to achieve the vision. But when more facts are collected, the product manager needs to drive the team based on deduction. The product manager should use the facts to modify the vision, if necessary, and switch back to mobilize the team via the vision. Think of vision as the Yin and fact as the Yang. The interaction of these two extreme polarity allows the product manager to guide and mobilize the team to realize a vision that is practical and achievable.

- **Divergence Thinking and Convergence Thinking:** Diverging thinking is a process that explores many possibilities as solutions for a problem. This process opens the mind to various directions in search of possible solutions. Converging thinking is a process of determining a most effective solution from a set of possible solutions. The interaction of these two processes can help strike a balance between looking out for new possibilities and determining the most effective solution. In innovation, exploration, searching the whole sample space, is using diverging thinking process and exploitation, exploiting the promising area found, is using the converging thinking process.

- **Consensus Building and Making Hard Calls:** In managing a cross functional team with different perspectives and value judgements, it is important to build consensus as much as possible. But if a consensus cannot be reached because of diverse opinions and it is time critical to make a decision, the product manager needs to make a hard call based on opinions and perspectives expressed by the group.

- **Internal Focus and External Focus:** In exploring what value propositions would be accepted by customers and what products/services would realize the value propositions, product manager needs to guide the team to focus externally to generate more possibilities. In exploiting the promising areas found, the product manager needs to focus internally to provide analysis and recommendation.

- **Stubborn in Vision and Flexible in Execution:** When the team has adapted a product vision that all can embrace because it is meaningful, achievable and bring value to society, the product manager needs to stick to it even if the short term results do not turn out as expected. In executing the plan in reaching the vision, the product manager needs to be flexible in adjusting the plan, pivoting on the facts that are revealed while executing the plan.

- **Developing Hypothesis and Validation Testing:** A very common approach in scientific discovery is iteration between developing hypothesis and validation testing. A hypothesis can be viewed as an educated guess. A hypothesis assumes cause and effect relationship between variables based on limited samples. Validation testing is collecting enough data on the variables and performing statistical testing on whether the assumed relation is true. For example, consider the hypothesis that young drivers are more reckless. Collecting driver history data and do A/B testing to validate whether this is true or not. Very often, the validation testing does not give enough confidence as to whether a hypothesis is true or not. If that happens, repeat the process based on more observed data, modify the hypothesis and test again. The ability to design an experiment cheaply and quickly to test a hypothesis is an important skill that a product manager needs to have.

In 1-N product expansion, product manager needs to manage product lines extension in order to be competitive in the market place. 1-N linear expansion requires strategic thinking and managing quantifiable uncertainties. The product manager needs to be sensitive and find proper ways of response to possible disruption, and also needs to grab opportunity to initiate 1-N exponential expansion. This would require skills in product strategy formation and management of unquantifiable uncertainties. A great product manager must have competence to switch from one mode to another at proper timing. Through repeated practice in 0-1 and 1-N developments, a great product manager gradually develops an innovation culture in the team.

# Discussions:

1. What is the common characteristic of a cool product? Can you give an example of cool product outside the tech industry?
2. What is a successful product? Cool product? Good product? Great product?
3. Give a simple one sentence description of a cool product, a good product and a great product.
4. Is the Macintosh a cool product or a good product? Is Uber a cool product or good product?
5. Describe the type of risk one faces in a 0-1 product innovation.
6. What is the value proposition of an electric car? What problem it is solving? Who are involved in solving the problem? Value to whom?
7. What is the ecosystem supporting electric car? Can you identify the ecosystem members in the supply side and in the demand side? What influences the strength of the ecosystem?
8. In a 0-1 product innovation, what mind-set would lead to a cool product and what mind-set would lead to a good product?
9. What makes a great product? What mind-set would lead to a great product?

# 2

# New Product Idea

The starting point of a new product is a new product idea. A new product idea is good if the new product based on it has the potential to be a good product. There are many anecdotal stories on how a new product idea led to a new good product. In fact, what is interesting is that many of the ideas tended to emerge unintentionally. Brian Chesky and Joe Gebbia lived in an apartment in San Francisco. Their monthly rent went up and they faced financial difficulty. There was a conference held in San Francisco organized by Industrial Designers Society of America in October 2007. This was a big conference and it was anticipated that the hotel capacity near the conference location would be in short supply. Their apartment location was not very far from the conference location. They came up with the idea of renting out air beds in their apartment with breakfast service to conference attendees during the conference period to earn some income. They quickly developed a website to promote this idea and had three customers with very different backgrounds and financial statuses. In the few days that these three stayed in the apartment, Brian and Chesky interacted with them extensively and discovered that there would be a high demand for short term rental to support conferences. They believed that if they could organize the supply side (people like them that desire to rent out space in short period), then it would a good business opportunity. They recruited Nathan Blecharczyk to join as the technical lead and three of them started Airbnb in 2008. In March 2008, South by Southwest Festival was held in Austin, Texas with large attendees. They helped to book short term renting near the Festival location. Chesky was one of the bookers and through his interaction with the property owner, he learned the needs and concerns of the short term rental suppliers. The actual experience of being the supply side and demand side of short term renting lead the team to develop a website that served as a platform to attract both supply side and demand side to participate and the web would do the matching of supply and demand online. Airbnb was born. This created a product category that enabled it to establish a strong market position in vacation rental online market place.

Another interesting case is Facebook. A movie was made based on this story. A "face book" is a directory consisting of individuals' photographs and names. In particular, it denotes publications of this type distributed by university administrations at the start of the academic year, with the intention of helping students get to know each other. In 2003, Harvard had a paper version with private online directory. On February 4, 2004, Mark Zuckerberg, a Harvard student, developed a website "TheFacebook" that would facilitate Harvard students to interact socially online. Three Harvard seniors Cameron Winklevoss, Tyler Winklevoss, and Divya Narendra sued Zuckerberg for stealing their idea. They had planned to develop a social network website called HarvardConnection.com. Zuckerberg said he could help to develop the website for them quickly, and so, they shared their idea with him. They claimed that Zuckerberg took their idea and developed TheFacebook. The lawsuit was settled later in 2008 for 1.2 million of Facebook shares. When TheFacebook was launched initially, membership was restricted to Harvard students. Within a month, more than half Harvard undergraduate students had registered. In March 2004, membership expanded to Columbia, Stanford and Yale, then later expanded into Ivy Leagues and other universities. In 2005, the company dropped "The" from its name and became Facebook.

One commonality across both cases is that the new product idea in each of these cases is not actually new. In the Airbnb case, the new product idea is based on a value proposition of offering efficient arrangement for lodging, primarily homestays, or tourism experience. This value proposition is old and many bed and breakfast inns offered this value proposition before the creation of Airbnb. What is new is that it leveraged the Internet to scale up the service by organizing property owners who desire to rent out their spaces occasionally that greatly increase the supply side, as well as matching the supply and demand sides of the vacation rental market. Before internet infrastructure was widely adapted, their value proposition would not have led to a big market. Similarly for Facebook, the idea of social networking is not new. What is new is that through Internet, this activity can be scaled up so that many more people enjoy and derive value. Another commonality across both cases is that the founders had first hand experiences in appreciating their new value propositions.

In the Airbnb case, the founders accidentally conceived the new idea while solving an urgent financial problem they were facing. In the Facebook case, it was not clear who had the new idea first. Most likely, the new idea was already floating around in Harvard and Zuckerberg quickly acted on it to exploit the new idea.

Insight from cases like these can help us to develop a new product idea to start the new product development, especially for a new startup. This case-based approach can be very helpful but not very effective, especially if there is not a very large case data base. This Chapter will describe a systematic framework to guide product managers to find a new product idea with good business potential. A product is a means to deliver value proposition. Instead of trying to develop a new product idea, start with a new value proposition and develop a new product idea from it.

## Old to New: the Concepts of Cross Time and Cross Region

Two products that realize the same value proposition will be different if the supporting infrastructure, government policy, technology status and demographic demand are different when they are developed. The same value proposition can give rise to different product ideas under different circumstances. This means that no value proposition is completely new. In the Airbnb and Facebook cases, an old value proposition can become new in present because we have advanced technology and improved communication infrastructure. In general, an old value proposition that was embraced in the past can transform into to a new value proposition with improved infrastructure and advanced technology. Since the old value proposition led to a good product, the new value proposition will potentially also lead to a good product (but one that is completely different from the old product). For example, consider the iPod as the Walkman for the Internet era – they have the same value proposition. The Walkman was developed in the analog era while iPod was created in the Internet digital era. This phenomenon is called "**Cross Time**". This can be applied to develop a new product idea. Popular old value propositions can be combined to develop a new value proposition leveraging new technology. The iPhone's value proposition is a combination of hand phone value proposition, iPod value proposition, personal computer value proposition and other services offerings.

A value proposition that is well embraced in region A can be promoted in region B. The value proposition in region A is old. If the supporting infrastructure, government policy and demographic demand structure in region B are different from those of region A, then the value proposition in B will be new because the resulting product that deliver this same value proposition in B will be different from that in region A. Since the old value proposition led to a good product in region A, the new value proposition could potentially lead to a good product in region B. Instant messaging in US and QQ in China had the same value proposition, but the product attributes of these two were very different. In 1998, people engaged in instant messaging in US had their own computers, while in China most people did not have a personal computer. Adapting to different market conditions, instant messaging in the US was designed to have messages sent between two personal computers while QQ was between two servers. Internet Café sprang up in China to support the QQ's value proposition. Similarly, Google in the US and Baidu in China, Amazon in the US and Alibaba in China, Uber in the US and Didi in China. This is called "**Cross Region**". When a product is expanded globally, it should not just adjusted the product to fit a foreign market but instead a "Cross Region" concept should be applied to get a new product idea in a new country.

## Fulfillment of Hierarchical Needs

**Maslow's hierarchy of needs** is a theory in psychology by Abraham Maslow. Maslow's hierarchy of needs is described by a pyramid with five levels: "physiological", "safety", "belonging and love", "social needs" or "esteem", and "self-actualizations". See the figure below.

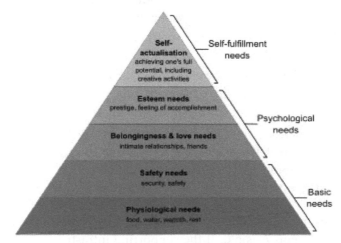

**Maslow's Hierarchy of Needs Pyramid**

Maslow argued that needs lower down in the hierarchy must be satisfied to a certain level before individuals can start to think about needs in the next level. So, when the majority of people in a region are satisfied with the needs at a certain level, the next level needs becomes these people's latent needs. A new value proposition addressing the next level needs would potentially have high demand if the price is right. But whether the company can develop a product that can deliver such value proposition cost effectively would depend on the supporting infrastructure, government policy, and technology status in that region. Therefore a new value proposition addressing the next level would be a good idea for a company if it has the core competence to realize the new value proposition with the given supporting infrastructure, government policy and technology status cost effectively.

Henry Ford successfully introduced his mass-produced, mass marketed Model T in 1908 to fulfill the value proposition of a "car for everybody to provide safe transportation". Safe transportation is a basic need. He focused on product simplicity and a single model: the Model T, only in black color. He created the production line concept and developed a workflow that could achieve economy of scale. By 1914, Ford held 48% of the market. William Durant was another entrepreneur who proposed a different solution to fulfill the same vision. Durant bought up many car companies to form General Motors. Durant could not achieve economy of scale because each of his acquisitions produced a different car model, and thus a different production line. By 1920, General Motors nearly collapsed, Durant was ousted by GM's investors and Alfred Sloan was brought in to run GM. At that time, many Americans had bought basic cars and some of them were getting rich. The rich people aspired to have a car that could represent their wealth. This means that different car models for people in different economic and social status became a latent need. GM, with multiple car production lines was perfect to meet this latent need. A new value proposition "different cars for different economic and social classes" was a good idea for GM to tackle. GM established different car brands that helped customers to derive an identity from the brand of the car they drove. Chevy people saw themselves as different from Cadillac people, and both were proud to be associated with their chosen car brands. Ford on the other hand was not able to respond because it had been perfecting economy of scale. Very quickly, GM surpassed Ford and dominated the U.S. car market.

Maslow's theory has little scientific base. Like many theories of human development psychology, it describes the stage of growth in human. Human's desire is unbounded. When people reach a certain level of satisfaction, they aspire to reach the next level. The lower levels of needs are basic (also known as deficiency) needs and the upper levels as nice to have (also known as growth) needs. Motivation to fulfill basic needs is stronger the longer it is not fulfilled, but it will go away when those needs are satisfied. Then people start aspiring to next level needs. Nice to have needs, on the other hand, continue to be felt and may even become stronger once they have been engaged. For example, most people only take pain killers when there is a pain but take vitamin every day once they believe it would help to maintain their health. Basic needs are more objective but nice to have needs are more subjective. A product that solves customer's pain problem will find quick acceptance. A growth path is taking the product to solve the same problem in other parts of the world with similar supply structure. However, the product may not be sustainable if the pain it's addressing does not occur frequently. A product that addresses the nice to have needs may take time for people to accept, but once it is accepted, the demand may even grow in time. However to expand such product globally may be a lot more complicated because the nice to have needs and the supply structure may be very different in countries around the world.

An external disruption may instantly change people's needs level. In 1998, Richard Liu founded JD as an electronics retailer business in Beijing by renting a retail space in one of Beijing's technology parks. The growth was very slow because it addressed the growth needs of people in Beijing aspiring to have new technology products. In 2003, SARS hit Beijing and the whole city was under a lockdown. Suddenly the ability to buy daily necessities online became a basic need. Richard decided to move its business online by setting up JD.com to sell and deliver people daily needs products. During the SARS period, JD provided a solution to people's basic needs and the customer base grew quickly. After the SARS period, JD's customers got used to do online shopping on JD.com and continued to shop for basic daily needs and other nice to have products to fulfill their higher-level needs. JD grew to become the second largest e-Commerce company in China with its own express delivery service.

Analyzing the fulfillment of hierarchical needs is a good approach for product managers to find a good value proposition at a new startup, a company that wants to get out of its stagnation, or a company that wants to diversify its growth in a new area.

## Ride the Wave

When a new product with a new value proposition is starting to gain market momentum, there is an opportunity for other companies to join in and ride the wave to promote the same value proposition. The fact that the new product is gaining market momentum implies that the new value proposition is getting acceptance in certain market segments and the grabber holder dynamics is in motion to develop a new ecosystem to support the new value proposition. More players enter to promote the same value proposition helps to accelerate the formation of a strong holder to support the new value proposition. It would therefore be a good idea for a new startup or a company in related industry to be a follower promoting the same value proposition. Note that the recommendation is not to promote the same or similar product, but to promote the same value proposition. If the follower focuses on same or similar product, there is a tendency for the follower to focus on product attributes and lose sight on strengthening the holder. If the focus is on value proposition, then the follower can focus on where the first mover is weak in terms of developing the holder strength and design a different product that is more conducive to developing a stronger holder to overtake the first mover. Also as people are more or less satisfied with the value proposition, they start to aspire to the next level of needs. The company would be better prepared to grab the next opportunity if its focus is value proposition instead of product attributes. This is a very good approach for companies engaging in the emerging market.

The car industry started with steam car with external combustion engine in 1818. The value proposition is a "horseless carriage to provide transportation". To fulfill this value proposition, the government needed to build pave road within a town or a city. More entrepreneurs entered the steam car market, which exerted pressure on the government to build more roads. When the battery was invented, electric cars appeared in the market in 1886 to promote the same value proposition. With the invention of the internal combustion engine and the discovery of a gigantic oil field in Texas, gasoline cars appeared in the US market in early 1900 promoting the same value proposition. In early 1900, cars in US were 50% steam cars, 35% electric cars, and 15% gasoline cars. It was the total car industry that gave pressure to government to build more roads within and between towns. This also led to community developments with clusters of shops, and stores sprang up to support a new way of living. Instead of just moving within a community, people had a new desire to move around and visit communities in other towns and cities. With more oil fields discovered all over the world, oil companies had the vested interest in growing the gasoline car market. Henry Ford started Ford producing only gasoline car. Ford also persuaded oil companies to develop gasoline refilling infrastructure in the US by building gasoline station in towns and along road sides between towns. This infrastructure made gasoline car a much better option to fulfill the new desire of traveling between towns and cities. General Motor and Chrysler joined forces to promote gasoline car as a better option to fulfill this new higher-level value proposition. This triggered a positive feedback loop between gas station network and gasoline car sold. The growth in gasoline car provided higher investment in the technology in gasoline cars. Gradually gasoline cars overtook electric cars and steam cars and dominated the US car market. Recharging infrastructure for electric cars is still very weak in US.

A follower may promote the same new value proposition by developing a complementary product that enriches the holder structure. The history of the personal computer in the computer industry has shown us that there are many cases where followers promoting the same value proposition won out by building a stronger ecosystem and not by having a better product. These cases show that those who rode the PC wave by focusing on building an ecosystem became a winner. Whereas the one that focused on product lost out in the competition. Here are some case examples:

- When the Altair 8800 had a successful launch, Bill Gates and Paul Allen provided Basic to promote Altair 8800 value proposition. The Altair 8800 promoted the value proposition "a rewarding experience in building your own personal computer". This had a limited market and even though it had a smashing success in the initial launch, its growth was limited. The Apple I was a product similar but better than the Altair 8800 addressing the same market. Apple leveraged on this success and introduced the Apple II that promoted a new value proposition "help people to process and manage personal information" which addressed a next level need. The Apple II was successful in breaking open the personal and professional usage market. As Apple II was gaining market momentum, VisiCorp provided VisiCal to support Apple II's value proposition. VisiCorp rode the Apple II wave and became the world's fifth largest microcomputer-software company in 1984.

- Even though IBM, Intel and Microsoft worked together to develop the IBM PC, each of them had a different perspective. IBM's perspective was to deliver a better personal computer than Apple II, Intel's perspective was to act as a component supplier, while Microsoft's perspective was to embrace the value proposition "help people to process and manage personal information". Microsoft had been writing computer language programs and application programs for the Altair, the Apple II, and other personal computers within the period 1975-1980. It realized that the abundance of software application programs is one of the key factors to fulfill "help people to process and manage information". Microsoft actively engaged in providing training to software developers to develop applications under DOS. With IBM being the dominant player in the computer industry and trusted by large US companies and Microsoft offering training support, a lot of software start-ups and companies developed applications running in DOS. Lotus Development Corporation released Lotus 1-2-3 running only in IBM PC-DOS that combined spreadsheet calculation, database functionality and graphical charts (thus 1-2-3). Very quickly Lotus 1-2-3 overtook VisiCal and became a killer application for IBM PC-DOS. The IBM PC quickly overtook the Apple II and became the market leader in personal computer. In this process IBM PC developed a strong ecosystem. Lotus and many PC board producers in Taiwan were winner in supporting the growth of the IBM ecosystem. Lotus was later acquired by IBM in 1995 with a valuation of $3.5 billion.

- Steve Jobs fell in love with the graphical user interface (GUI) and led a team in Apple to develop the Macintosh with GUI, with the objective of defeating the IBM PC. He called it an "insanely" great machine. His focused on box design, plug and play, point and click, and packaged with Mac software to show off GUI. Steve's passion for the product led him lose sight on the key factors that would help people to process and manage information: computation speed and software applications. Even though some software companies like Microsoft and Adobe developed applications for the Macintosh, most software developers developed applications for the IBM PC because the cost of developing applications for the IBM PC was much lower and the IBM PC had a much larger market share. Even though the Macintosh had a smashing success in its initial offering in early 1984, its sale declined in the later part of 1984. Sales continued to decline in 1985 and Jobs was pressured to resign. It was Scully that put the focus on delivering the value proposition to a specific group of users that saved the Macintosh.

- Don Estridge, the product manager for the IBP PC, died in a plane crash on August 2, 1985. His boss, William Lowe, took over responsibility for the IBM PC product line. In 1985, the IBM PC dominated the personal computer market. As a manager for the IBM PC line, Lowe had a product focus and looked for ways to increase market share and profit margin. DOS was co-developed with Microsoft and so they both owned half of DOS. The royalties from DOS were split evenly between the two companies. Because the IBM PC was an open system, its success attracted new startups like Compaq to enter the market offering with IBM PC compatible machines, referred as PC clones. At that time IBM had the dominant market share and IBM believed that this would continue. In 1985, Lowe agreed to a deal proposed by Bill Gates where Microsoft would kept all the royalties on DOS that they sold to clones, and in exchange, IBM paid nothing for DOS on the IBM PC. Lowe thought this was a good deal for IBM as he believed the IBM PC would continue to dominate the market. Gates saw this as an opportunity to allow him to grow the PC clone market by low loyalties for DOS and made money in software applications. The low loyalties for DOS triggered a flood of PC clones that eroded IBM's market share and profit. With a product focus, IBM's response was to develop a closed system with a new operating system OS/2 that it had full control of. The new operating system would include many advanced new features: GUI, multi-tasking, and be able to link with IBM mainframe. But OS/2 was not compatible with DOS, and so when it was initially released, practically no applications were available. IBM did not have a usable version of OS/2 with adequate applications until 1992.

- While IBM was busy in developing a new product to solve the clone problem, Microsoft spent its major effort in developing Windows that many considered an imitation of Macintosh's GUI. Windows was running under DOS, and Microsoft invested in training DOS software developers to develop applications ran under Windows to assure there would be a lot of applications running under Windows. Offerings of Windows 1.0 and 2.0 were not very successful because the chip was not powerful enough to support a GUI. Windows 3.0 released in 1990 became phenomenal success when Intel released 486 – a chip that was powerful enough to support Window's GUI. Microsoft, Intel and Compaq picked up the ecosystem that the IBM PC had built but left behind, and they worked together to continue growing the ecosystem to support the personal computer value proposition. Microsoft and Intel became big winners in the personal computer race. HP, Dell and many companies in Taiwan and China rode the wave producing PCs with Intel's chip and Windows became winners. HP's printer, Microsoft Office, many application software developers and peripheral producers also became winners by riding the Window-Intel wave.

To ride the wave in an emerging market, pick a player that has developed a momentum in building an ecosystem and develop a product/service to strengthen this player's ecosystem.

## Variations of Value Proposition

Take a product category with a good size market with many players (smartphone, car, drone, personal computer, and TV, etc.). Companies competing for market share typically think about developing product variations and focus on product attributes to derive differentiation. For example, for smartphones it would be a longer battery life, a bigger screen, and better reception, etc. The question is which attribute to improve and how much improvement? This is not an easy problem. Instead of focusing on variations of product category, focus on variations of value proposition within the product category. Variation of value proposition comes from considering how the value proposition is experienced and realized by different people in different context. Here are some concrete examples to illustrate this.

In the late 1990's, hand phones were very popular in China. Motorola, Nokia and Ericsson collectively owned 70% of the market share in China; Siemens, Samsung and Panasonic collectively owning 20%. There were more than 12 Chinese local hand phone companies, each had less than 1% market share. The Chinese firms had inferior technology and could not compete in functionality or performance. They could only compete in pricing and many of them were struggling to survive. One of my Ph. D. students, George Guo, was a product manager in TCL Mobile Communication Ltd. (TMC) in Shenzhen. The company was formed in 1999 with TCL, one of the largest consumer electronics company in China, as the major shareholder and some venture investors from Hong Kong as minor shareholders. The total registered investment was US$10 million. TMC's main business was in hand phone production. Like many other Chinese hand phone companies, they engaged in low price competition. Players like Motorola and Nokia successfully captured the high end premium market and they leveraged their income from the high end market to penetrate the low end market. This put great pressure to Chinese hand phone companies. By 2000, TMC found itself in a desperate situation. It was not profitable in the low end market and the $10 million investment was running out. TMC could not find new investments with the current business model. What should TMC do? Through George, I learned what had actually happened in a critical decision making that saved TMC.

The CEO of TMC, Mr. Wan, loved Rolex watches. He visited Hong Kong very often and he found Rolex watch with diamonds was very popular in Hong Kong. The owner like to show off his/her Rolex watch with diamonds as a symbol of his/her social position. Wan reasoned, since a hand phone, like a watch, is something people carry with all the time, would inlaying a diamond or jewelry on mobile phone be a good idea? Successful people, especially in the second and third tier cities in China, could use this to show off their success to friends and relatives living in the first-tier cities like Beijing and Shanghai. The idea was debated and there was a lot of disagreement. The proposed idea was finally accepted because there was no other obvious alternative. Successful people in second and third tier cities in China were not technology savvy and so all they needed was a basic mobile phone that they can make and receive calls with. They did not need to have a hand phone with the latest technology. The focus was a slick design inlaying a diamond or a jewelry and premium pricing (US$1,500) to reflect the wealth of the owner. TCL had a good connection with a jewelry wholesale distributor and had a strong distribution network for consumer electronic products in second and third tier cities in China. The product was released in October 2000 and was extremely successful. By 2002, its sales passed US $1 billion and captured 8% market share in China. TMC mobile phones were highly profitable with a gross margin of 60%. TMC replaced Ericsson as the third largest mobile phone supplier in China in 2002. Despite its initial great success, TMC's jewelry phone did not sustain very long in China's market. However, TMC leveraged jewelry phone's success to buy out Alcatel, a French mobile phone company, and entered the worldwide market. TMC pursued a variation of value proposition approach by focusing on how the successful people in second and third tier cities in China would want to derive value from a mobile phone.

TMC's success brought forth a new insight that Chinese mobile phone companies could take to compete with more advanced mobile phone companies like Motorola and Nokia, etc. Instead of focusing on product functionality and performance, they focus on variations of the value proposition: how people with different professions, social status, ages, and backgrounds derive value from using a mobile phone in different context. The Chinese mobile companies had a definite competitive advantage on this over foreign mobile companies on addressing the growing hand phone market in China. After TMC's success, many Chinese mobile phone companies adapted this approach to develop mobile phones that captured specific niche markets in China. Chinese mobile phone companies gradually gained market share in China although they did not match up with Motorola, Nokia and others in terms of technology advancement and sophistication. One interesting case that George told me was a mobile phone developed for construction workers. China was going gangbuster in real estate and infrastructure building in 2000. The construction environment was very busy and noisy. Construction workers very often missed important calls because they could not hear the ring tone or feel the vibration. Even they picked up a call, the environment was so noisy that they could not hear from the other side clearly. One mobile producer came up with a phone with very loud ring tone and heavy vibration and also increased the speaker volume. This was very well received by people working in the construction business. But unexpectedly, this was also well received by old people who had hearing problems. Even though product based on this had little barrier to entry and therefore may be not sustainable in a heavy competitive environment, many small hand phone producers in China quickly moved to other user groups to sustain its operation.

In 1984, PCs was a very big market with many big players including IBM, HP and Compaq. They all sold their products through electronic retail stores channels with specific product configuration. This is a "**build to stock**" business model. Dell entered the market by letting the customers specify their preferred configuration and made products to order. This is called "**build to order**" business model. This is a variation of value proposition based on people's experience in ordering the product that they desire instead of buying a ready-made product from store. To support this variation, Dell had to build a very different ecosystem to support its value proposition. Instead of having suppliers all over the world, Dell needed to have the suppliers close by. Instead of having a planned production, Dell needed to have a flexible production capability. Instead of selling through the existing retail channel, Dell had to build efficient channel for one-to-one direct sales. Fax machines were gaining market momentum in the late 1970's and by 1984, all companies and many individuals owned a fax machine. This became the main direct sales channel for Dell. When Internet came along, Dell was one of the first to launch a direct sales website in 1996. Dell's sales surged very quickly with Internet direct online sales. Dell is now the third largest personal computer producer in the world.

The most interesting case example of variation of value proposition is Xiaomi. It started with a variation of the smartphone value proposition and ended up with a broader value proposition. Smartphone market was growing in China in late 2000. The market was very crowded with big players like Samsung, Apple, and Huawei. In 2010, Xiaomi entered the crowded smartphone market. Le Jun, one of the founders of Xiaomi, had a big young fan base that were enthusiastic about smartphone technology. They were very vocal about desiring smartphone functionality and usability. Xiaomi developed a platform for these fans to give their suggestions and Xiaomi tried to incorporate their suggestions and offered weekly updates on their progress. A user was notified if their suggestion was adopted in a new update. This gave the user a sense of achievement and a strong sense of ownership. Jun's fan base was Internet savvy, so Xiaomi only sold the product online through its website. Xiaomi attracted tech savvy youngsters, a group of people that is homogenous and have similar preferences. They could engage in social networking and buy software and services related to Xiaomi's phone as well as an array of products like hats, dolls and many other products that appeal to their emotion on Xiaomi's website. Xiaomi sold its high-spec smartphone at cost to capture its fans and make money from software, services and an array of products. Xiaomi released its first product in 2011 with great success. By 2013, Xiaomi's revenue reached US $4.3 billion and profit $56 million. In 2019, Xiaomi ranked fourth in the smartphone world market.

The "variations of value proposition" approach is appropriate for widely accepted consumer products. Variation based on specific user group may lead to the development of a niche market. Variation based on user's purchase and experiences may lead to disruption in the mainstream market.

## Value Proposition not Product

Products are the means and value propositions are the end. There is a tendency to focus on a product because it is tangible while value proposition is abstract. But too much attention on the product can mean losing sight of the end purpose of the product. In many cases, this is a major reason of product failure in a competitive environment. So instead of looking for a good product idea, it's better to start by looking for a good value proposition. Depending on the competitive environment the company is facing, the product manager can choose the appropriate methods to develop a proposed value proposition that is proven to have a good potential market. If working with a new technology, "old to new" or "fulfillment of hierarchical needs" (or both) may be applicable. If considering entering an emerging market, "fulfillment of hierarchical needs" or "ride the wave" (or both) may be applicable. If entering or competing in a mature market, "variations of value proposition" may be applicable. If company is in stagnation and looking for a way to breakthrough, "Fulfillment of hierarchical needs" may be applicable.

Is the proposed value proposition right for my company? To determine this, the product manager should first "own the gaps" for the proposed value proposition: identifying all the missing or incomplete supporting infrastructure, government policy, technology and complementary products/services that people can have good experience in realizing the value proposition. Then the product manager should lead the team in brainstorming to determine whether the company have the competence and the competitive advantage to reduce the gap. If the team has confidence that they could effectively utilize the company's resources to reduce the gap, then the proposed value proposition would be potentially good for the company. The process can be represented by a cyclic flow diagram below. Red arrows are possible entry points to the cycle. An idea, market, or capability can all serve as starting points.

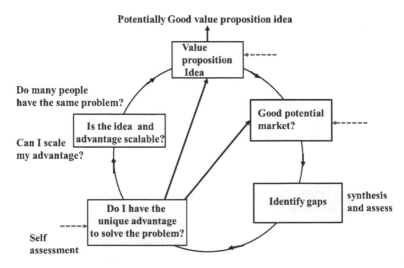

**Cyclic Flow Diagram: Potentially Good Value Proposition Idea**

What if someone strongly proposes a "good product idea"? The product manager should ask him/she what is the value proposition and to whom that this product would deliver. By going through discussions and analysis, the product manager leads the team to come up with a value proposition of the product. Then go through the process described above to quickly assess whether this value proposition idea will be potentially good for the company.

This proposed value proposition is just the first cut on a potentially good idea. This needs to be validated by converting this idea into a testable prototype that can be validated by actual market acceptance. This is a sequence of iterative diverging and converging processes. During this process, the proposed value proposition may be adjusted and modified to find the match between supply and demand to realize the value proposition.

The discussions above are mainly for B2C (Business to Consumer) products. Consumers' desires change dynamically and the ways to fulfill their desires will be different with advancement in technology, changes in supporting infrastructure, demographic shift and many other exogenous changes. The number of consumers is large and this ultimately leads to more intense competition. Therefore promoting a good value proposition (good market potential and compatible with the company's competence) is an important first step in designing a good B2C product. For B2B (Business to Business) products, the value proposition is simply "make your customer successful". The product is upstream of a value chain to a consumer product. The potential customer base is more stable and the number is limited. Therefore, the focus is to choose the right industry and respond to the dynamic changes in downstream needs in that industry and actively provide new product to make them successful. Riding the wave is the key factor in choosing the right industry. Take Intel as an example. It left the memory business and chose to ride the personal computer wave in 1985. Anticipating that PC consumers would continue to desire faster speeds, better graphical displays and more software applications to fulfill their nice to have needs, Intel's focus shifted to designing a faster chip that would help the personal computer companies successful. Now as a thought experiment, what do you think Intel's focus should be when the PC industry has reached saturation point? Mobile phones? Drones? IOT?

# Discussions:

1. Apple's iPhone can be considered as combining the hand phone, iPod and PC while also introducing the additional value of having service/games/etc. available on your hand. What other examples you can think of having this characteristic? What are the old value propositions and the new value proposition?

2. When Uber was released in India, they had to pursue various unconventional strategies to compete with Ola, India's version of Uber. See https://www.linkedin.com/pulse/ubers-uber-cool-unconventional-marketing-strategy-india-malpani/. Given the specific demographics of Indian consumers, technology availability, and the fact that most people do not have a bank account, how do you think the value proposition of Uber might have been different in India vs the US? How about the difference in Europe where affordable public transportation is more accessible? How would this effect your product's design and marketing approach to these market?

3. Why is Maslow's theory a good approach in coming up with a new value proposition idea? How would you apply this? Can the theory be applicable to B2B?

4. What is the broader implication of JD case? Can we apply JD case to COVID-19 situation in the US?

5. Can you think of other examples of companies riding the growth of a certain value proposition, where they help to build up the ecosystem around that value proposition? Can you think of a novel application of riding a trend today to provide adjacency value to an emerging ecosystem?

6. Does knowing the facts as to why electric car failed in the past provide context for Tesla's strategy in developing its refueling infrastructure? What risk will Tesla be facing in this strategy?

7. Would new startup or existing company find variations of value proposition useful in coming up with new value proposition idea? Give some examples.

8. Give one example (not mentioned in this chapter) of companies/products that derived new value proposition idea using the following methods:
   a. Old to New: "Cross Time"
   b. Old to New: "Cross Region"
   c. Fulfillment of Hierarchical Needs
   d. Ride the wave
   e. Variations of Value Proposition

# 3

# Turn Idea into Solution

Even though the value proposition derived using the method suggested in the last chapter is based on logical reasoning, to believe that it is a good idea is still a leap of faith. Before validating it does actually lead to a good product in the real market, this remains as a hypothesis. Before the proposed value proposition is actually well received in the market place, it is hard to persuade people to join and participate in turning the idea into solution from a rationality perspective. The product manager needs to arouse the interest and excitement of its team from an emotional perspective. The first thing that they need to do is to make sure that the value proposition is meaningful. This means that the value proposition would deliver value to society that people care about and that realization of the vision proposition would be within reach. This would be the North Star that provide a direction for navigating the process to find a solution. A visionary statement should express this in a way that arouses people's excitement, and recruits people who also feel passionate to join the team. Then, lead the team to work collectively to identify the gaps for the value proposition and lay down a plan to reduce the gaps to realize the value proposition. This will help focus the team's effort to work synergistically towards finding a path to realize the vision. If the team members know where they are heading and understand their roles in making the vision a reality, it will give them a sense of belonging and make them feel they own the project. Product managers should also set up short milestones. When a milestone is completed, have a simple celebration party to keep up the team spirit. This is very important especially if the period between the start of the product development project to market launch is long.

Note that the end goal of the product manager is a solution that may include more than just a product. It would also include a road map on how the gaps for the value proposition could be reduced over a period of time. For example, in the Dell case, the solution of "build to order" included basic personal computer specification, different configurations that the customers can customize, a road map on building supply chain structure and flexible manufacturing process that would effectively support build to order, and a road map on developing infrastructures to support direct sales. In the Tencent case, the solution to fulfill the instant messaging value proposition in China in late 1990s was an instant messaging program designed to communicate between servers, a plan to build up the network of messaging service, and a plan to attract users to engage in messaging activities through the service network.

If one anticipates that the gaps would increase or decrease because of current trend, then the road map should reflect a plan that factor in such trends. In other words a solution should include not only the product/service, but also a road map on how the product/services can be purchased, delivered and how it can be used to fulfill people's needs.

A design is a plan for the construction of an object, a system, or implementing an activity. Design thinking refers to the cognitive processes by which design concepts are developed. Design thinking as a way of thinking in solving wicked problems can be traced back to Herbert Simon (1969). The practice of design thinking in consulting to help companies in industrial design was initiated by IDEO in 1990's. The executive chair of IDEO once said: "Design thinking is a human-centered approach to innovation that draws from the designer's toolkit to integrate the needs of people, the possibilities of technology, and the requirements for business success". In 2005, Stanford University's d.School began teaching design thinking as a generalizable approach to technical, social and business innovation. There are many variants of design thinking and they range from having three to seven stages, phases, or modes, but all variants have the same basic principle: an interactive process to understand the user, challenge assumptions, redefine the problem, and identify strategies and solutions that might not be apparent with our initial understanding. The process does not necessary give the best solution but it may yield a good solution that may otherwise not have been thought of.

# Design Thinking Process

Stanford's design thinking process has five modes: Empathy, Define, Ideate, Prototype, and Test. It is a nonlinear process in the sense that these modes are not sequential. They can occur in parallel and repeat iteratively. The following diagram describes how the activities in one mode better prepare for other modes. The arrows do not represent process flow. An arrow represents how the activities in one mode can provide better information for you to better engage in another mode. Iteration is the key for good design. Iteration can happen by cycling a subset of these modes or iterating within a single mode many times. While taking multiple cycles through the modes, the scope narrows and moves from tackling the broad issues to the nuanced details of the solution.

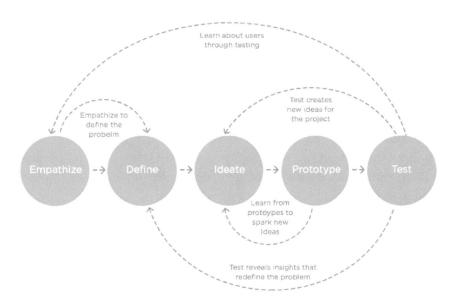

**DESIGN THINKING:**
A non-linear process

- **Empathize:** To realize the proposed value proposition, to find the match between the supply side and demand side of that proposition is needed. Demand side refers to people who will find such proposition valuable. Supply side refers to economic agents that collectively deliver the value proposition cost effectively. Understanding the demand side gives a better idea as to whether the proposed value proposition will have customer buy-in. Understanding the supply side gives a better idea as to whether the economic agents in the supply side would be willing to participate. Understanding both the supply and demand sides allows finding the gaps for the value proposition. Working in empathize mode helps to understand all those people and economic agents on the demand side and supply side for the proposition. It's important to understand the way they do things and why, their physical and emotional needs, how they think about the world, and what is meaningful to them – this can happen through observing, engaging, watching and listening.

- Observe their behavior through their activities. Notice any disconnect between what they say and what they do, and how they create work-arounds to overcome problems. These observation provide information that may not emerge from normal conversations.

- Engagement can be viewed as a technique of "interviewing". Interview with prepared questions tend to drive people to give information that you are looking for, but it does not allow the interviewee to express what they think or feel. Engage with people to make them feel more like they are talking to a friend. Prepare some questions but only be loosely bounded to them. Let the conversation decide the flow, and occasionally steer the conversation to the questions you prepared when appropriate. "Tell me your story" and always ask "why?" are good ways to get a thorough understanding of people's needs and the values they hold. It is also a good way to build relationship and trust.

- While observing and engaging, try to do less talking but more watching and listening. Have them to tell you why they are doing what they do. Have the conversation in their comfortable environment, like their homes or workplaces, which would be conducive for them to tell you their personal stories.

Empathizing is a diverging process. You are reaching out to understand the supply side and demand side of the value proposition. In empathize mode, no conclusions are made and the main focus is absorbing facts from the real world. Use a note book to record what was seen and heard without any personal opinion or conclusion. Conclusions are deferred to define mode. One important issue is how big a net to cast in this diverging process of empathizing. Casting a big net is costly. Cast a small net initially, and based on conclusions made in define mode, cast another non-overlapping net and repeat iteratively. The product manager needs to have a strategy on how big a net to cast iteratively based on information collected and conclusions made.

- **Define:** The focus of the define mode is to bring clarity and focus on the problem that needs to be solved. The goal is to determine whether the proposed value proposition is meaningful, and if meaningful, determine the gaps for the value proposition and craft an actionable problem statement that guides the team to develop a path or a roadmap to reduce such gaps. This statement is referred as point-of-view (POV). A good POV should capture the essence of the problem being solved, inspire the team, have a criteria for evaluating possible solution, and empower the team to work synergistically to develop the solution.
  - Here is an example on how a team uses the information collected during the empathize mode to determine whether the value proposition was meaningful. "Design for Extreme Affordability" is a class offered by Stanford's d.School. Students in the class formed teams to develop solutions for daunting, real-world problem. A team of four students had an assigned project "Design a low-cost infant incubator for use in the developing countries to save lives of premature babies". At first glance, this looks like an engineering project, and the focus should be a new incubator design that reduces the cost by minimizing parts or using cheaper materials, etc. But the course emphasized the application of the design thinking process. The team was encouraged to "empathize with the user". The user of baby incubator is a hospital. One of the team members received funding for a trip to Nepal to understand the needs of incubator in hospital. He visited a hospital in Nepal and noticed that there were many denoted incubators, but they were all empty. He asked the doctors and nurses why. A doctor explained that the incubators were empty because the babies who needed them were mostly born in villages far away, and the road infrastructure was so poor that mothers could not bring their babies to the hospital.

    This was a wake-up call to the team. The problem they were asked to solve was not the true problem because of the poor road infrastructure and the distance between village and cities. The gap for the value proposition is too large and cannot be reduced by the team's effort. Instead of reducing the gap for the value proposition, a better approach is to modify the value proposition so that it is meaningful and reachable. Incubators are a means to an end. The real problem is to save life, not make a cheaper incubator. The team met and discussed the findings. Through an iterative process, they adapted a new and meaningful value proposition: "Help parents in remote villages increase their babies' survival rate", and the POV would be "a baby-warming device that would help baby to survive". This guided the team to develop a low cost (99% less than a traditional baby incubator), easy to use medical device product: Embrace Infant Warmer. The team turned a class project into a real-life product.

If one of the team members came from under-developed countries and was familiar with the environment, they might have immediately noticed that the original problem was not meaningful. But the fact that a device like Embrace was not available in the market place implies that people then had the mind-set that incubators was the solution to increase a baby's survival rate. Very often, people are stuck with a certain mind-set because of their experiences, their training, their living environments and their cultural background. The iterations between the empathize mode and define mode can help to unstuck and expand the mind-set.

- Another case is Tencent's QQ development. Instant messaging (IM) technology offers real-time text transmission over Internet. In 1997, AOL released AOL instant messenger (AIM) - a software program that can allow registered user to communicate in real time if both sides were connected online. AIM was popular in North America from late 1990s to late 2000s. In late 1990s, AOL and many Chinese local companies started to promote IM in China. Because IM was successful in US, they all adapted the same value proposition for Chinese market. All of them, except Tencent, perceived that the gap for the value proposition was only language translation. The founder of Tencent had the view that the gap was beyond just language translation, the other gap was that most young people in China did not have a personal computer. This difference led to two different solutions: messages sent between two personal computers and messages sent from a personal computer to a server with a receiver to retrieve the message in a public Internet Cafe. Note that all IM players could get access to market data on the percentage of young people in China that owned a personal computer. The fact that all except Tencent did not include this knowledge in assessing the gaps implied that they either did not try to get access to this data, or they got the data but ignored it.

The define mode is a converging process. It synthesizes the information collected from empathizing and people's feedback revealed through testing to determine whether the value proposition is meaningful, and if meaningful, articulates the gaps to be reduced to realize the value proposition. This is a subjective judgement process that depends on the background, experience, and knowledge of the team members. An insightful person on the team would greatly enhance this mode.

- **Ideate:** In the ideate mode, the focus is in idea generation. It is a diverging process of combining rational thoughts, imagination, out of box thinking, and challenges of the status quo to generate many ideas of how a specified problem is to be solved. There are three levels of problem to undertake in order to reduce gaps for a specific value proposition. The first level is to determine the set of problems to be solved to deliver the value proposition and to achieve a competitive position in a certain market segment. The second level is to generate hypothetical solutions that would solve the problems determined in the first level to reduce gaps in the value proposition. The third level is define the roadmap that addresses when these problems will be solved. At an earlier iteration cycle, ideate to address the first level problem. Then ideate to address the second level problem, and finally ideate to address the third level problem in later iteration cycle.

- Take the Dell case as an example. The problems to be solved is to achieve a competitive position under the "build to order" vision that would consist of (1) the customized options that customers can select in ordering, (2) the ease of ordering, (3) the maximum lead time between receiving orders and shipping the product to customers is less than the maximum lead time the customer can accept between ordering and receiving, and (4) cost effect direct sales channel.

    The maximum lead time between receiving order and shipping the product to customers can be further broken down into sub-problems: modular design with some modules "build to stock" and some modules "build to order", locations of the suppliers to "build to order" modules, lay out assembly process to reduce production time, and cost effective delivery of a single product. Modular design, locations of suppliers, and production process are interrelated. Customized options can influence the maximum lead time the customer can accept between ordering and receiving.

    In an early cycle, generate ideas for an independent problem at each iteration. For problems that are related, group them as one problem. In later cycles, generating ideas separately for the roadmap in developing the supplier network, direct sales channel and the customized options at each iteration.

- In 1956, the founders of Honda had a vision of "two-wheelers for everyone in developed and developing countries, in urban and rural areas". At that time, Honda was in the motorcycle and clip-on bicycle engine businesses so this vision was within reach. After World War II, many roads were destroyed and Japan was under construction, so roads were narrow and a practical two-wheelers would be ideal. Honda first targeted the Japan market. The problems to be solved to achieve a competitive position in Japan's market were (1) a reliable, simple to maintain, simple to use, safe, easy to handle two-wheelers, (2) efficient distribution channel, and (3) advertising message to attract customers. At an earlier cycle, generate ideas for each problem in each iteration. At later cycles, generate ideas for user group expansion and a roadmap for developing a distribution network.

- Alibaba was in B2B business since it was founded in 1999. Its business was to help companies all over the world to source suppliers in China. The business was growing slowly. In 2003, SARS hit China and many countries issued warning for businessmen traveling to China. Because of this, Alibaba's online B2B fell drastically in the SARS period. Jack Ma grabbed the opportunity and set up TaoBao, a B2C business within Alibaba, that year. At that time eBay was the number one B2C platform in China. Within two years, Alibaba overtook eBay and eBay left China in 2006.

To understand why Alibaba could overtake eBay, examine the problems that need to be solved to reduce the gaps for B2C e-Commerce in China. At that time, China did not have a nationwide credit system. Even though China UnionPay started issuing credit cards in 2002, only high net worth individual were issued credit cards. Most people could not make payment through credit card in a B2C e-Commerce platform. Moreover, China had weak consumer protection law and no return policy in retail transaction. Therefore the problems to be solved to establish a market position in B2C e-Commerce in China consist of (1) build trust between buyers and sellers on e-Commerce, (2) provide secured transaction on e-Commerce, (3) attract buyer to the platform, (4) attract sellers to the platform, (5) protect both buyers and sellers, and (6) cost effective delivery service.

In 2003, all B2C platforms in China addressed problems (1), (2), (3), (4) and (6). Even though eBay addressed problems (1) and (2) using a US solution, they were not effective when adapted in China. Alibaba addressed problems (1), (2) and (5) explicitly and found solutions compatible to Chinese culture. This is an error that US companies often made when expanding a product/service to a foreign country with a completely different culture, infrastructure and law.

Note that the first level in identifying the problems to be solved is bounded. The problems to be solved are related to the product offering, production, sales, distribution, and ecosystem loyalty. However with specific value proposition, infrastructure status, technology status, and cultural background, some problems have more impact on the likelihood of success. Like in the Alibaba case, identifying the right problems to be solved win half of the battle. To generate a good idea requires insightful observations and logical thinking. Getting an insightful person who is knowledgeable about the environment under which the product/service will be delivered can be extremely helpful in generating a good idea.

The second level in solving specific problem is a lot more open ended if the value proposition is new and people have no prior experience with it. For example, before the iPhone was introduced, who would imagine a phone with no keypad? Honda developed Supercub, a two-wheeler that fulfilled its vision, but found that the traditional motorcycle distribution channel was not an effective channel. It developed new channels that included sport shops, super markets, university book stores, and bicycle shops. Alibaba set up Alipay to solve the payment security problem that protected both buyers and sellers. When it was first started, Alipay worked like an escrow service with no transaction fee. When someone decided to buy some product on Taobao platform, they made payment to Alipay. When the payment was received, Taobao notified the seller to ship the item. When the buyer received the item, they had 7 days to decide whether they wanted to keep the item. After the buyer notified Alipay that they liked the item within the 7 days, Alipay paid the seller in full with no service charge. If the buyer complained and appealed for return, they could ship the item back for free and get 100% refund. Alipay earned interest income of escrow money to support its service. Alipay has changed many times and evolved into the world's largest online and mobile payment system.

Open ended problems require out of box thinking: "going wild" to think what is unthinkable and to challenge the mainstream status quo is helpful to generate surprising solutions. To achieve this, a brainstorming session is commonly used. Since idea generation is highly dependent on each person's knowledge, experience, mind-set, and creativity, getting the right people to engage in brainstorming is crucial. Getting someone with "think outside the box" mentality engaged in the brainstorming session would be very helpful. In a consulting exercise, brainstorming is conducted in a formal setting. Someone is assigned to be the moderator to control and guide the session. A good moderator should know the problem to be solved and drive the team to think creatively. The group should consist of people with open minds, and have different backgrounds and experiences related to the specific problem to be solved. The group is encouraged to go beyond what is obvious and let everyone express freely what comes into their minds. One rule is no one can say "no" to other's proposed solution but can build on it. The moderator should avoid group thinking, and encourage ideas that may go against what has been proposed. The main theme is to generate as many ideas as possible and defer judgement on these ideas. In so doing, it unlocks creatively and imagination. Hopefully, through this process, some unexpected solutions may surface. These activities also help to harness the perspective and strength of members participating in the brainstorming session. Each brainstorming session should put a time limit to control cost.

Brainstorming session for different problems may involve different people. Brainstorming can also be carried out in an informal manner with a few key people in a room or an open space. The quality of a brainstorming session is not measured by the numbers of people engaged or ideas generated, but measured by the numbers of surprising or unexpected ideas generated. Since idea generation is subjective, the quality of brainstorming is determined more by the right people engaged than the process.

The third level in defining the roadmap is also bounded, and we need more insightful observations and logical thinking than out of the box thinking.

- **Prototype:** The Prototype Mode is to build something that a user can interact with to bring out more emotions and responses. Consider a hypothetical solution of a particular problem that can reduce the gaps for the value proposition. For the hypothetical solution to be a good solution, certain assumptions related to users' acceptance need to be verified. For a particular assumption, build a prototype to elicit useful feedback to verify whether the assumption is correct or to learn more about users' attitude toward the problem. A prototype can be anything that people can interact with. It can be a physical object, a drawing, a storyboard, or a role-play activity. Build a prototype with the assumption and the user in mind. What information you hope to find out? What assumption you want to verify? What would motivate the user to interact with your prototype? These are the questions to be addressed in building the prototype. A prototype also provides opportunity to have direct conversation with people to receive meaningful feedback in the testing phase.
  - In the TMC case, their problem is to design a hand phone with an inlaid jewelry that would appeal to high income group in second and third tier cities. The product team built a simple prototype of a flip phone style casing with a jewelry inlaid on top of the clamshell. The assumption to be verified was whether rich people in second and third tier cities would desire a basic hand phone with inlaid jewelry. The prototype was not a functioning phone, just a hand phone casing. The slick design gave it an aesthetic look and gave user a good feeling when carrying the phone and use it to make calls. The jewelry was easily noticeable, whether the phone was just being carried around or people were making a call with it. They showed it to some rich people in the second and third tier cities. No one asked about the functionality of the phone. They only cared about whether the jewelry would be exposed when they were making call and the pricing.
  - In the Dell case, there were certain assumptions that needed to be verified. One assumption was whether fax machines would be a good medium for direct ordering from customers. A good prototype to verify this could have been an interactive story board articulating the ordering process through fax. Another assumption was whether it could attract suppliers to locate close by Dell's assembly plant. A good prototype would be a role play with some suppliers using a map with the location of the assembly plant marked out on it, and asking them whether they would relocate nearby if the sales volume reached a certain level.
  - A YouTube clip "Speedee Service System" features how the McDonald brothers built a prototype for a fast make-to-order system for hamburger. They used a tennis court to represent the kitchen space and white chalk to mark the kitchen layout. The brothers and the kitchen crew role-played the production process as "orders" came

in. They "moved" the layout around to increase the speed of production. Through many iterations, they had a final kitchen lay out for McDonald's Speedee Service System. This clip is in the movie "The Founder", which is a biographical drama firm on McDonald's. Whether the clip showing the prototyping for the Speedee Service System is actually what McDonald brothers did or not is not important. What is important is that it shows how a cost effective prototype can be built to verify whether an assembly layout would be efficient. https://www.youtube.com/watch?v=jTageuhPfAM

- For many software app and mobile app products, an interactive story board or a video is a good prototype to get people's feedback.

A prototype as an artifact that one builds to either verify an assumption or elicit more information from users. Iterating through prototyping stages can verify an assumption. In the early stage, create cheap and simple prototype to validate certain hypothesis made about the solution and use it to elicit useful broader information that can help to develop more refined prototype in the later stage to elicit more details. Prototype mode is a converging process of consolidating the ideas generated from the ideate mode to build an artifact to test the validity of an assumption in a hypothetical solution. Building prototypes is a creative process of finding a solution within "a box". Building a good prototype to address an assumption depends on the background, experience, knowledge and "within the box" creativity of the team members.

- **Test:** The Test Mode is to verify, from users' feedback on the experience with the prototype, whether the assumptions are valid and to learn more about the users. In the early iterative stage, test mode is an opportunity for you to gain empathy and better understand the economic agents' attitude towards the value proposition. In early stages, focus on asking "why" to learn whether there is a meaningful proposition, to determine the relative importance of gaps to realize the value proposition, and help to generate new ideas. If the prototype is a physical objective, have the users take the prototype with them and use it. Watch how they use it or have casual conversation with them on their experience of using it. If the prototype is a story board, solicit feedback and have casual conversation during the story telling. If the prototype is a role-play, try to create a scenario in a location that captured the real situation. Observe how they respond in the role-play and have a casual conversation.

Design thinking is not a sure way to come up with a good solution to a specific problem. It is a process to open up our minds to understand people more, encourage collaboration of people with different skills and mind-set, and work collectively to generate innovative solution to solve some of the hardest problem. Iteration is the key in design thinking, but iteration also involves generating ideas and judgement that are both subjective. Insightful observation, logical thinking, "go wild" out of box thinking, and "within the box" creativity are required to deliver an effective design thinking process. Therefore getting the right people engaged is more important than the process itself.

## Problem Space Thinking vs Solution Space Thinking

The problem space of a person is the set of problems that the person is facing. These may be their pain point, desire, jobs to be done, etc. People would attach a value to each problem in their problem space representing how urgent and important it is to them if the problem is solved. A person's problem space and the value attached to solving the problem are dynamically changing as the external environment changes.

The **problem space thinking process** is a process that a product team uses to navigate from an initial value proposition idea to POV. In this process, the team would think through what would be a value proposition that would address many people's urgent and important problem and then articulate a POV to guide the product development to deliver the value proposition. This process consists of two iterative sub-processes. The first process is a discovery process where the team, through empathy, find out what people's urgent needs and important problems are, how they are dealing with such problems right now, and what pain point remains. The second process is a converging process were the information collected is synthesized to determine whether the value proposition is meaningful, and if meaningful, articulates the gaps to be reduced to realize the value proposition. Note that in this process, the discovery process is the thinking surrounding people's problem space and the converging process is synthesizing the information to articulate a POV.

The solution space of a POV is the set of all possible implementations to build a product, to deliver services, etc. that would reduce the gaps for the value proposition. Associated with each implementation, there is cost to the company and benefit to the customers.

The **solution space thinking process** is a process that a product team uses to navigate from a POV to a prototype for testing. In this process, the team thinks through what the implementation would be that reduces the gaps for the POV in the most cost-effective manner. This process consists of two iterative sub-processes. The first process is a discovery process where the team brainstorms possible implementations that would reduce any gaps. The second process is a converging process where the cost effectiveness of each generated implementation is evaluated, and one is selected to build a prototype for testing. Note that in this process, the discovery process is thinking surrounding POV solution space and the converging process is assessing the cost effectiveness of a solution and build a prototype based on it.

Having a good understanding of customers' problem space before proceeding to product design is the key to product success. Unfortunately, most customers cannot articulate all the problems they are facing, and it's hard for customers to talk about specific benefits they require and their importance. Experience tells us customers are much better in giving feedback in the solution space. If the customer is shown a new product or design, they can respond with what they like and don't like. They can compare it to other solutions and identify pros and cons. Hence, building a prototype and having solution space discussions with customers through testing is much more fruitful in developing a better understanding of customer's problem than trying to ask customers their problems explicitly. To get a higher chance of building a product that solves customers' problem, one can start with a hypothesis of problem space, navigate the problem space thinking to get a POV, then use solution space thinking to test and improve the problem space hypotheses -- then iterate.

Design thinking can be viewed as an interaction between problem space thinking and solution space thinking. The test is to have solution space discussion with customers to help the product team to have a better understanding of the problem space. The problem space thinking process to derive a POV gives a problem framing for product development. The diagram indicates that proper problem framing for product development is through an iterative process. This is the double diamond iterative process.

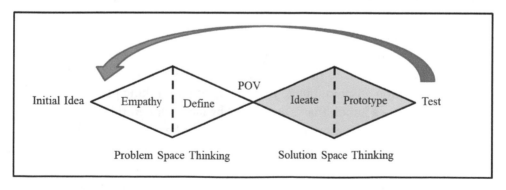

**Iterate between Problem Space and Solution Space**

There are many failed products in the market. The main reason is usually because the product team focus on the specific solution rather than the problem, and thus developing a product that does not meet customer needs. "Design a low-cost infant incubator for use in developing countries to save lives of premature babies" is a solution space thinking. A POV is fixed, and the team's responsibility is to go through solution space thinking to find a solution. However, the proposed solution may not solve the underlying problem. "Helped parents in remote villages to increase babies' survival rate" was the resulting POV after the student team went through problem space thinking.

Many successful US products failed in China. The main reason is that the product team failed to understand the problem space in China which is very different from that in US because the two countries have different culture, infrastructure and government policy. They took the problem space in the US for granted and modified the product that was successful in US slightly to adapt to the local Chinese market environment. Without having a good understanding of the problem space in China, the product failed to address the real problem local people are facing. AOL, eBay and Uber are a few examples.

## Manage to Reduce Unquantifiable Uncertainties

In the process of turning an idea into solution, many unquantifiable uncertainties that a product manager encounter comes from the human response to new situation. Which market segment would like the product? Who would be willing to distribute the product? Will the team be strong? How to build a strong supply chain? Why other agents are willing to offer supplementary products? Design thinking is not just a process to come up with a good product design, it can be viewed as risk management to reduce unquantifiable risks in the process of turning an idea into solution: 0-1 innovation. The major theme when facing with unquantifiable uncertainty is to not draw conclusions from mainstream belief, subjective mindsets, and common wisdom; but go through a design thinking process to explore and discover an innovative solution that is supported by facts. Design thinking can be applied in the development of a new product, establishment of a beach head for market entry, solidifying position in a market segment, and expanding the market to achieve profitability. In order words, a product manage can use design thinking as a tool to reduce unquantifiable risk in the process of turning a value proposition idea into a good product. Every time a product manager faces an unquantifiable risk situation, they need to identify what the problem space is and use a "diamond" iterative process to frame the problem to be solved and then use another "diamond" iterative process to determine a possible solution. Iterative between these two "diamonds" to arrive at the final solution.

There are four risk levels associated with 0-1 product success, with first level being the highest risk and as the level goes up the risk decreases. The first level is "market entry risk" where the concern is whether the product can find a market. The problem space is customers' pain point. This risk can be eliminated if the product is accepted by a few customers in a particular market segment. The second level is "value proposition risk" where the concern is not enough people buying into the value proposition. The problem space is the concerns of players on the demand side and supply side of the value proposition. This risk is eliminated if there are enough buyers for the product. The third level is competitive market risk where the concern is that the product is not competitive and cannot sustain itself in the market. The problem space is the impact of existing and new competitors on market expansion. This risk is eliminated if the product has established a sizable market position. The fourth level is the scale-up risk where the concern is that the company cannot scale up the operation to create economy of scale to establish a dominant position in a large market. The problem space is what the different ways to scale up the operation are. This risk is eliminated when the product has sustainable growth in the market and the market potential is large. The four level of risks can be illustrated in the diagram below. The lowest level is unquantifiable and has the highest risk.

**Hierarchical Levels of Risk**

The job of the product manager is to find a cost effective way to mitigate and eliminate the risk at each level starting from the lowest level.

1. **Eliminate the Market Entry Risk:** A team may have a great idea for a new product. Until there is proof that someone is actually willing to buy the product, this remains just an idea. Investing in an idea is very risky and not many people are willing to do so. Only a few that share your vision may be willing to invest. Even so, the cost of investment is very high. The product manager needs to spend the least amount of efforts to eliminate this risk. The goal is to develop a product with minimum features that can provide enough value to your first targeted customer segment (market entry) and successfully sell to a few customers in that group to eliminate this risk.

2. **Eliminate the Value Proposition Risk:** The fact that a product sells to a few customers in a certain market segment implies that it may sell to other customers in that segment – reducing the risk for product success. To further reduce risk, it needs to be proved that the product can be sold to other customers in that segment. To do so, economic agents may be needed to provide a strong holder for that segment to buy into the value proposition and support outreaching to this segment cost effectively. For example, sales and distribution channels, reliable suppliers, etc. may be needed. Instead of just focusing on the product, the product manager needs to focus on building a strong holder to reach out and capture enough customers in that segment to eliminate the value proposition risk.

3. **Eliminate Competitive Market Risk:** When the value proposition risk is eliminated, competitors will enter the market to promote the same value proposition or a better value proposition. The risk is that you may not be able to defend yourself in the market place against the new competitors. The holder needs to be strengthened (includes improving the current product) and it needs to build an ecosystem loyalty program for the current segment to solidity the current position. Expanding the holder structure (includes adding new features to the current product) will support growing into other segments. The expansion can be across different market segments in a region, or to the same market segment in a different region, or both. When a sizable total market can be maintained, the competitive market risk is eliminated.

4. **Eliminate Scale-up Risk:** The ability to scale up economy of scale allows for the establishment of a strong position in the market. The main focus here is to make sure that your product is scalable and build capacity ahead of time to handle any exponential growth resulting from a strong holder structure with loyal ecosystem members. The first player to build a strong holder structure with loyal ecosystem members will have the ultimate competitive advantage. When sustainable growth is achieved in a very large market, the scale-up risk is eliminated.

In each of these stages, the product manager faces different types of unquantifiable risk and needs to apply different double diamond iterative processes starting with a different problem space to reduce risk. In the first stage, the risk is product-market match. The focus is to use the least among of effort to develop a minimum marketable product and sell the product to a few customers in a targeted market segment. In the second stage, the risk is whether the product can be sold to other customers in the same segment. The focus is building holder structure to support penetration into the targeted market segment. In the third stage, the risk is the ability to protect the current market and expansion to other markets. The focus is building loyalty in the current segment and expanding the holder structure to enter and be competitive in other market segments. In the fourth stage, the risk is the ability to become a strong player in the market. The focus is to assure that the product is scalable and to build up capacity to handle exponential growth. Using design thinking at each stage keeps the product manager alert on the possible outside changes that they need to take into consideration in real time. Very often, a product that has early success fails because the product manager takes the outside situation for granted and fails to take appropriate actions to deal with exogenous changes in a timely manner. This would be the case of a cool product that fails to turn into a good product.

The effectiveness of the design thinking process depends on whether the problem one is facing is open ended or bounded. If the problems is open ended, then the risk of not finding a good solution is high and thus the design thinking process may be less effective. If the problem is bounded, then the chance of finding a good solution is high and thus the design thinking process is very effective. The information, knowledge, and experience gained in the earlier stages should be used to bound the problems in the later stage and thus increase the effectiveness of design thinking process. For example, if there is a large customer base, empathizing can be a lot more effective by developing a customer engagement program that enables learning more about customers and develop closer relationship. Customer behavior could be predicted better and thus would help bound the problem. Also, leveraging the information and knowledge derived from historical market data on similar and related products will help bound the problems to be solved and thus increase the effectiveness of design thinking process.

# Discussions:

1. Think of a product that inspires you. What was the roadmap to reduce the gaps for the value proposition? What would be the roadmap for the product to evolve and why?
2. Often, in interviews, product managers have to translate between solution space thinking and problem space thinking. Can you think of examples from your own experience where you or others have phrased the problem in the solution space rather the problem space? What would be the implied solution? What was the fundamental problem?
3. When eBay went to China, did they have solution space thinking or problem space thinking? Is this a common theme for companies when they expand into foreign market?
4. You are asked to design a wallet. What value proposition you are addressing? Among all the solutions that would address the value proposition, what problems you address to come up with your design?
5. Legend has it that during the height of space race in 1960s, NASA engineers realized that pens cannot function in space. They needed to figure out another way for astronaut to write things down. So, they put years and millions of taxpayer dollars into developing a pen that can put ink to paper without gravity. But their crafty Soviet counterparts, so the story goes, simply handed their cosmonauts pencils. Treating these as facts, comment on NASA's thinking process and Soviet counterparts' thinking process.
6. However, the facts are actually very different. NASA astronauts actually used pencils. NASA ordered 34 mechanical pencils and paid $128.89 per pencil in 1965. NASA had main concerns: that the tips flaked and broke off, drifting in microgravity, and could potentially harm an astronaut or equipment, and also that pencils are flammable. Paul Fisher and his company invested $1 million to develop a space pen that was patented in 1965. The pen does not rely on gravity, instead pressurized with nitrogen to push the ink towards the ball at the pen's tip. NASA and Soviet space agency bought the space pen for $2.39 per pen. What lesson you learn from facts and fiction?
7. In a brainstorming session, if you find most ideas are from within a box thinking, what should you do?
8. Minimum Viable Product (MVP) is a type of prototype with a specific objective: an artifact that enables the collection of the maximum amount of validated learnings about the targeted customers with the least amount of effort. Here are a few examples of MVPs: https://softwarebrothers.co/blog/15-examples-of-successful-mvps/#facebook. What are some characteristics that are common throughout them?
9. How did Airbnb go about overcoming the four levels of risk? What can you learn from their process? Think about a product or company that you like. How did it overcome the four levels of risk?

# 4

# Lean Startups

Back in 2017, Tesla had an interest in producing its models in China and selling them in China and other parts of the world. The Chinese government was promoting electric cars and there were more than 400,000 middle class in China at that time. Tesla's models are loved by many in the US and were gaining acceptance in China. These factors meant that Tesla had great potential in the Chinese electric car market. Production in China would greatly reduce cost and improve profitability. The decision problem that Tesla was facing was not whether they should produce Tesla models in China, but rather how to make it happen. Tesla followed the right path and started conversations with the Chinese government to get a license to produce and sell cars in China. At the same time they wrote a business plan articulating the size of the market, the problems to be solved to produce cars for global market, and how to enter the China electric car market aggressively. The investment community judged Tesla's investment project based on the assessment of how well Tesla would meet its plan. For decades, this business plan-centric approach was the conventional wisdom for starting a business. Prior to 2010, most technology startups wrote a business plan, pitched it to investors, assembled a team, introduced a product, and sold as aggressively as they could. Many large companies used this model to start new initiatives. The result was hit-or-miss. Research statistics in the early 2010s indicated that 75% of startups failed.

The basic underlying assumption for the business plan-centric approach is that the value proposition of the product is known and accepted by many people. Like in the Tesla example, the problem is how to fill a void in the market place. The purpose of a business plan is to articulate what are the known problems to be solved and how to solve them. But for a new startup or a new initiative, it is not clear whether the proposed new value proposition is meaningful or what problems need to be solved. To write a business plan for a new business where the real problem is unknown, the problems to solve and how to solve them have to be made up. This is why the business plan centric approach is not suitable for new technology startups and new initiatives in large companies. When dealing with 0-1 innovation, there is a discovery problem followed by an implementation problem: discover what is needed to deliver a value proposition that many will buy into and implement a plan to deliver this value proposition. A business plan deals with the implementation problem. For 0-1 innovation, the discovery and implementation problems need to be integrated.

Scientific method had been used since the 17th century to address the problem of scientific discovery. The method starts with an insightful observation of things happening in the world. Based on this, a hypothesis is formulated. Then experiments are designed to do measurement-based testing of deductions drawn from the hypotheses. Based on the experimental findings, the hypothesis can be refined, altered, expanded or even rejected. The process involves going through iterative cycles until a particular hypothesis becomes very well supported by observation data; and when that happens, a general theory may be discovered. The design thinking process is very much like a scientific method that can be used to discover the right problem to be solved through problem space thinking, and how to solve them through solution space thinking in 0-1 innovation. Both scientific method and design thinking process include observing, forming hypotheses or making assumptions, designing tests to determine the validity of the hypothesis or assumption, and then iterate to refine the hypothesis or assumption to discover the solution. The differences between these two are in the hypothesis formulation and design testing stages.

One of the most important problems in 0-1 innovation is product-market fit. Another problem is selecting the entry segment. According to Andreessen, product-market fit means being in a good market with a product that can satisfy that market. Once an entrepreneur discovers a new product-market fit potential and finds their entry segment, they can write a credible business plan to implement the solution. In other words, 0-1 product innovation should look for the right business plan in the process of turning an idea into a solution. This is the underlying theme in "Lean Startup", an approach that is gaining popularity amongst Silicon Valley startups over the last ten years. It is a holistic approach to create a new business that combines new product-market fit discoveries, business plan development, stage financing, go-to-market strategies, and market expansion.

# Minimum Viable Product (MVP)

Suppose you have a product idea that you are passionate about, should you immediately share it with others to see how they respond or should you develop a prototype before you share? There are pros and cons if you disclose your idea too early or too late. If you share your product idea early you can get feedback from potential customers which increases the chance of getting product-market fit, but you run the risk that someone may take your idea and enter the market ahead of you. Facebook is an example. On the other hand, if you keep the idea to yourself and work hard to turn your idea into product, then you run the risk of not getting product-market fit and may even run the risk of losing a business opportunity. An example is Digital Research Inc. losing the deal to develop an operating system for the IBM PC because its lawyer recommended not signing IBM's NDA which was a requirement for IBM to release its business intention. Depending on who you talk to, the advice will be different. If you talk to a lawyer, they would tend to stress the IP right issue. If you talk to an entrepreneur, they would tend to stress the importance of getting early customer feedback. For a new product, product-market fit risk is much more important than IP risk because if you get the wrong product, who cares about IP risk!

Therefore, the focus should be to **maximize the chance of product-market fit while reducing the IP risk as much as possible**. This means try to engage with the customer as early as possible while protecting the product idea as much as possible. One approach is instead of focusing on the product idea, turn the focus to the value proposition of the product. One can elicit people's response to whether they like a certain value proposition without giving away the product idea. For example, in the TMC case, you can explore, in a casual conversation, whether a certain group of rich people would want to own a basic hand phone that can show off their social and economic status. People can give you their preferences but they have no idea how you are going to achieve this.

Start to engage potential customers who may buy into the proposed value proposition early. Before there is a concrete product idea, sell the value proposition and the team. This not only gives the opportunity to learn more about potential customers, it also helps the team to build rapport and trust with customers. Through early iterations in the design thinking process, develop a product idea with a value proposition that a targeted customer segment would buy into. Through engagement with some people in the targeted segment, develop a buyer persona. This is the description of someone in the targeted customer segment: their goals, pain points, aspirations, and buying patterns. Then design a prototype with a specific objective; an artifact that enables the collection of the maximum amount of validated learning about the targeted customers with the least amount of effort. This validated learning elucidates whether the targeted customers find value in the product, and if not, enables learning their preferences. This is referred to as a **Minimum Viable Product (MVP)**. The word "product" in MVP may be a bit misleading because it does not necessarily have to be something close to what is commonly referred to as a product.

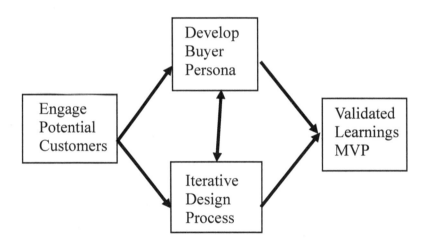

**Early Engagement with Potential Customers**

- **Ceres Imaging:** Ceres Imaging was founded in 2014 and is now a company delivering solutions for irrigation and nutrient management, and pest and disease prevention. The founders had originally looked for funding to build a drone with a hyper-spectral camera to fly over farm fields collecting hyper-spectral images. They wanted to then process these images with the company's proprietary software and tell farmers their plants' health. The founders were excited by the technological possibilities, but found through engagement with the farmers that they were neither excited about the drone technology nor the hyper-spectral camera at all, but only in how the software can interpret the images to provide the health status of their plants. The farmers even told Ceres' founders that given there were already crop dusters flying over the fields, they could mount their camera on the crop dusters to take the images.

To validate their value proposition, Ceres' founders mounted the hyper-spectral camera on a crop duster, took images of the field, and explained to farmers how their software can interpret images to assess the field's health. The MVP was an imaging system on a crop duster to generate data for analysis. Engaging with the farmers, they worked out a price structure for the service. Ceres found a way to validate the value of its service with the least amount of effort. It also found a distribution channel to deliver the value proposition. Instead of raising money to build drones with hyper-spectral cameras, the founders raised money to build a service business leveraging the existing crop dusters business, which was already well developed in US.

- **Aerobotics:** Aerobotics was founded in 2014 and is based in Cape Town, South Africa. The company combines aerial imagery obtained from satellites and drones with its machine learning algorithms to provide early problem detection services to farmers: helping them monitor their crops, get early warnings of potential risks, and optimize yields. James Paterson, one of the cofounders, grew up on a South African citrus farm and Aerobotics' first customer was his father's farm. They built a drone with a sensor system to take aerial images. They combined the aerial images from satellites and drones with its proprietary software to help farmers monitor their crop health over time. Their early clients were neighbors in the area. For each client, they built a new drone with a custom sensor system. Building custom drones was a slow and expensive process, and so they re-examined the value of their product offering. The core value was the software algorithm that analyzed the raw data to provide actionable information to help optimize yield. They switched to buying commercial drones from DJI and attaching sensors made by a French company instead of building their own custom drones. They worked out a pricing structure that was based on the area that needed to be analyzed and additional features that could give economic gains to the farmers.

- **Dropbox:** Dropbox was founded in 2007 and is now a company that offers cloud storage, file synchronization, personal cloud, and client software. The founder, Drew Houston, conceived the Dropbox concept when he was a student at MIT. He was working on multiple desktops and laptops and very often forgot to carry the USB flash drive that he kept his working files. So, he came up with the idea to bring files together in one central place by creating a special folder on the user's computer. These folders are synchronized to Dropbox's servers, and computers and devices where Dropbox's application was installed. This solved Houston's problem of repeatedly forgetting his USB flash drive. Houston believed that this was a problem many software developers would face. At that time there were many data backup companies, but Houston did not use their services because he had encountered problems with transferring data across firewalls when the file was too big or when there were too many files. He figured that if he could solve this problem, then he could succeed in competing in this growing market.

He recruited Arash Ferdowsi, also an ex-MIT student, to work on the idea. They created a prototype that worked on Windows PCs. The next thing was to verify the assumption that "software developers would also want such a product". The conventional practice in the software industry was to find beta customers to try out the software and provide user feedback. The beta customers could very well be early entry customers and the purpose was to litmus test to see if they found the product useful. But they could not follow this conventional practice because their product dealt with file transferring, and before the code was 100% reliable, no one would try out the prototype. Instead, Houston came up with an innovative MVP to achieve the same goal. Houston produced a video with three minutes of a product demo. He uploaded this video on Hacker News, a website for software developers.

He got a lot of feedback from developers on the functionality of the product. Through this video feedback, they learned what to change as they completed the product. The video also connected Houston with Paul Graham who is the founder of Hacker News and co-founder of Y Combinator. Dropbox received seed capital, mentoring, and workspace from Y Combinator in April 2007. With the feedback from the video, the founders of Dropbox decided to build a version that would target individuals, both consumers and businesspeople. They would use this as an entry point to penetrate into the enterprise market, because enterprise sales typically have long sell cycles. In other words, the personal use would be a Trojan horse to break into the enterprise market.

Dropbox got first-round financing from Sequoia Capital in September 2007. With the funding, they completed the product development for both Windows PC and Macintosh clients and planned to deliver its service through Amazon's cloud storage platform. They created a beta testing program for interested people to register through a landing page. Beta testers would receive 2GB Dropbox for free. To generate demand for beta testing, they produced a second short demo video and posted it in March 2008 on Digg, a very popular social news website with over 200 million visitors at the time. The video was also sprinkled with content that attracted a tech-savvy audience. Overnight, beta registration jumped from 5,000 to 75,000.

- **Zappos:** Zappos was founded in 1999 and is now an online shoes and clothing retailer. It was acquired by Amazon in 2009 with a $1.2 billion valuation. In 1999, Nick Swinmurn, the founder of Zappos, had the idea to sell shoes online. Looking back to 1999 with a modern perspective, this would seem like a good idea since Amazon was not in this segment yet. But from their point of view at the time, this was not clear. At that time, Amazon was growing but losing money. Amazon was only selling books prior to 1998 and began selling music and videos in 1998. It was not clear then when Amazon would become profitable (Amazon first turned profitable in the fourth quarter of 2001). The Internet was at its peak, and many expected the Internet bubble to burst within a few years. Selling shoes online could be a risky business. Validating the business without making investments in warehouses and inventory stock would be a challenge.

Swinmurn came up with a clever MVP. He developed a website to handle sales, went to close by shoe stores, and took pictures of the shoes with a high-resolution camera. He posted the shoe pictures on the website with prices. When people clicked to buy a shoe on the website, he went down to the store to buy the shoe and shipped it to the customer. As far as the customer was concerned, this was a fully functional online store selling shoes. After validating that there were actual customers buying from the site, he went to raise money to build the business.

Among the above four cases, only Aerobotics had an actual product as its MVP. For the other three cases, the MVP was an innovative design of a prototype that helped them discover whether their product idea was viable, and through an iterative process helped them to achieve product-market fit potential. Knowing the persona of the targeted customer group is helpful when designing an effective MVP. Note that the **design of MVP is focused on users' experience in deriving value, and not so much about the product features and functionality**. One very important thing to keep in mind is that the cost of developing MVP should be very low. Finding out whether a product idea is credible or not should not be costly. In the Aerobotics' case, they actually had a buying customer, so they could build the product to conduct validated learning. The MVP should enable learning from users to determine the minimum feature requirements to provide enough value to targeted customers, and also help to determine the initial offering price. Iterate the MVP validation cycle and incorporate customer feedback in each cycle to develop a product that could be sold to a few customers in the targeted segment at a certain price.

## Business Plan and Stage Financing

Once there is a marketable product sold to a few customers in the targeted segment, a credible business plan can be created to articulate what the market size for the product would be and how to eliminate the risks in the process of business development to achieve the market potential. There were four risk levels outlined in the last chapter: entry risk, value proposition risk, competitive market risk, and scale-up risk. Entry risk is eliminated once the new product is sold to a few customers in the targeted segment. The business plan is to articulate how to eliminate value proposition risk, market risk, and scale up risk. In any new product venture, financing is necessary; whether financing from VCs for startups or internal financing for new corporate initiatives. It is prudent to do stage financing. The objective of first stage financing is to provide enough funds to enable the company to eliminate the value proposition risk, the second stage is to eliminate the competitive market risk, and the third stage is to eliminate the scale up risk. The business plan for first round financing should be focused more on eliminating the value proposition risk.

Investors are balancing risk and returns. Therefore, they tend to invest in large and growing markets. To describe the market potential, market sizing is commonly used. The acronyms TAM, SAM, and SOM are used to describe the potential of a business venture.

- **Total Available Market (TAM):** It is also known as **Total Addressable Market**. It refers to the combined revenues of all the companies in a specific market on an annualized basis. For example, TAM for shoes would be the sales of all shoes companies in a year. This data can come from a credible marketing research company like Gartner, Forrester, Dataquest, IDC, Meta, and Yankee Group to estimate TAM. A bottom-up approach can also be used by adding up sales of leading shoemakers and assuming they capture a large percentage (say 80%) of the total market. There are several methods to cross check the validity of the estimates. An investor may want to know the TAM in the US, or North America, or the rest of the world, and its potential growth over the next five years. For an entirely new product, TAM can be calculated by adding up the current products that it would substitute. For example, when the iPhone was first introduced to the market, Apple could have added up all hand phone sales, land phone sales, and walkie talkie sales to estimate TAM for the iPhone.
- **Served Available Market (SAM):** It is also known as **Service Addressable Market**. SAM is a subset of TAM. It is the size of the total market that your company can provide a solution to serve. It represents the market size of the product category. SAM can be specified for regions. For example, worldwide SAM for Nike is the total sales of athletic shoes all over the world. The growth of SAM/TAM represents the expansion of the product category into TAM. For example, the growth of SAM/TAM for online retail represents the expansion of online retail into the total retail market.

- **Share of Market (SOM):** It is also known as **Serviceable Obtainable Market**. It refers to the sales a particular company is planning to achieve in short term (e.g. five years). This plan should be credible and within reach consistent with the company's business plan. By definition SOM is a subset of SAM.

The diagram below shows the relative relationship between TAM, SAM, and SOM:

**TAM, SAM, SOM**

TAM and SAM represent market potential. Typically, TAM is a very big number. It represents the ultimate size of the market that may be captured by expanding current business practices. SAM is the market that can be captured with current business practices. Small SAM/TAM (SAM divided by TAM) represents high expansion potential. Amazon started selling books online. Should it use the total size of the book market as its TAM or the total size of the retail market as its TAM? Since Amazon is positioned as online retail selling, it could sell books and other products online. Therefore, its TAM should be total retail markets, both online and offline. SAM is the total online retail market. SAM is a very small percentage of TAM, indicating a great expansion potential. As online sales outpace total retail sales, SAM/TAM for Amazon increases, indicating a decrease in expansion potential. SAM/TAM has been steadily growing and in 2018, online retails was 9.9% of total retail sales. For a bookstore chain, TAM is the total book sales, SAM is the total book sales near its network of store locations. This means that if we compare the SAM/TAM, Amazon had a much lower percentage than a bookstore chain at the time Amazon started. In order words, even though both were in the business of selling books, Amazon had a much higher expansion potential compared to a bookstore chain.

SOM represents the share of the market the company plans to capture in five years. Setting a target for SOM reflects how the company intends to penetrate the market over the next five years. The credibility of this target hinges on successful implementation of a business plan detailing how resources are utilized to support a go-to-market strategy to reach this target goal. A company's SOM/SAM represents the competitive advantage of the company in the same product category. For a product category with fast growing SAM, to achieve a high percentage at the end of five years the company would need a very aggressive plan that may reduce profitability. In developing a five-year plan, a company needs to balance capturing high market share and profitability. A product category with growing SAM/TAM and low SAM/TAM attracts investors because it is growing and has a lot of room to grow. A company with a product in this product category should have the balance tilted more towards capturing high market share, or a high SOM/SAM ratio since it could raise money to support the operation even if it is not profitable. On the other hand, if SAM/TAM is stagnant and/or the SAM/TAM is high, then the balance should be tilted more towards profitability.

Take the Amazon case example. Its SAM/TAM ratio was very low, so it kept its emphasis on building market share without much concern for profit. It finally turned profitable in 2001. On the other hand, Barnes and Noble, a bookstore chain competing with Amazon in the book sales market, had to be concerned about profitability because its SAM/TAM ratio was high. Barnes and Noble also offered online book sales in 1997, but it was confined to only book sales. The SAM/TAM ratio remained high and thus it had to be concerned about profitability. When Amazon scaled up with more investment, Barnes and Noble lost its competitive advantage and in 2018 reported a loss of $17 million.

Consider the Zappos case. When it entered the market in 1999, should it position itself as an online retail sales business or an online shoe sales business? If it positioned itself as an online retail sales business, then Amazon and Zappos have the same TAM and SAM. This means they both have the same expansion potential for all time. As Amazon had already built up online sales momentum and warehouse structure for expansion in 1999, Amazon would outpace Zappos in online retail sales in the future. So, its SOM/SAM ratio projection would be decreasing as compared to that of Amazon over time. This means that even though it would have the same expansion potential as Amazon, it would be losing competitiveness to Amazon more and more over in time. This might threaten Zappos' survival. But if it positioned as online shoes sales, then its TAM is the total shoes sales, and its SAM is the total online shoe sales. Projected out ten years, its SAM/TAM ratio projection might be higher than Amazons, meaning much less expansion potential. But its SOM/TAM ratio would be very high because of first mover advantage.

The significance of TAM, SAM, and SOM is that estimating these metrics forces a company to think through its positioning, its market potential, and sets a proper target goal for the five-year business plan. To achieve the target goal, there are two major risks to overcome. One is the value proposition risk and the other is the competitive market risk. The first risk is whether there are enough people buying into the value proposition. When the company is successful in opening the market, this would indicate that many have bought into the value proposition. New entrants may come in offering the same or similar value proposition. Then the second risk is whether the company will be competitive in the marketplace. Cautious investors who think the proposed value proposition has market potential would want to reduce its risk exposure by breaking the investment into two stages. The first stage is to invest enough for the company to eliminate the value proposition risk. If the company is unable to meet its goal, then the investors will not continue to invest. If the company meets its goal, then they will further invest and invite other investors to join in to make enough investment for the company to eliminate the competitive market risk. As the value proposition risk is eliminated, further investment is less risky and it will therefore be easier to attract additional investment. See diagram below for stage financing.

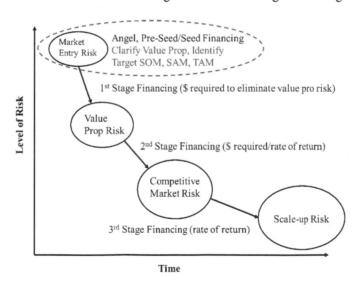

**0-1 Risk and Stage Financing**

# Go to Market Strategy

A go to market strategy for a new product is the way an organization utilizes internal resources to shape the grabber-holder dynamics to develop a strong market position in a targeted segment and be ready for expansion. This would enable the company to deliver the value proposition to customers and achieve its competitive advantage in the targeted segment. Through the MVP iteration cycle, a product is developed that a few users express interest in and are willing to buy or test. This is when a go to market strategy should be developed to support the writing of a business plan to secure the first round of financing. The strategy will also guide the tactical implementation of utilizing inside and outsides resources to develop a viable business.

In the conventional approach, go to market strategy starts after a product is ready to sell. The focus is pricing, channels development, and customer acquisition. Lean startup approach advocates going to the market before you have a 100% ready to sell product. Early customers can be used to help further refine the product. This helps in building up channels and new customer acquisition. Building loyalty in your early customers also helps tremendously in new customer acquisition. So in a lean startup approach, go to market strategy should be a combination of product refinement with customer feedback, channels and sales development, and building customer loyalty. Product refinement would be important in the early part of go to market strategy. Building customer loyalty should be in parallel with channel development because it will create positive feedback between the two activities. Proper balancing among these three activities will greatly increase the product success rate.

Securing a few customers would seem to indicate that a product-market fit is found, however there are still a lot of uncertainties and a lot of problems to be solved before it can be concluded that there is market for the product and a position can be secured in the market. Would the product be accepted by those other than the few who have bought the product? How can the customers that would have an interest in buying the product be reached? How can a strong market position in the targeted segments be developed? How will the customer acquisition cost change after expanding beyond the easiest and most loyal customers? A grabber-holder model can guide the development of a go-to-market strategy.

## Entry Segment and First Targeted Segment

Why are the first few customers willing to buy or test a product? The reason is because, very often, the product either solves their pain point or satisfies a need they aspire to fulfill. The first step in the strategy is to learn through engagement with these customers to find out the primary reason they bought the product. Is it helping them to solve a certain pain they are having? Is it giving them more convenience in solving a problem they often face? Is it allowing them to satisfy a higher aspiration? Finding out the primary reason for them to buy or test the product allows the identification of the needs of these people. Modify the product accordingly to further meet their needs and determine a price for the product. It is reasonable to expect that people like those few customers would find the product valuable and be willing to pay the price.

There can be a difference between the entry segment and the first targeted segment. The segment that is first approached to gain new product acceptance is the entry segment. Very often, this is the people who are similar to the few that have initially bought the new product. But for a product like the iPod or Google, the entry segment can be in the supply side. If the entry segment is in the supply side, then the entry segment should be leveraged to identify a large enough demand segment to be the first targeted segment. Apple first approached a record company to get their approval of downloading music to the iPod before launching the iPod. So, the record company was the iPod's entry segment. With the rights to download music titles legally, Apple identified the Apple customers who love music as their first targeted segment. Google first got enough people to use Google search for finding information on the web before it could launch a business in online advertising. So people searching information on the web was Google Search's entry segment, and the first targeted segment was the medium and small companies who wanted to do online advertisement.

If the entry segment is on the demand side and is big enough, then it can be the first targeted segment. If the entry segment is on the demand side but is small, then, in addition to capturing more from the entry segment, identify a large enough demand segment to be the first targeted segment, develop additional features, and leverage the captured entry segment to gain acceptance in the first targeted demand segment. In the personal computer example, the entry segment was the hobbyists. This segment was on the demand side but it was too small and therefore should not be considered as the first targeted segment. Even though Altair had the first successful product in capturing this segment, it was eliminated from the personal computer market race early in the game. Apple developed the Apple I to capture customers in the entry segment, and then updated the packaging and included new features to upgrade it to the Apple II, thereby providing value to forward-looking personal computer users who wanted to manage and process their personal information. In this case, hobbyists were the entry segment and forward-looking personal computer users were the first targeted segment. Apple's success in the early personal computer market was because it entered the market through the entry segment identified by Altair, but instead of focusing on competing with Altair in the entry segment, it identified the first target segment and quickly evolved the Apple I into Apple II to develop a value proposition for the first targeted segment.

## Get Committed Agents to Buy-in

For a new product, discovering an effective channel to sell to the first targeted group is a critical step. Very often, the established conventional channels may not be very effective, especially for new startups. Either they are expensive or they do not want to deal with an unproven product and/or unknown company. The potential ecosystem members for a value proposition fall into two groups: committed agents and opportunistic agents. The committed agents are customers on the demand side and economic agents on the supply side who are "grabbed" by the excitement of the value proposition and are willing to participate in promoting the realization of such proposition before seeing the actual benefit. Hobbyists, forward-looking personal computer users, some software programmers (like Bill Gates), some small electronics companies, some electronics magazines (like Popular Electronics), some electronics retail stores and some early VC investors were the committed agents in the personal computer example.

The opportunistic agents are customers and economic agents who embrace the value proposition after they see others deriving benefit from the value proposition. Companies that use personal computers to improve their productivity, large IT retail stores, third party software developers, computer-peripheral product producers, many service providers in the PC industry, and late-stage private equity investors were the opportunistic agents in the personal computer example. In general, there are a lot more opportunistic agents than committed agents. It is the committed agents that work together to get enough people buy into the value proposition, but it is the opportunistic agents that shape the development of a sustainable ecosystem that support the value proposition. In other words, securing enough committed agents makes the value proposition vision a possibility, while getting the opportunity agents to engage makes the value proposition vision a reality. The focus of a go-to-market strategy is to acquire as many committed agents as possible to make the vision a possibility, and the focus of a market expansion strategy is to attract opportunistic agents to build up a strong ecosystem to make the vision a reality.

Convincing the committed agents to buy-in is hard because they do not yet see the benefit. You are selling the future, a vision, and ideals. You need a concentrated effort instead of a shotgun marketing approach. You need steady progress, though slow, in acquiring more committed agents. This can be achieved by grabber-holder iterative dynamics. When the product is ready, design a launch that can stir up excitement and grab the attention of the targeted customer segment on the demand side and committed economic agents on the supply side that would benefit from the value proposition. This does not have to be a high-profile launch event like Apple did with its Macintosh. The launch can be a concentrated effort to attract some early adopters from the targeted customer segment and convince some committed economic agents of how the value proposition vision can benefit their business. When the Altair 8800 was featured in Popular Electronics it grabbed the attention of hobbyists, Bill Gates, and many small electronics companies – this is a good example of a soft launch that grabbed the attention of the committed agents. Another example is the beta test program that Dropbox developed to get some early adaptors to try out its product. As it turned out, some of these early adaptors became Dropbox's primary distribution channel.

The early adaptors and economic agents acquired through a launch effort serve as an origin of a diffusion process. The early adaptors, if they find the product satisfactory, will be very helpful in recruiting like-minded customers through word of mouth. Setting up an effective referral program will be a good channel to recruit like-minded new customers. Identifying and acquiring like-minded committed economic agents will be easier as more is learned about how they could benefit from supporting the value proposition. To get more people to buy into the value proposition, product refinement should not be focused on improving product attributes but on increasing the basic value proposition and getting more committed agents in the supply side to support the value proposition. With more early adopters wanting the product, committed agents are attracted to support the value proposition of the product. Those who focus on product attributes may lose out to those that focus on value proposition.

Apple introduced the Macintosh in 1984 with an exciting graphical user interface (GUI) operating system and a plug-and-play feature. The GUI operating system required a lot more computing power to support and with the microprocessor technology at that time, the Macintosh's processing speed was slow. Most software application developers were familiar with text-based user interfaces and only a few had the skills to develop application programs under GUI and thus very few application software was available. To provide the plug-and-play feature, the Macintosh adopted a closed architecture that further discouraged third parties from providing complementary products. Apple over-emphasized product attributes and lost sight of the basic value proposition that the Macintosh could deliver. Apple focused on product attributes instead of value proposition.

In comparison, the IBM PC was a lot more focused on value proposition but not so much on product attributes. The IBM PC had a text-based user interface which is less intuitive to users, and it needs installation before it can be used. But users were already accustomed to text-based interfaces and many of them did not want to learn a new user interface even though it was more intuitive. Text-based user interfaces required less computing power and so the IBM PC's processing speed was much faster than the Macintosh's. As the IBM PC became popular, many electronics retail stores did free installation to promote more sales. The IBM PC had an open architecture design which enabled software developers and peripheral producers to add value to personal computing. So IBM's focus was to increase their value proposition by facilitating and promoting more software developers to develop software applications and hardware producers to develop IBM PC compatible peripherals. Thus, the IBM PC was providing more basic value than the Macintosh. As a result, the Macintosh had strong sales after its initial launch, but a rapid decline after a few months while the IBM PC dominated the PC market in 1985.

The Macintosh case shows that before computing power is up to a certain level, the value of a GUI operating system won't be appreciated by users. If the primarily concern is to increase the value proposition, then it's important to first have a microprocessor and an operating system that supports the development of language programs to deliver the value of a personal computer that would attract hobbyists and sophisticated high techies to write their own application programs. With a basic personal computer with CPU, operating system and language programs, software engineers could develop application programs to further increase its value proposition. Also, adding peripherals like more memory, a disk drive, etc. would add more value. This would attract forward-looking professionals and students that use personal computers to help them in their daily work. Hence, the development roadmap to increase the value of a personal computer should follow a support-push dynamics. First start with a basic machine that includes CPU and an operating system. Use this as a pivoting support to develop language programs to provide an effective push towards increasing the value proposition. Then use the basic machine and language programs as a pivoting support to develop application programs to provide an effective push towards increasing the value proposition. The support-push dynamics for the personal computer can be represented by the diagram below.

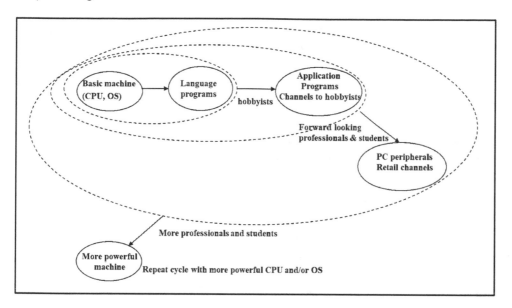

**Support-Push Dynamics for Personal Computer**

In the diagram, the oval shapes represent supports and the arrows represents pushes. The push is to get more customers buying in which then attract more relevant economic agents to provide the next push. The new buy-in customers are indicated below the arrow and the relevant push agents are in the pointed oval. As indicated by the dashed oval, the collective committed agents provide the support to the next push. With each support-push cycle, more committed agents buy into the value proposition. When the push runs into diminishing returns, the next support-push cycle begins.

Note that some of the support may be provided by committed supply side agents: third party software developers, PC peripherals producers, and retail stores. A product roadmap to introduce new product features and improve product attributes are geared towards enhancing the support-push dynamics effectively. In the PC case, this would be system design, support, and pricing that incentivizes the committed supply side agents to buy into supporting the value proposition.

In the early stage of 0-1 innovation, discovering the support-push dynamics and the roles different economic agents play in shaping the dynamics is the key to develop an appropriate development roadmap that prioritizes the tasks that the company should implement to acquire more committed agents to buy-in and build a holder structure to secure a strong market position in the first targeted segment.

Concurrent product improvement based on customer feedback and building loyalty of acquired committed agents would also help the acquisition of new customers and new economic agents. One-step acquisition accumulation dynamics is represented by the diagram below. The plus sign indicates positive influence. Assuming the acquired customers and economics agents remain loyal, the one-step cumulated acquired customers equals the acquired customers plus new customers and the one-step cumulated acquired economic agents equals the acquired economic agents plus new economic agents.

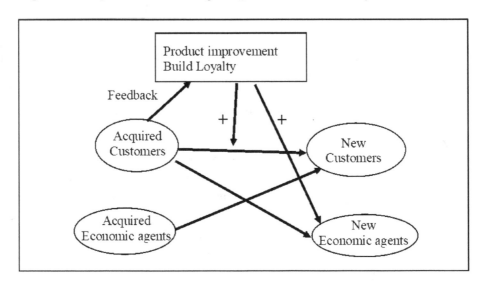

**One-Step Acquisition Accumulation Dynamics**

The combined support-push dynamics and acquisition accumulation dynamics create a ripple effect that steadily builds an ecosystem consisting of committed agents. In the beginning, this ripple effect is slow, but will pick up steadily. The growth is linear in the sense that growth is proportional to the effort you put in. The proportion slowly increases. Even though there may be customers outside the targeted segment, the main focus should be the targeted segment. The objective is to build a strong market position in the targeted segment. Competitors may enter the market, but they will not constitute a competitive threat.

Instead, they will help to promote the value proposition and thus help to eliminate the value proposition risk. Therefore, the focus should not be on the competition but to try to capture committed agents and build ecosystem loyalty.

## Go-to-Market Case Examples

One of the below case studies is a B2C product and the other is a B2B product.

- **Dropbox:** Dropbox felt it had found potential product-market fit after its tremendous success in releasing its second video. It was ready to launch the product in September 2008. Users received 2GB for free, and an additional 50 GB for $9.99 a month or $99 a year. Dropbox secured $6 million Series A financing in October 2008. After the initial launch, their service grew rapidly mainly through word of mouth referral and viral marketing. So they focused on ease-of-use, reliability, and better pricing to reflect value to users. They set up a support forum, Votebox, and A/B testing to gain insight on users' preferences and user experiences. Analyzing usage data and statistics, they discovered many users had untouched files stored in Dropbox. As they had more untouched files, the cost went up quickly. To provide more user value to subscription users, they offered 30 days of "undo" history free of charge. Unlimited undo history cost $39 per year. This increased user loyalty. They set up a referral program whereby an existing user would receive 250 megabytes per new referral. Additionally, new users would receive 250 megabytes on top of the 2GB free upon sign-up. They also improved their viral marketing tools. Dropbox captured 4 million users through word-of-mouth, referral programs, and viral marketing efforts by January 2010. Growth was slow in the beginning of 2009 but picked up towards the end of 2009. It surpassed 1 million users in April 2009, 2 million in September, and 3 million in November. This represents the period of growth represented by the grabber and holder iterative cycle when capturing the committed agents. In May 2010, Dropbox had millions of users and was ready to capture more committed agents. Dropbox developed a mobile API that allowed software developers to access files within a user's Dropbox. They began talks with PC and smartphone manufactures about pre-installing Dropbox on their devices to help their businesses. Dropbox was considered the leader in serving the individual users. But in the small-medium business and enterprise segments, Dropbox encountered much stronger competitors like Mozy (founded in 2005) and Carbonite (founded in 2006).
- **Aerobotics:** The founders of Aerobotics were engineers. They thought drones were automated and easy to operate. They figured they could sell each farmer a drone with

an attached sensor and the farmer could fly the drone to collect data for them to analyze. When they went to sell, they quickly discovered two problems. The first problem was that the farmers were not tech-savvy and they did not want to operate a drone. The second problem was that getting a farmer they did not already know to listen to their value proposition was not easy. After going through an iterative discovery process, they developed a partnership agreement with South African Cane Growers' Association. Through SACGA, Aerobotics could reach up to 23,866 independent sugar cane growers, many of them small farmers. Aerobotics developed a sophisticated machine learning algorithm with drone imagery to provide detailed information on the health of crops. Also, data could be aggregated and provide information to do a performance comparison between farms. SACGA offered this as a new service to its members. This also helped SACGA attract new members. The partnership with SACGA would solve the second problem. To solve the first problem, Aerobotics had to build a fleet of drones and hire people to operate the drones. This would create a bottleneck problem. Looking to solve this bottleneck problem, they found that drone service providers (DSP) were emerging everywhere to offer drone flying services to collect all kinds of data, including imagery data, for companies. So instead of building a drone fleet and hiring people to operate them, they developed a program to screen and select high quality DSP partners. This also allowed them to grow in countries with DSPs. With the scaling problem solved, they grew by reaching some large farmers through their website and developing additional partnerships with organizations that would allow them to reach an even larger number of farmers. Examples would be banks and loan and insurance companies offering services to farmers. Aerobotics now operates across hundreds of farms in 11 countries throughout the world, including Australia and the United States. Aerobotics has a lot of competitors all over the world and most of them started in the last five years.

These two case examples show that a go-to-market strategy is a discovery and implementation iterative cycle process to refine a product to get a better product-market fit and to develop the proper channels to reach the targeted customers. In the Dropbox case, the value to the customer is hard to quantify because it is subjective. This is the case for many B2C products. What is the value of convenience? What is the value of a faster car? To do proper pricing requires a lot more interaction with customers. In the Aerobotics case, the value to the customers is economic gain that can be estimated. An economic model can be developed to estimate the gain to set the price. Feedback from customers is needed to fine-tune the price but the iteration needed is much less. This is the case with most B2B products. Both cases need third party services to make the business scalable. In the Dropbox case, it needed the cloud services. In the Aerobotics case, it needed DSPs. Notice that in their go-to-market strategies, they did not pay much attention to competition but instead focused on building their businesses as if they were the only ones in their market. In the Dropbox case, it was trying to change people's behavior in handling file storage. More competitors with similar offerings would help in changing people's behavior. In the Aerobotics case, more farmers knowing about similar service offerings would help Aerobotics to convince farmers to take its service. The main goal of a go-to-market strategy is to eliminate value proposition risk. More like-minded competitors entering the market accelerates this process. They are more like "partners". However, when the value proposition risk is eliminated, they turn into severe competitors.

## Market Expansion and Concluding Remarks

When enough people buy into the value proposition, opportunistic agents will join in. This would be the time to get a second round of financing to build a strong position in a competitive market. With the opportunistic agents rushing in, the growth of the total market is exponential because of networking effects among the opportunistic agents. Companies that were "partners" in promoting the value proposition before now become major competitors. The rapid growth attracts new competitors to the market offering the same or similar product. Also, the established companies offering products/services that the new proposition would replace would find ways to compete by introducing more valuable value proposition. Therefore, intense competition in a new market structure is the new problem the company would have to face. Focus should switch from the targeted customer segment to expanding into other segments. This requires the development of an extended holder structure to support the expansion strategy. Another set of discovery and implementation iteration cycles is needed to capture the opportunistic agents to build a strong ecosystem that supports the new value proposition. Failure to do so could lead to the company either falling into a death valley or remaining as a minority player in a growing market. Companies that can successfully do this will be able to experience a hockey stick growth. Below is the hockey stick growth chart for Netflix.

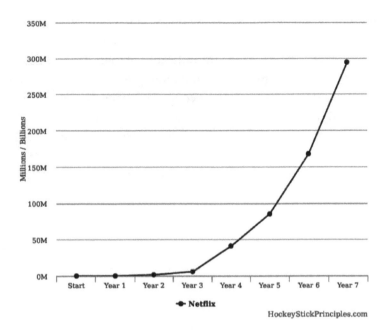

Starting a new venture is risky. Many of these risks are unquantifiable. An effective way to manage an unquantifiable risk is to spend as little as possible to learn as much as possible and iterate the process to discover the right solution before developing a plan to implement it. This is the iterative discovery and implementation cycle process. The spirit of a lean start-up is to apply this process whenever the company faces a new situation. This can be applied to a new startup and can also be applied to an established company. For 0-1, the first new situation is discovering the product-market fit. The next new situation is discovering the proper holder structure to build a strong market position in the targeted segment. After that, the next new situation is expanding the holder structure to support the expansion into other market segments and develop a competitive advantage. At each junction when the company is facing a new situation, it must shift its focus and initiate a new iterative discovery and implementation cycle process to address the new problem. The idea of using the lean startup approach is to discover the right business plan through the process. The business plan changes dynamically as more is learned through execution. This keeps the company agile, flexible, and alert to new external changes that may have big impact to the company's growth.

# Discussions:

1. Think of how Airbnb and Facebook engaged with customers in an intuitive and direct way before they even had a concrete product idea. If your targeted customer is in the enterprise space, how would you engage with your customer before you have a concrete product idea? Can you give an example?

2. Zappos' MVP is an excellent example of how one can test a value proposition and potential product-market fit without having to develop a complicated or complete prototype. In the world of software (apps, games, etc.) what are different ways you can imagine building credible MVP's for those products without *writing* code? Think of some of the apps you use on your phone and imagine how they could have built an MVP to test with users.

3. The question of how to position the SAM/TAM and SOM/SAM ratios is also related to how companies think of their mission/vision. Google's mission is to "organize the world's information and make it universally accessible and useful". This offers it a huge TAM from within to execute in, in which it's been most successful in search and in software products like Google Suite and Android. Consider Facebook or another company of your choice. What are their mission statements? How do you think their SAM/TAM and SOM/SAM ratios have changed over time and why?

4. Lean startup advocates engaging early with customers before you have concrete product idea and going to market even when your product is not 100% ready, but it does not advocate launching your product before it is ready. What are the differences? Why? Forbes has an article (https://www.forbes.com/sites/forbesagencycouncil/2017/04/14/too-soon-how-to-avoid-a-tech-product-launch-fail/?sh=6759bcc86aa1) which details some considerations when releasing a product early and why one needs to be careful. League of Legends and other games are an excellent example of how delaying official launches (games that stay in beta for years) can sometimes be the right strategy to build a community and the product expertise necessary to succeed (a related and interesting podcast https://www.npr.org/2020/12/10/944978668/riot-games-brandon-beck-and-marc-merrill). When would be the right time to launch your product? Does a successful launch guarantee product-market fit? Give some examples.

5. Think of Uber, when it first got started, who were the committed agents and who were the opportunistic agents? Why is it important to distinguish these two groups?

6. In the early entry stages, how do we rank priority in improving attributes? Let's say you have two attributes A and B: A would increase the basic value of the product's value

proposition and B would delight your customers. How would you rank them in terms of priority and why?

7. Draw the support-push dynamics for the electric car.

8. In the early entry stage, what is the objective of a pricing strategy? To make profit, to prove viability, or something else? Why?

9. What risk is an MVP trying to eliminate? What risk is a go-to-market strategy trying to eliminate? If you are successful in go-to-market strategy, do you have product-market fit? Give some examples.

# 5

# Data Analytics, Metrics, and Models

Data analytics has been increasingly important to new product success. It is not necessary for producer managers to possess this skill, but they must know the role that analytics plays in managing the success of product development and market penetration. The word analytics come from the Greek word *analytika*, which means "science of analysis". In the context of product management, it is taking large sets of product data, market responses, and sales data and putting them through statistics, mathematical models, and computer software to support product-market fit, go to market, and market expansion. Now with the increased use of different measurement devices, many types of data are available to analyze (digital, voice, imagery, etc.) With the improvement and expansion of the Internet and mobile infrastructure, collected data can be made available anywhere, anytime. With advancements in statistical methods, optimization algorithms, and AI machine learning, more powerful tools are available to uncover hidden knowledge embedded in the massive amounts of data. Therefore, it is expected that data analytics will be increasingly crucial in product management in the future.

Data analytics is a growing field of discipline. For the purposes of product management, its significance is in managing the success of product development and market penetration. Data on its own is not valuable. Its value is unlocked in how it is used to help solve problems.

Since data collection can sometimes be costly, it is important to know what data should be collected, how often, how useful the data is in helping decision making, and the cost of data collection so that a cost-effective data collection system can be designed.

A company can get a lot of data regularly through their typical business operations. For example: a daily sales history, customers' payment records, marketing and sales spending, etc. can be collected directly from business operations. To support its business operations, a company can setup a website so that customers can engage to inquire information, make complaints, place orders, etc. Depending on the nature of the business and the stage of product development, a company may need to design a cost-effective data collection system to collect data regularly that would be useful to help to achieve the business objective. In the early stage, the business objective is to achieve product-market fit and secure a strong position in its targeted market segment. In the development stage, the business objective is to expand target reach and achieve profitability. The data collection system that would support the early stage may be different from the one to support the development stage. In addition to the data collected regularly through the data collection system, a company may also want to collect relevant data to support a specific purpose. For example, in preparation for a product launch, it would make sense to collect a lot of market data to ensure a successful launch. Another example is when determining the product price, conducting market testing to understand buyers' behavior would be helpful. Designing a cost-effective and relevant data collection campaign is also important.

There are three major problems a successful product manager needs to know how to handle. The first problem is how to create product-market fit. The second problem is how to create and build a strong targeted product market segment. The third problem is how to expand into new product market segments in an intensive competitive environment. The focus of data collection and analysis is different when solving each problem. Also, solving each of these problems consists of a discovery phase and an implementation phase. The use of data analytics in each of these two phases is different. In the discovery phase, data analytics is used to guide iterative experimentation. A cost-effective data collection campaign should be designed to collect relevant data to support the discovery process. In the implementation phase, data analytics is used to adjust an implementation plan based on feedback. Sometimes it is helpful to collect specific data to supplement data from the regular data collection system to get a better assessment of the market situation to support implementation process. For example, companies conduct customer surveys after a product is introduced to the market for a period of time to assess customers' satisfaction levels with the new product. This data, together with sales and website feedback data, helps to refine the product and improve product-market fit.

Metrics are numbers that indicate important facts about the past and present situation. Metrics are obtained by analyzing historical data and computed via a mathematical model. The historical data is a collection of regular data from the everyday data collection system and specific relevant data collected on customers and the market. Key metrics, also known as Key Performance Indicators (KPIs), are numbers obtained from past statistical data that measure the performance of the product and current business activity. Product PKIs provide useful feedback to help product managers assess customer satisfaction with the product, and improve the product so as to achieve a better product-market fit. Business KPIs provide useful feedback to help product managers assess past business performance and provide information that can help to develop product strategies to improve performance. Metrics are a reflection of facts in the past, but they may not represent what will happen in the future. To project into the future in a new situation, a model that represents an understanding of the cause and effect relationship among all the variables would be helpful. This model could also be used as a guide to develop KPIs for the new situation. The iterative flow among data, metrics, and performance improvement is illustrated in the diagram below. The red dashed arrows indicate the feedback flow of how the new situation would require development of new KPIs.

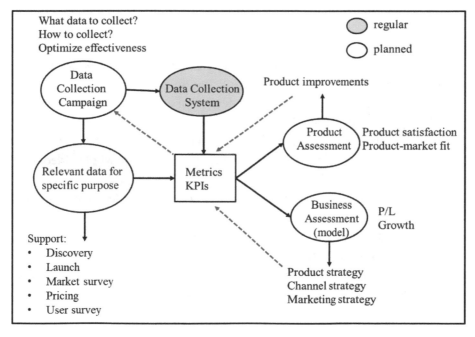

**Data, Metrics and Performance Improvement**

# Data Collection Campaign

Reaching many potential customers and getting high-quality feedback data from them is essential in getting product-market fit. Creating an MVP is the first phase in the product-market fit discovery process. In this early discovery phase, the question to be answered is what product features would meet the targeted customer needs. Begin with an assumption on the product features and verify these assumptions by getting feedback data from potential customers. But what data do we need? How do we get this data? How do we entice people to give us the data? How do we get this data cost effectively? These are important questions to be addressed in designing an effective data collection campaign for creating the MVP in validated learning.

Take the Dropbox example. It wanted to get users to provide data on whether the product would satisfy their needs and wanted the user to provide feedback to improve their products. But it could not get the product into users' hands and have them try it because it was still buggy. What did Dropbox do? It designed a short video of a product demo and put it on a website for potential users to watch to solicit their feedback. But there were still other important questions to answer to have an effective data collection campaign.

- First, Dropbox had to consider what group would provide the most useful feedback information that it needed. This would be the group Dropbox should focus on soliciting feedback from, referred to as a targeted solicitation group.
- Once the targeted solicitation group was determined, the next question was how to create a video that would entice their target audience to watch all the way through. If they did not watch the whole video, then they would not get a feel of the product and they might not provide useful feedback. Even if they watched the whole video, what would entice them to give Dropbox feedback?
- The next problem was how to write a description of the video that would attract the targeted solicitation group to click on it.
- Finally, where should Dropbox post the video to reach the targeted solicitation group?
- Suppose they were not satisfied with the feedback from the video; how would they determine what went wrong? Was the feedback data not useful? Did not have enough targeted people watch the video? What if enough targeted people watch the video but only a few of them give responses?

Analyzing the number of responses and the response content, another data collection campaign can be designed to get more useful data. In most startups, they would do the MVP validation learning process using trial-and-error iteration by first reaching a small sample of potential user first, learn from them and increase the sample size of potential users in later trials. In large companies, they may develop a data collection campaign to facilitate the MVP validation learning process.

There are many situations where a data collection campaign may need to be designed to collect useful data to support decision making. Before an official product launch, it makes sense to design a data collection campaign to obtain useful data that would optimize the impact of the product launch. After the product starts selling in the market for a period of time, data collection campaigns can be designed to engage with customers in regular intervals. The campaign can be directed to customers' feedback with the product experiences, announcement of events hosted by the company, announcement of next generation of the product, etc. Other situations where one may want to design data collection campaign to help in decision making includes exploring new market segment opportunity, product pricing, new product discovery, etc.

In designing a data collection system, an initial data collection campaign may be launched to find out what would make a cost-effective system. For example, in designing a website to collect feedback data, it is important to consider how to design the webpage such that it is the most effective in getting people to be more engaged and provide the desired information.

There are several methods that are commonly used to design an effective data collection campaign. The trial-and-error iteration method mentioned above is commonly used. Another method that is commonly used is A/B testing. A/B testing is a way to compare the subject's response to two variants: A vs B. For example, two webpages are created with the same content, but one with a response button on the right (A), and the other with the response button on the left (B). To test which variant is more effective in getting a response, half of the participants receive variant A, and the other half receive variant B. If variant A gets more click-through, then variant A is more effective. Likewise, if variant B gets more responses, then it is more effective. Obviously, if the difference in the number of responses between the two variants is too small, then the test is inconclusive. The process may be repeated many times to get statistical validation. Psychologists tell us that people's response to the same information could be different if the same information is presented in different ways. This is the framing problem: the same information framed differently could get different response. A/B testing can be used to find out the proper way to frame a question to get higher a response rate. Simple A/B testing assumes the group is homogenous. If the group is heterogeneous, then it is possible that variant A is more effective in certain segments, and B is more effective in other segments. A/B testing can be done with small samples from each segment to see which variant is more effective for each segment. In the final round of testing, different variants should be sent to different segments to maximize the response rate. A/B testing is widely considered to be a simple controlled experiment. It may be done before rolling out a final campaign to reduce costs. It is recommended to do a small set of sample experiences to find out which roll out method is more effective before the final, large roll out. A/B testing is commonly used in determining product pricing structure, assessing the potential popularity of product features, web designs, and email campaign.

There are professional experts that have many tools that can help in designing an effective data collection campaign to get more responses from a targeted group, but it is up to the product manager to identify what data would be most useful to collect to improve product-market fit and business performance. Depending on the situation and budget constraint, data collection can be conducted internally or outsourced to outside professionals.

## KPIs for Product Management

Key metrics are quantifiable measures used by a product management team to detect problems, set goals, and make informed decisions to improve product-market fit and business performance. Below are some of the most commonly used metrics in various product and service industries. They are by no means inclusive. Some specific industries only use some of them, and some may define their own to fit their businesses. They are grouped according to the intended use. The first group of metrics is used to assess product/feature popularity and help increase customer engagement level. Many of these metrics are related to web or mobile app products. These days all products should take advantage of the internet and the popularity of mobile devices to connect with customers, get them to engage, and solicit feedback. Designing an effective website and mobile app to connect with customers is very important to product success, and this should be considered as part of a one-time purchased product. This group of metrics are also known as product KPIs.

- **Customer Satisfaction Score (CSAT):** This is calculated for a particular product feature. The customers are asked to give a number 0 to 10 to reflect their satisfaction level with a particular feature. Sum the scores of all respondents and divide by the total respondents. The customer may also be asked to put a weight for each feature that representing their ranking of the feature's importance to them. It is required that the weights sum up to 1. For each customer, multiple the weights with the corresponding scores for each feature and sum them up to get a score for the product. This score is subjective and may be biased. If the distribution of the scores is not unimodal, then it implies the customers surveyed are not in the same segment. The weights customers give to each feature can be used to determine market segmentation. With enough data AI learning can be applied to help to determine and define distinct market segments. Sum the scores of all respondents in the same segment and divide by the total respondents in that segment will give the satisfaction score for the product in that segment. Survey design and the right timing to do the survey to get high responses are important to get an accurate measure.

- **Customer Effort Score (CES):** Like the Customer Satisfaction Score but is directed to a particular customer experience with the product. How easy is it to use the product, what is the purchase experience, how is the support service, etc.

- **Net Promoter Score (NPS):** This is a measure that reflects how current customers' experience might convince others to buy the product. This is commonly done via a survey asking the customer to give a score from 0 to 10. Those that give a score 9 or 10 are considered promoters. They like the product. They exhibit positive behavior towards the product. They may say good things about the product, remain loyal for a longer period, and buy more of any related products. Those that give a score 0 to 6 are considered as detractors. They dislike or even hate the product. They exhibit negative behavior towards the product. They may complain and even bad-mouth the product. They will likely switch if they find an alternative. Those that give a score 7 or 8 are considered neutral. Their behavior may fall somewhere between the promoters and detractors.

$$NPS = \% \text{ of Promoters} - \% \text{ of Detractors}$$

If there are more promoters than detractors, **NPS** is positive. What this implies is that current customers are highly likely to have a positive impact on others buying the product. If **NPS** is negative, current customers are having a negative impact on others to buying the product. It is also very important to conduct the interviews at the right time. Surveys conducted right after the product is sold may be different from the surveys conducted a while after the product is sold. Another consideration is survey design (i.e. how to design the survey so as to get a high enough response to make the estimates statistically significant).

- **Daily Active Users (DAU):** This is the number of unique active users per day. An active user is one that engages with the product and performs some valuable activity. What constitutes "valuable activity" depends on the business definition. For example, creating an account, buying something, viewing product information, and giving feedback could be considered as valuable activities. This number reflects how many unique people are engaged with the product in a day. In most cases, people take the average of DAU for a month when they refer to DAU.
- **Monthly Active Users (MAU):** This is the number of unique active users in a month. A user that engages more than once in a month is still considered as one user.
- **DAU/MAU:** This metric reflects some degree of stickiness. This is obtained by dividing the average DAU by the MAU for the same month. Getting 20% is considered to be good.
- **Average Session Duration:** A session starts when a user lands on the website and ends when either the user leaves or takes no action for 30 minutes. The session duration for a user is the time the user spends interacting with the website. Average session duration of a group of users is calculated by summing up the total session durations of these users and dividing it by the total number of users.
- **Bounce Rate:** This is the percentage of users who visited only one page of a website and left. Depending on the objective of the landing page, a high bounce rate may or may not be bad. If the bounce rate is higher than what was expected, the landing page may need to be redesigned to engage visitors, and hopefully to retain them. Average bounce rate range is different for different website categories. Bounce rate also depends on the traffic source. The traffic source can be email, referral, paid search, organic search, display, etc.
- **Exit Rate:** Exit rate for a specific page is the percentage of people that leave the website after viewing that specific page. Getting this may give some idea of what engages the customer.
- **Retention Rate:** The retention rate is the percentage of customers remaining engaged over a period of time. The plotting of retention rate vs time gives the retention curve. The retention curve is generally decreasing for as time goes on. The concept of engaged customers is discussed in the next session on product market fit.
- **Churn Rate:** There are two types: customer churn rate and revenue churn rate. Customer churn is the number of customers lost in a period of time. Revenue churn is the estimated amount of revenue lost due to customer churn. Customer churn rate is calculated by dividing the number of customers who have left by the total number of customers at the beginning of this time period. Revenue churn rate is calculated by

dividing revenue churn (i.e. revenue lost from existing customers in the given period) by the total revenue at the beginning of the period.

- **Number of Sessions per User:** This metric measures how often users come back and use the site. For a particular group of users, this is the average number of sessions per user per month. A high number of sessions per user implies that people are enticed to come back more often. According to a benchmark study by Littledata updated May 3, 2020, having a score above 1.6 is in the best 20% of sites and less than 1.2 is in the worst 20%.
- **Number of User Action per Session:** This keeps track of the number of times a user performs certain actions in a session. This can also be used to perform A/B testing to help in making decisions on certain features and understanding customer behavior.

The second group is used to assess business performance and help to forecast the business success of a product. These are business KPIs.

- **Monthly Recurring Revenue (MRR):** This is typically used by monthly subscription service businesses. To calculate, take the **MRR** at the beginning of the month, add gained revenues from new subscribers and upgraded current subscribers, and subtract churn revenues from lost customers and downgraded current subscribers. For businesses like Uber where income stream from customers is unknown and fluctuate, MRR is calculated differently. This is discussed in the next session on product-market fit.
- **Average Revenue per User (ARPU):** Divide **MRR** by the total number of customers to arrive at **ARPU** per month. When there is a change in pricing structure for the service, **APRU** can be calculated for new customers and **APRU** for existing customers before the change and compare these two to see the impact of the change in price structure.
- **Customer Lifetime Value (LTV):** For a subscription business, this is the average duration of a customer's "lifetime" with the company. Average gross profit per user (**AGPU**) is obtained by subtracting the cost associated with making and selling a product to a user from **ARPU**. **LTV** is **AGPU** multiplied by average customer lifetime. This gives a measure of average gross profit attributed to the future engagement with the user. For a business like Uber, the concept of average customer lifetime is not well defined and difficult to measure. Just because a customer does not use Uber for one month does not mean they will stop being Uber's customer. Maybe they went out of town for a long vacation and will use Uber again when back. Retention rate and money discount rate can be used instead of the average customer lifetime to reflect the profit attributed to customers' future engagement. The retention curve would tend to a value $\delta$ as time increases. Let $r$ be the annual discount rate for money. Then, LTV is given by

$$LTV = AGPU \times 12 \times \sum_{i=0}^{\infty} \delta \left(\frac{1}{1+r}\right)^i = AGPU \times 12 \times \frac{\delta}{r}$$

So effectively $12 \times \frac{\delta}{r}$ represents average customer lifetime in months. For example, if yearly retention rate is 40% and annual discount rate is 8%, then $12 \times \frac{\delta}{r}$ =60 months or 5 years.

- **Customer Acquisition Cost (CAC):** This is the cost of acquiring a customer. Take the total sales and marketing spending in a period of time and divide it by the number of new customers acquired in the same period. An example of the composition of **CAC** is given in the diagram below. This measures the effectiveness of the current sales and marketing program. By comparing **LTV** and **CAC**, the profit picture can be assessed to see if the current trend will continue. If customer lifetime value is less than customer acquisition cost, then the sales and marketing programs need to be improved, and/or the product should be improved, pricing should be increased and/or more money should be raised. But what to do and how to do it is left to the product manager and the company's executives.

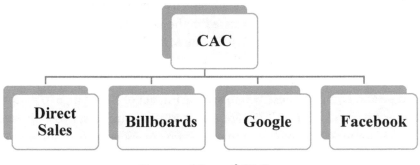

**Composition of CAC**

- **Lead Conversion Rate:** This is the percentage of leads converted to an account. Generating leads is the responsibility of marketing and converting those leads is the responsibility of sales. Getting good leads increases the lead conversion rate. Therefore, this metric directly reflects the effectiveness of the sales team, but it also indirectly reflects the effectiveness of the marketing team. Lead conversion rate from a website is the average customers captured through the website divided by the average number of visitors in a month. Lead conversion rate can be calculated based on each source where the visitors come from to determine which referral channel is more effective. Getting quality leads may incur higher costs but lead to a higher conversion rate, so depending on the business objective, multiple tests can be done to find an effective sales and marketing program.

# Product-Market Fit

Product-market fit is more than customer satisfaction with the product. First, there must be more than a few people interested in buying the product. So, getting a few people buy the product only indicates a good potential for product-market fit. When successfully selling too many customers, then product-market fit is closer. To achieve product-market fit, it's crucial to be competitive in the marketplace. There are two metrics that can give an idea of how good the product-market fit is – customer satisfaction and customer loyalty. Give each of them a scale of 0 to 10, with 0 being very low and 10 being very high. If there is more weight put on loyalty than satisfaction (say 2 to 1), then there is a matrix with product-market fit measure as below.

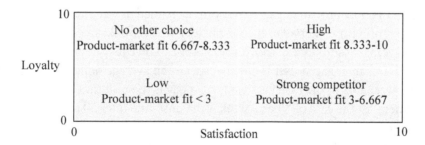

If the satisfaction level is low, but loyalty level is high, then it means that customers complain but they can tolerate whatever issues there are and will continue using the product because there is no other choice. This is not a very good fit, but customers are giving a window of opportunity to improve the product. This might be the situation for new product category just introduced into the market or products that have a monopolistic nature. If the product satisfaction is high but loyalty is low, this is more troublesome. The implication is that there must be a strong competitor that is drawing satisfied customers away. If the metrics measure falls on the left side of the matrix, the product needs to improve. If the measure falls in the right lower corner, loyalty needs to be built. The objective is to drive the metrics to the upper right corner. For a new product, it will most probably not be in the lower right corner. A strong competitor emerging to offer the same value proposition will cause the metric to move from the upper right corner to the lower right corner. It's crucial at that point to build loyalty, or else it may be difficult to defend the already captured market, even though customers are currently satisfied with your product.

By combining two product KPI metrics (**Customer Satisfaction Score (CSAT)** and **Customer Effort Score**) a number can be assigned from 0 to 10 to represent the level of satisfaction. Focus on the segment that reports the highest satisfaction levels. How is customers' loyalty measured? For a frequently used product, like Uber, Facebook, and Netflix, the retention cohorts are a good proxy for loyalty measure. For a regular subscription service like Netflix, to compute the retention rate, subtract the number of new subscribers from the total number of subscribers at the end of the calculated period, divide by the total number of subscribers at the start of the calculated period and multiply by 100%. The calculated period can be quarter or year and be computed for one period, two periods, and so on. The curve retention rate vs period gives a good proxy for measuring loyalty.

For products like Facebook, Uber, or SaaS, retention rate is hard to define. What is considered a customer? Would someone that signs up and has no activity be considered a customer? Depending on the business, an engaged user can be defined as one that has a certain average engagement per unit time interval over a threshold. For Facebook, an engaged user is one that has a certain average visits per day above a set number. For Uber, since it receives an income stream from users, an engaged user is one that spends an average dollar amount more than a threshold per week. So, in the case for Facebook, a day is the unit time interval, and one visit is an engagement. In the case of Uber, a week is the unit time interval and a dollar spent is an engagement. For software services, a month may be the unit time interval and a dollar spent is an engagement. The choice of unit time interval and engagement depends on the specific business. It should reflect the vague notion of what an active user is. For any customer, an engagement level can be assigned which is the average engagements per unit time interval from the time they became a customer to the present period. Let us define

$$x(i; p) = engagements\ of\ customer\ p\ in\ the\ unit\ time\ interval\ i$$

$$z(n; p) = average\ engagements\ per\ unit\ time\ interval\ for\ n\ unit\ time\ interval\ for\ p$$

$$= \frac{1}{n} \sum_{i-1}^{n} x(i; p) = engagement\ level\ for\ p\ for\ n\ unit\ time\ interval$$

The engagement level for customer $p$ can be updated for each unit time interval by the formula

$$z(n + 1; p) = z(n; p) + \frac{1}{n + 1}(x(n + 1; p) - z(n; p)); n = 1, 2, \ldots;$$

$$z(1, p) = engagements\ in\ the\ remaining\ first\ unit\ time\ interval$$

This metric reflects the engagement level of an individual customer. It is calculated from the time that the customer signed up with the company.

With this running engagement level for each customer, **MRR** can be calculated for a business like Uber where the income stream from customers is unknown and fluctuates. If a month is taken as the unit time interval and dollar as the engagement, then the equation for $z(n;p)$ is the average spending of customer $p$ after it has been a customer for $n$ months. This is also the average revenue the company can derive from this customer. Summing up the average revenue from all customers gives **MRR**. One can calculate **MRR** $(n)$, where $n = 1, 2, 3\ldots$ This gives a trend on the monthly recurring revenue.

This running engagement level for a customer can also be used to determine whether this customer is active at any time unit: if greater than a threshold then assign it 1 representing an engaged user, and 0 if less than the threshold. The table below shows this calculation.

| Threshold | 5 | | | | | | | | | | | |
|---|---|---|---|---|---|---|---|---|---|---|---|---|
| Month (i) | 1 | 2 | 3 | 4 | 5 | 6 | 7 | 8 | 9 | 10 | 11 | 12 |
| x( i; p) | 10 | 8 | 5 | 7 | 4 | 2 | 3 | 2 | 2 | 4 | 3 | 5 |
| z( i: p) | 10 | 9 | 7.667 | 7.5 | 6.8 | 6 | 5.571 | 5.125 | 4.778 | 4.7 | 4.545 | 4.583 |
| Engaged user | 1 | 1 | 1 | 1 | 1 | 1 | 1 | 1 | 0 | 0 | 0 | 0 |

By having a running engagement level for all customers, the number of engaged users can be computed at any unit time interval. To calculate the retention rate over a period of time, first subtract the number of new engaged users from the number of engaged users at the end of the calculated period, then divide that number by the total number of engaged users at the start of the calculated period, before multiplying by 100%. The plotting of retention rate vs time gives the retention curve.

Note that this depends on how the threshold was set. The threshold should be set to reflect what is considered a "serious" customer. The next question is how to turn a curve into a number. One option is to use eyeball estimation to assign the number from 0-10 based on the shape of the retention curve. This depends on the industry benchmark. In general, a steep downward slopping retention curve indicates a low loyalty level. If the curve is decreasing but leveling off at a certain level, then that level indicates the loyalty level. If the curve decreases for a short period and then moves up, then that indicates a high loyalty level. The curves below give some examples. The numbers are a subjective judgement based on the shape of the curves and the industry under consideration. As time moves forward but the window remains fixed, the shapes of the curves changes, indicating changes in loyalty.

The retention rate may fluctuate indicating that engagement is not uniform. For example, for an Uber customer, it may be up and down depending on the seasons, any traveling activities, and external events like Covid-19. Looking at the curve and matching with any external situations, a possible fit between the customer and the product can be assessed. This is where AI learning can be applied with enough data. Knowing which customer segments have declining engagement levels can prompt finding out why and improve the product and/or services to regain the customers.

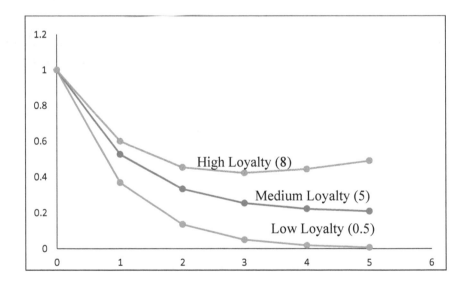

**Customer Retention Curves**

It's not immediately intuitive why the retention curve can move up as time increases. This is possible for businesses like Uber. In the beginning there may be some glitches, or in Uber's case there may have been reservations about the safety of getting a ride from someone unknown, and so the service is not used often. The engagement levels may be lower than the threshold. But as Uber's services improves and people are getting used to the idea of a shared driving service, engagement level goes up and gets above the threshold. So, in the beginning users are counted at 0 and later counted at 1. This gives rise to the retention curve moving up as time increases. For subscription services, the retention curve always moves down and levels off like the lower two curves shown in the chart above. In all cases, retention curves tend to reach a steady state level as time increases.

For a one-time purchased product like smartphones and cars, the percentage of re-purchase is a good measure of loyalty. But this cannot be measured before the announcement of a next generation product, and by that time, it is too late. Another metric is needed that can act as a proxy for customer loyalty in between product generations to help the product manager in product generation planning. When Xiaomi entered the crowded smartphone market, it developed a website that not only allowed them to sell their products online, but it also served as a platform for its targeted customers to engage in social networking, discussions on Xiamoi's smartphone, buy software and services related to Xiaomi phones as well as an array of other products, and enable them to give their suggestions on product revisions. Xiaomi tried to incorporate some of their customer's suggestions and provide weekly updates. The frequency of users' engagement in phone revision discussions, suggestions, and buying phone-related products on this website could be a good representation of customer loyalty level. Engagement can be defined as a certain set of activities customers do within a unit time interval. Then the above model can be used to define retention and get a proxy for a loyalty measurement. For a one-time purchased product, it makes sense to develop something similar to Xiaomi's website to get an estimate of each customer's engagement level. The idea is to associate the one-time purchased product with specific events that customers will engage in if they remain loyal to the product. Customers' engagement history can be used to estimate their loyalty level. Besides a website, regular forums for product news and social events could be another idea. In such gatherings user feedback can be gathered. The focus is to design the website and regular events to optimize getting useful data cost effectively to assess customer loyalty.

# Improve Product-Market Fit

The product-market fit is represented by a point in the satisfaction-loyalty matrix. A product roadmap strategy that would steer the point of the product-market fit upward or upper right would be a good strategy that would improve the product-market fit. The point is represented by two metrics: customer satisfaction and customer loyalty. Break these metrics into actionable inputs like product features, customer support, distribution channels, and price etc. so that changes that are made directly influence the value of these metrics. Then design experiments to find out the impact of changing these actionable inputs on the movement direction of the point in the satisfaction-loyalty matrix. Usually there is a small set of actionable inputs that are most influential to steer the point movement in the satisfaction-loyalty matrix. These are the key drivers to improve product-market fit. Identifying the key drivers and understanding how they influence the direction of point movement greatly helps to develop a cost-effective product roadmap strategy to improve product-market fit.

The relative weights that customers put on each product feature represents their ranking of the feature's importance to them. Therefore, it is probable that improving the features that have relatively higher weights would increase customer satisfaction. Customers can be classified into segments where each segment has a similar weight distribution, and a mathematical model can be built to relay feature improvement to **SCAT**. Using this model, cost benefit analysis can be done to derive optimal feature improvement. This provides a guide to design an experiment to validate the hypothesis of which features are most important and find out the impact of feature improvement on **SCAT**. The same can be done to assess the impact of improvement in customer support, distribution channels, etc. to **CES**. Combining these results in the impact of actionable inputs to customer satisfaction metric.

To find out the impact of actions on customer loyalty is a bit more complicated. First, decide what would be a good proxy for the customer loyalty metric. This is highly dependent on the nature of the product. Take Netflix as an example: is the retention of subscribed members a good proxy for customer loyalty? It may not be. There are many subscribed members that are not active in watching programs on Netflix, but they don't cancel the subscription either because they forget to do so or because the subscription rate is low enough that they keep it just in case. Take myself as an example. I am a subscriber of Netflix for many years. I do not watch Entex frequently, but my grandchildren who had been visiting me frequently watch Netflix. I keep the account just for them. Now my grandchildren are visiting me less because they are growing up and have many outside activities. I am now considering whether I should cancel the subscription. What may be a better proxy for loyalty is the number of hours a subscribed customer watches Netflix within a weeklong period. Then define an engaged customer as one that spends more than a certain number of hours within a week and develop an engagement model as described in the last section. Experiments can then be defined to find the relationship between actionable inputs to this engagement metric.

The right choice of proxy may depend on the pricing policy. Use Netflix as an example. Since its pricing is based on subscription, the revenue is dependent on subscribers' retention. An active user is more likely to remain a subscriber so the retention rate of an engaged user as defined above would be a good proxy to represent loyalty. However, if Netflix adopted a charge per view pricing model, then maybe average view per user would be a better proxy. Note that pricing is usually one of the key actionable inputs on customer loyalty metric.

# Product Strategy and Growth

The business KPIs reflect past business performance. By using averages of past statistics as metrics implicitly assume that the business environment is rather stable. In the early stage and the development stage, new metrics need to be developed to reflect whether the market has been growing and be able to provide guidance to develop product strategy to enhance growth.

According to the grabber-holder model, there are two groups of potential customers. One is the emotional group that responds to exciting marketing campaign, advertisements, and sales efforts. The other group is the rational group that responds to favorable user feedback. The dynamics goes as follows: cool product features and marketing attracts some of the emotional group. Some of them will find value in the product and become engaged customers, thereby influencing some of the rational group people to buy the product, and a percentage of that group become engaged customers.

$x(k)$: *number of customers from the emotional group in time period k*

$y(k)$: *number of customers from the rational group in time period k*

$z(k)$: *number of engaged customers in time period k*

$u(k)$: *sales and marketing effort in time period k*

$x(k) = \theta u(k)$

$y(k + 1) = \alpha z(k)$

$z(k + 1) = \delta z(k) + \beta x(k) + \gamma y(k)$

$\theta$: *cool product features and effectiveness of sales and marketing effort*

$\alpha$: *word of mouth effect through referral or review by engaged customers*

$\delta$: *retention rate of engaged customers*

$\beta$: *% of emotional turned engaged after the customer used the product*

$\gamma$: *% of rational turned engaged after the customer used the product*

The parameters $\{\theta,\alpha,\delta,\beta,\gamma\}$ depend on the strength of the product-market fit, effectiveness of the sales and marketing program, any referral programs, and characteristics of the targeted group. These parameters will change slowly during market development. The metrics defined in the previous sessions can be used to estimate these parameters. For every new customer, track whether they came from sales and marketing efforts like TV commercial advertisements, email marketing, the company's website, and sales events; or from word of mouth through engaged customers and their referrals, customer reviews, and social media. This separates the new customers into two groups: one from sales and marketing efforts and one from word of mouth. Those come from sales and marketing would be the emotional group, those come from word of mouth would be the rational group. Take the sales and marketing spending in the period divided by the total number of new customers through the sales and marketing effort to give an estimate of $\delta$. Take the number of new customers from word of mouth divided by the total number of engaged customers to give an estimate of $\theta$. The one period retention rate for engaged customers gives the estimate of $\beta$. The one period retention of new customers for the emotional group gives the estimate of  The one period retention of new customers for the rational group gives the estimate of $\gamma$

If there are enough data points, these parameters can also be estimated using the least square estimation method. In every time period $k$, the number of new customers is

$$n(k) = x(k) + y(k)$$

Linear least square method can be used to estimate the parameters in the following equation:

$$n(k + 1) = \delta n(k) + \alpha\gamma n(k - 1) + \alpha(\beta - \gamma)\theta u(k - 1) + \theta u(k + 1)$$

Cross check estimates obtained by both methods.

This model reflects that the lifetime value of a customer is much more than what is defined above. If network effects are included then getting a new customer would result in getting more new customers in the future through the dynamics. So, a better measure of the lifetime value should include the dynamic effects of getting new customers in the future but discount the income stream from these new customers. Also, it is helpful to divide newly acquired customers into two groups: from sales and marketing efforts and word of mouth. Define **CACM** as sales and marketing spending divided by new customers obtained through sales and marketing efforts (not including new customers from word of mouth). This is a true measure representing the effectiveness of the sales and marketing program, with smaller **CACM** representing a more effective sales and marketing program. By definition, **CAC** < **CACM** and the difference reflects the effectiveness of referral program.

The grabber-holder dynamic mathematical model is a system of linear difference equations. The dynamic behavior of this system can be analyzed using mathematical theory in difference equations. It can be proven that if $u(0) = u$ and $u(k) = 0$ , $k = 1,2,...$ then $z(k)$ and $n(k)$ will grow exponentially if $1 - \delta < \alpha\gamma$; will grow linearly if $1 - \delta = \alpha\gamma$; and will plateau if $1 - \delta > \alpha\gamma$. Conceptually this implies that if the launching program is successful, and no more spending on sales and marketing in the future, the inherent grabber-holder dynamics are completely determined by the metrics $(\delta,\alpha,\gamma)$. The term $1 - \delta$ represents the churn rate or the leakage of engaged customers in the dynamic system. The term $\alpha\gamma$ represents the organic new customer acquisition rate: the rate that is self-generated within its engaged customer ecosystem. **So, the inequality $1 - \delta < \alpha\gamma$ implies that the system induced organic growth rate is higher than the leakage rate, or the net organic growth rate is positive.** This will induce an exponential growth even with no sales and marketing effort. Sales and marketing effort would further boost the growth. If the two terms are equal, then the net organic growth is zero. The growth is proportional to the sales and marketing efforts. If $1 - \delta > \alpha\gamma$, then the net organic growth is negative. The effort of sales and marketing will have diminishing returns and thus the growth will plateau off. The other two parameters $\theta,\beta$ do not influence the inherent growth characteristic (exponential, linear or plateau). They influence the speed of exponential growth, the slope of the linear growth, or the plateau leveling off. The curves below display the dynamic trajectories for $z(k)$, $n(k)$, $y(k)$, and $x(k)$ by assuming the parameters are constant and the sales and marketing effort is constant. Note that in the situation where the organic growth rate is positive or zero, engaged customers will surpass new customers, whereas if organic growth rate is negative, engaged customers will always below new customers. The parameters $\{\theta,\alpha,\delta,\beta,\gamma\}$ are slowly changing over time, and thus estimate-able by assuming they are constant. The estimated values can be used to guide decision making.

Having a cool product to grab emotional customers is important to kick start the grabber-holder dynamic. This is achieved by developing a product with product-market fit po-

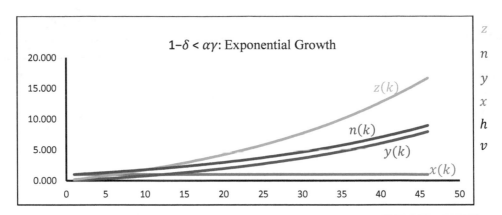

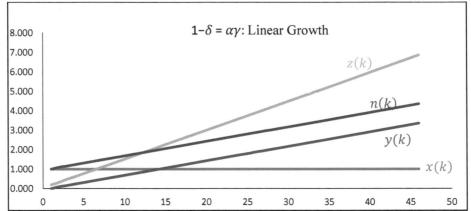

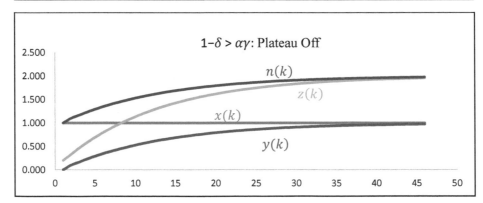

**Net Organic Growth Rate and Growth Characteristics**

tential and an effective marketing and sales program ($\theta$, $\beta$ would be high). Once this is achieved, the focus should turn to increasing its intrinsic growth. For intrinsic growth, the key metrics are retention rate ($\delta$), conversion rate to engaged customers ($\gamma$), and engaged customer word of mouth effect ($\alpha$). The retention rate is highly dependent on whether customers find lasting value in the product, competition intensity, and the ecosystem loyalty program. Conversion rate to engaged customers is highly dependent on satisfaction level and user experiences.

A measure of how competitive the product is in a competitive environment can be represented by ($\theta$,$\beta$) and the net organic growth rate. Large ($\theta$,$\beta$) would mean a short-term advantage in capturing emotional customers whereas larger organic growth would imply a long-term advantage in retaining loyal customers. A positive net organic growth rate also implies perpetual growth with little or no sales and marketing efforts. The effort in improving $\theta$ would level off, and thus the long-term strategic goal is to bring the net organic growth rate to positive.

The effect of engaged customer word of mouth may depend on what specific word-of-mouth program is setup for engaged customers to communicate their user experiences with like-minded customers and product prices. The product strategy is to do proper resource allocation to the product development roadmap, develop a word-of-mouth program, and develop a loyalty program to balance the short-term and long-term advantage in the early stage, with a slight emphasis on short term advantage. This is a grabber strategy. Once the market captured is up to a certain level, product strategy should set its goal to achieve a positive net organic growth rate as early as possible. This is a holder strategy. Through engagement with customers, find out what product features or attributes to improve that will increase net organic growth rate cost effectively. This will help determine a product roadmap for the next few years.

The customer acquisition cost (**CAC**) is inversely proportional to the effectiveness of the distribution channels. The effectiveness of a channel is determined by the average cost of acquiring a customer through that channel which is equal to the average lead conversion rate through that channel multiplied by average cost of getting leads through that channel. In the beginning when the product is relatively unknown, it is hard to attract effective distribution channels and **CAC** is high. As the number of engaged customer increases, it's possible to attract more effective distributors and reduce **CAC**. With the same amount of sales and marketing expenses, more new customers can be acquired, and thus more engaged customers. This will induce a cross network effect between distribution effectiveness and engaged customers that will speed up growth.

The model can also be used to estimate revenue and gross profit projection for short-term (3-5 years) projection. With a given pricing structure and cost structure, one can estimate revenue and gross profit projection for future time periods. For example, if the business has revenue streams from engaged customers, then revenue in time period $k$ is $z(k) \times$ **ARPU***(k)* and gross profit is $z(k) \times$ **AGPU***(k)*. If it is a one-time purchase product, then revenue in time period $k$ is $n(k) \times$ product price and the gross profit is $n(k) \times$ gross profit. Combining this with engineering, marketing, and administrative expenses can give an estimate of P/L projection. Using the spreadsheet model, parameters can be selected based on the industry standard to build a base case for comparison. Then you can vary these parameters over time according to the proposed strategy. Using this model will allow for a better defense of the projection for SOM and P/L because the model is based on a logical argument of dynamic consumer behavior and metrics that are familiar to investors.

# Concluding Remarks

An effective way to manage unquantifiable risk in the exploration phase is through the design thinking iterative process. An effective way to manage quantifiable risk in the implementation phase is through using feedback to make informed decisions. In both phases, the design of an effective data collection campaign to get useful data to support informed decisions is important. In the implementation phase, KPIs are feedback data to support making informed decisions. The grabber-holder dynamics model tells us that the product success hinges on the degree of product-market fit which is measured by the net organic growth, and the cross-network effects between distribution effects and engaged customers. So, in the implementation phase, the focus is using KPIs as feedback data to support making informed decisions on the product roadmap, distribution strategy, and building ecosystem loyalty that would drive up the net organic growth (improve product-market fit in the targeted market segment) and develop strong cross-network effects between distribution effectiveness and engaged customers that would speed up capturing of market share in the targeted market segment.

In the expansion phase where the focus is expansion into other market segments, KPIs can be defined for each segment and the network effects between segments. This is where big data and AI technology can be applied to develop new KPIs that would be helpful to develop a successful product strategy to enhance penetration into other market segments.

# Discussions:

1. Suppose you are a smartphone producer; how would you assess the loyalty of your customers?
2. What other KPIs can you think of to assess business performance? Think of KPIs that are company-specific and how such metrics reflect a company's business operating performance.
3. What other KPIs can you think of to assess product/feature popularity and increase customer engagement level? Think of product/feature specifics and give an example.
4. Can you give examples of products in each of the quadrants in the satisfaction-loyalty matrix?
5. Why would we expect CAC to decline faster during exponential growth compared to other forms of growth? What mechanisms are typically at work?
6. What metrics would be worth tracking to determine whether the net organic growth is positive, zero or negative?
7. What should you do if the net organic growth is negative? Give an example.
8. Why is the grabber-holder dynamic model a more nuanced encapsulation of CAC and LTV? How do they relate to each other? An LTV/CAC ratio of 3 or above is often desired for startups, but could there be situations where this blanket threshold does not make sense? Give an example.

# 6

# Cool to Good

Aerobotics had successfully developed a business that combines aerial imagery obtained from satellites and drones with its machine learning algorithms to provide early problem detection services to farmers, helping them monitor their crops, get early warning of potential risks, and optimize yields. Aerobotics started to provide services to farmers in South Africa in 2014 and had cornered 40% and 20% of South Africa's macadamia nut and citrus markets respectively, by 2019. In the last six years, Aerobotics expanded its operations to provide services to hundreds of farms in 11 countries throughout the world, including Australia and the United States. The new challenge Aerobotics faced revolved around expansion. When Aerobotics started the business, the challenge was to convince the farmers that their service provided them value. Now that the value proposition is accepted by farmers, the challenge is to determine how to compete with competitors offering similar service to farmers all over the world. Should Aerobotics expand by targeting macadamia nut and citrus markets one country at a time? Or should Aerobotics expand into many farming sectors in many countries simultaneously? Or should Aerobotics expand its data services to financial institutions that provide loan or insurances to farmers to enable them to make better risk assessment while they are doing business with farmers? What Aerobotics faces is a new problem. To address this new problem, Aerobotics needs to go through a new discovery and implementation iterative process.

In his book "Crossing the Chasm", Geoffrey Moore argues that there is a chasm between early adopters and pragmatists in high technology products because they have different expectations and different skill levels. Early adopters would be grabbed by the excitement of the new technology and have the skill to derive value from the early version of the technology product. Most pragmatists, on the other hand, do not have the skill level to derive value and would want to wait until the technology is matured and someone with the same skill level has benefited from the product. The success of a new technology product hinges on whether the company can improve the product and develop a market strategy that would "cross the chasm" between the early adaptor and the pragmatists. For those who cross the chasm, the one that can first create a strong bandwagon effect would become a de facto standard and would dominate the market. This theory was originated from the studies of IT technology products in the personal computer revolution era where disruptive technology innovation occurred frequently in this period. Whether this is applicable to general 0-1 product innovation is questionable. In a general 0-1 product innovation, something similar to crossing the chasm is applicable, but the chasm is not in market segment but in product team's mind-set.

As discussed in an earlier chapter, there are four major risk levels associated with product success. The first is market entry risk, the second is value proposition risk, the third is competitive market risk and the fourth is scale up risk. When entering a new risk level, the product manager faces a new problem, and they need to change the team's mind-set to address the new problem. Dealing with the first level risk is pre-market while dealing with the second level risk is post-market. The separation is clear. When entering the second level risk, the product team would switch focus quickly from product development to capturing targeted market segment to validate the acceptance of value proposition by this segment. To help in eliminating this risk, competitors offering similar or same value proposition would be more like "partners" that help to eliminate the value position risk. Competitive market risk starts to emerge when there are enough customers and economic agents that buy into the value proposition. Those that were "partners" before slowly turn into competitors. New entrants with strong financial backing may enter to compete by offering similar value proposition or a more competitive value proposition. So, the market structure that the product team is facing is very different from what they faced before. In dealing with the competitive market risk, the product team would need to have a new mind-set with a focus different from what the team used to have before. A chasm is created in the mindset of the product team: expand the market by improving the product or respond to a new market structure with strong competitors. The success of 0-1 product innovation hinges on whether the product team can cross the chasm in the mind-set. This requires the product team to focus on expansion by initiating a new process to discover and build a strong ecosystem that supports the value proposition appealing to the mainstream market. There is no clear separation between the end of the second risk level and the beginning of the third risk level. And so many early successors may fail to see the structural change and continue their path in product improvement to expand the market. Among them, the one who can first see the change and successfully adapt a discovery and implementation iterative process to develop a strong ecosystem to support the value proposition would be the winner in the 0-1 product competition.

In the high technology product case, when the product team expand the product from the early adaptors to pragmatics, the team is facing a new market structure. Therefore, the team needs to switch the mind-set from expanding the early adapter market via product improvement to discover and develop a new strategy that would capture the pragmatists. This occurs when the value proposition is eliminated, and the competitive market risk starts to emerge. So, crossing chasm arises in all 0-1 product innovation, but the chasm is not in market segment but in the product team mind-set. To cross the chasm, the product team needs to switch its mind-set from product improvement to a new discovery and implementation process to build a strong ecosystem to support the value proposition. The successful first mover will miss the opportunity to become the final winner in the 0-1 product innovation if it fails to cross the chasm successfully. The following historical cases are used to illustrate this.

## Missing the Boat

An American company called Ampex was the first to introduce the video tape recorder in 1956. It was a very big "box" system and sold for $100,000 or more. The customers were the TV stations who wanted to record a program and broadcast the playback in a different city. Sony wanted to develop one for home use. However, the technology was not ready for the home use market and Sony decided to enter the industrial market to improve the video technology which would eventually be applied to the home use market. The whole concept behind the product was "time shifting": allowing people to tape the program at one time and play it back at a different time. For use in broadcasting, picture quality was the key factor. At that time, the "information contents" were TV programs that were normally half an hour to one hour long. Sony introduced an industrial product, and instead of using reel-tape, it used a cassette—hence the name VCR (**videocassette recorder**). Sony's product was very successful and soon overtook Ampex in the industrial use market. Sony's success in the industrial market allowed it to finance and further develop the VCR technology so that it could reduce the size and the price of the product. Eventually, Sony became the first to crack open the VCR home market in the US in 1975. The product was the Beta format machine which was reasonably compact, had good picture quality, and allowed up to one hour of recording (it had two recording speeds, the slower recording speed would allow up to two hours of recording but would greatly reduce picture quality).

The vision projected by Sony's advertising promotion was "watch your favorite TV programs at the time you want." This attracted a lot of electronic fans to buy the product. Many of them liked the product and this started to attract general consumers who knew very little about electronic products but wanted to take advantage of the "time shift" concept. As a first mover and with a strong brand name, Sony quickly dominated the US market with close to 80% market share. However, close examination of its market penetration would reveal its limitation for growth. For consumers to derive the benefit of time shift vision, they must be able to handle the auto-recording setting mechanism. For those people who are technology savvy, they would find the auto-recording setting function easy to handle. But for most general consumers, this was not very easy.[1] The "ease of setting auto-recording" is the important attribute that would limit the penetration of VCR into the general mass market. To engage in product competition, VCR producers would compete in developing new technology that could drastically improve the "ease of setting auto-recording" attribute. This was a technical bottleneck that Sony, or other VCR manufacturer, could not remove easily. This constraint had put a damper in the VCR market growth. The VCR market finally exploded not by Sony or another VCR producers solving this technical constraint problem, but by a non-VCR producer who introduced a totally different grabber vision.

When Sony introduced the Beta format VCR, Hollywood movie producers sued Sony for intellectual property infringement in 1976. Sony fought the legal battle and won. In the meantime, movie producers introduced a new grabber vision: "Watch your pre-recorded favorite movie at home." This proposition did not require consumers to do any recording at all, so the attribute of "ease of setting auto-recording" became irrelevant. Also, to make the proposition more valuable, movie producers would roll out new movie titles a few months after the movies finished their first view cycle in theaters. When Hollywood movie produc-

---

1. Even up to 90's, there were services that provide a 1-8 code for specific program auto-recording setting. Each code was attached to a specific TV program and was published in TV Guides to help general public in setting auto-recording easily.

ers first put their movie titles in VCR tape, the price per movie title was about $90, which was much higher than the price that people were paying to watch a movie in theaters. Therefore, consumers' decisions to buy a VCR was primarily based on realizing the "time shift" vision. When the movie producers had put enough new and old movies into pre-recorded tapes, and sold them at about $90/title, a new group of entrepreneurs created a pre-recorded video movie rental market. Video store owners used volume purchase to cut down the unit price for pre-recorded movies and rent them at about $9.90 per movie title per day, which was lower than $12.50 that people paid to watch a movie in theater. Since a rented movie could be enjoyed by the whole family, usually more than two persons, the emergence of video stores made the value proposition of "watch pre-recorded movie at home" much more attractive to their neighborhood consumers as compared to the "time shift" vision.

The ecosystem supporting this grabber vision "watch your pre-recorded favorite movie at home" comprises of three ecosystems: an ecosystem for the playback device, an ecosystem for the rental service, and an ecosystem for movie production and distribution. Also, the ecosystem of rental service consists of a collection of regional rental service ecosystem. When a video store owner opens a store in a crowded neighborhood, it would influence people in that neighborhood to purchase a device to watch movies at home. Since no setting of automatic time recording was required, ordinary consumers found a new use for the VCR in watching pre-recorded movies. Many people bought a VCR just for watching rental movies.

In 1977, a new VCR format called VHS was introduced by JVC in US market. The Beta and VHS were two incompatible formats with different convenience levels in playback. Sony was promoting the Beta format that had a one-hour tape length, and JVC was promoting the VHS format that had a two-hour tape length (both in fast speed mode). The Beta had a slightly better picture recording quality but both have similar playback quality. Movie titles were recorded in high speed in order to assure playback quality. A 90 to 120 minutes movie would have to be pre-recorded in two Beta format tapes but it could be recorded in one VHS format tape. Small video rental owners, with limited storage space, found it more profitable to stock movie titles in VHS format only because it could carry double the movie titles. Movie watchers that did not have a VCR would buy a VHS format VCR so that they could easily find new movie titles in their neighborhood video rental stores. Movie watchers that already had a Beta format VCR would also buy a VHS format VCR because they found most neighborhood video rental stores did not stock movie titles in the Beta format. JVC also adapted an extensive licensing strategy to allow many manufacturers to produce VCR with the JVC format. Due to the economy of scale, VHS was also cheaper than Beta. So, comparatively, people derived more value from the VHS format VCR than from the Beta format VCR. The increase in VHS owners induced more video rental stores with movie titles in VHS format only. This created an exponential growth in the VHS format VCR, and it dominated the US VCR market in 1979.

Eventually, Sony introduced a two-hour tape, but the VHS format VCR had already dominated the US's VCR market. By that time, tape length was no longer the critical factor. Instead, market share was the major factor that determined the outcome of the VRC competition. Sony could not reverse the tide and decided to discontinue the sales of the Beta format VCR in US and became a licensed VHS format VCR manufacturer.

Sony's Beta had the opportunity to be the standard for VCR because it was the first mover in the consumer VCR market. Sony missed the boat because it continued its pre-set product strategy and failed to respond to Hollywood's value proposition. The initial success of Beta triggered Hollywood to launch a new value proposition "watch movie at home" that would leverage on VCR machines. This new value proposition is much more attractive than Sony's "time shifting" value proposition and therefore, the VCR market was disrupted. From the product point of view, Hollywood was not a competitor of Beta. But from the value proposition point of view, Hollywood is a very strong competitor of Sony. When Hollywood launched a lawsuit against Sony, Sony should have anticipated that Hollywood would play some role in the VCR market. If Sony had gone through the design thinking process and conducted some brainstorming, they might have discovered that speeding up development of two-hour tape feature to support Hollywood's value proposition would be critical. If Sony had the two-hour tape Beta format in early 1978, it would have cross the chasm and the Beta format might have become the standard for VCR market.

A similar but different situation occurred when IBM, being a follower, emerged as a winner in the personal computer. Conventional wisdom is to reduce production cost to increase profit margin. IBM made a deal with Microsoft on DOS that led to a disruption in the PC market. The IBM PC-DOS was co-developed by IBM and Microsoft and therefore they would share 50-50 its licensing fee. Moreover, they had to both agree on the licensing fee to any PC clone producers. In 1985, Lowe (the product manager of IBM PC) agreed to a deal proposal by Bill Gates where Microsoft could set the licensing fee for DOS in clones without IBM's consent and keep all the fee; in exchange, IBM paid nothing for DOS in the IBM PC. Since IBM dominated the PC market at that time, this deal looked favorable to IBM from the surface. Since Microsoft was also a software application developer, it had the incentive to drop the licensing fee for DOS to clones and make up by selling more software applications. When Microsoft dropped the licensing fee to clones, this created a flood of clones into the market and caused a disruption. IBM responded to this by its traditional practice: cut off clones by taking control of the CPU and the operating system. The ecosystem members that had supported the IBM PC (Microsoft, Intel, Compaq, HP and other large PC clones producers, DOS application software developers) joined forces to continue the development of the ecosystem that IBM left behind. IBM could remain as the major PC producer if it explored to find new way to deal with the problem that it had not faced before. Instead, it adopted IBM conventional business practices that led it to miss the boat.

## Value Proposition not Product Features

Product is a means while a value proposition is the end. When people started to buy into a new value proposition, what they are buying is not the product but its value proposition. Hence, to develop a strong competitive position in 0-1 product innovation, the focus is on improving the value proposition and not simply developing new product features. Here are some examples in the history of the PC industry development.

The value proposition of personal computer was gradually accepted by individuals and business professionals from 1977 to 1981 due to the collective efforts of Apple, Radio Shack, Atari, Texas instrument, Intel, Motorola, Microsoft, Digital Research, VisiCorp and many other electronic companies. They formed the supply side of the ecosystem for personal computer: some produced personal computers, some provided microprocessor, some provided operating system, some developed software applications, some produced memory chips, and some produced peripherals, etc. Each member in this ecosystem understood the role it played in delivering the value proposition of personal computer. Take Apple as an example. Apple II was the means to deliver Apple's interpretation of how the value proposition of personal computer is realized. Rather than simply buying the product, customers of the Apple II realized the value proposition – "to help people process and manage information." To compete and expand the market, Apple would need to focus on exploring how to improve its value proposition to the current customer group and the potential customer group it plans to capture.

In 1981, IBM and other big established computer companies entered the PC market. The IBM PC had an open architecture that provided opportunities for software developers and peripheral producers to offer complementary products that would improve the value proposition of PC. In terms of features, the IBM PC was like all other PCs in the market. But its open architecture enabled it to deliver higher value in terms of "to help people to process and manage information". With IBM having a strong brand name and a strong relationship with big corporations, the IBM PC quickly became the standard office equipment in many large corporations. This enticed many large office equipment distributors and electronic retail stores to sign up to carry the IBM PC. In a few years, the IBM PC dominated the PC market. Despite its initial success, the IBM PC finally lost the market when it turned its focus to increase profit instead of increase value proposition to the customers.

Apple II lost market share to the IBM PC, and Apple launched the Macintosh with the objective of regaining market share from the IBM PC. The Macintosh focused on delivering two new features. One feature is the exciting graphical user interphase (GUI). The other feature is plug and play. The Macintosh adopted a closed architecture that further discouraged third party to provide complementary products. So, in terms of providing value in basic needs, the IBM PC is providing more value than the Macintosh (See discussions in Chapter 4). As a result, the Macintosh lost out to the IBM PC.

Microsoft approached its expansion strategy not by focusing on product features but on value proposition. GUI is nice to have, so users would aspire to have this when their basic needs are satisfied. Instead of a completely new GUI, Microsoft's Windows was a creative imitation of the Macintosh's GUI. Windows ran under DOS, and Microsoft trained the DOS software developers to develop applications that ran under Windows. The Windows 1.0 and 2.0 were not successful as the chip was not powerful enough to support GUI. They were more like beta versions to get user feedback. The Windows 3.0 released in 1990 became a phenomenal success when Intel released 486 that was powerful enough to support the Window's GUI. Microsoft also developed Microsoft Office running under Windows to increase the nice-to-have value to Windows users. Microsoft continued to improve the PC value proposition and its Windows was treated as a support to improve PC value proposition as opposed to an exciting new feature.

Building a strong holder structure for the value proposition should be the goal in this phase of product development. For the product to establish a strong competitive position, it must be viewed by many as one of the best products to deliver the value proposition. Decision on product features must be based on whether they would strengthen the holder structure that shape the development of a strong ecosystem where all members within the ecosystem can derive positive net benefit and the ecosystem is self-sustaining. The product becomes a good product when all members within the ecosystem can derive net positive benefit and the ecosystem is self-sustaining.

# Two-Sided Market Model

With enough people buying-in to the value proposition, opportunistic agents that were taking a wait-and-see attitude before would now want to ride the wave. With opportunistic agents rushing in, this then creates network effects between the supply side and the demand side of the value proposition. This can be represented by a two-sided markets model as illustrated below.

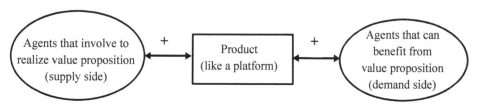

**Two-Sided Markets Model**

In this model, the product acts like a platform that links two groups of economic agents together: the demand side that will benefit from the value proposition, and the supply side that would collectively make the value proposition realized. The demand side is the customers that can benefit from the value proposition. The supply side is the economic agents that are involved in distributing the products and providing complementary products/services to enable the customers to realize the value proposition. As more customers benefit from the value proposition, word of mouth will go around and more people would want to enjoy the value proposition, and so the market demand for the value proposition will increase. This would draw in agents into the supply side to fulfill the demand. Moreover, the size of the demand size would in turn draw in new types of economic agents to provide products/services to further improve the benefit level of the value proposition. A mutually reinforcing cycle is set in motion to create a snowball effect. This creates network effects between the supply side and demand side. In the diagram above, the "plus" sign indicates that the network effects are positive in the sense that if one side increases it would induce the other side to increase. If the members in both sides are loyal and the cross network effects are positive, it would create a net positive growth among all ecosystem members.

The two-sided markets model emphasizes that the supply side economic agents should be treated as "customers". The market development strategy is not only focused in satisfying the demand side but also the supply side. Understanding the needs of the demand side and supply side "customers" would help to develop a strategy that would increase the network effects. A good market development strategy is one that coordinates product roadmap strategy and marketing strategy to create loyalty on both sides and "lubricate" the cycle of the network effects to speed up the development of the ecosystem. In other words, when it is noted that the ecosystem loyalty is decreasing and/or the cycle is sluggish, it is important to improve produce features and marketing efforts, with the focus on overcoming the obstacles that cause the problem. These obstacles may come from competitors, technology status, or external events.

For example, in the Beta case, movie rental stores preferred the VHS format because VHS with a two-hour tape would enable the store to make more profit, and a Beta customer would buy a VHS format VCR if most the rental stores stock up only VHS movie titles. Therefore, the ecosystem members for Beta are not loyal. In addition, the network effects cycle for the Beta format VCR was slowed down due to its one-hour tape as compared to its competitor with a two-hour tape. Sony could not come up with a two-hour tape format in time and thus completely lost out to JVC's VHS format VCR. In the Macintosh case, the Macintosh had a very loyal fan base, but its network effects cycle was sluggish because of the processing power and the fact that they did not have enough software application developers, while its competitor, the IBM PC, had many application software developers. The end result was that it was slow to build up a strong ecosystem as compared to the IMB PC and Apple faced financial crisis.

Loyal ecosystem members would retain the size of the ecosystem, but it is the network effects that would grow the ecosystem. Building strong network effects and loyal ecosystem members are both important; but, comparatively, building strong network effects are more important in growing the ecosystem. A mind-set that focuses on building a strong ecosystem is very different from a mind-set that focuses on product features. The winner would be the one that builds the strongest ecosystem, but not necessarily the best product.

One can get the snowball rolling by expanding the demand side or building up the supply side. Define metrics that would be a good representation of the network effects. Keep track of them and used them as feedback to guide product improvement and/or marketing strategy. Here are a few case examples to illustrate this.

- **Facebook:** Facebook started with a college campus and only opened its site to Harvard university students. Within two weeks, more than two thirds of Harvard students registered with Facebook. To most users, most of the value derived from joining the social network site came from their off network friends who were on the social network site. No matter how large a social network site is, if your friends are not on that social network site, it does not offer much value to you. For college students, most of their friends were from the same college or the same high school (these high school friends are at colleges too). For a Harvard undergraduate, his/her high school friends were most likely in other top universities in US. So, the logical move would be for Facebook to expand to Yale, Stanford, Columbia, and other Ivy League Colleges. After establishing a strong hold in the universities, Facebook then expanded to companies and other organizations. After Facebook had enough active users, it invited 3rd party application developers to build applications and make them available to Facebook users. This attracted more users to sign up with Facebook and spend more time in it. With more and more users, Facebook monetized its users by establishing its marketing platform, advertising platform, etc.

- **Apple's iPod**: Sony's Walkman was a very popular portable cassette player device to the teenagers in the 80s. Its value proposition is "carry the songs you like in your pocket". Most teenagers love pop music. At that time, many radio stations would play top ten songs every week. The teenagers would record the top ten songs in the cassette and with a Walkman they could enjoy the songs everyday while walking, doing homework, or engaging in other daily activities. So, to realize the value proposition, the key is how to get the songs you love into the device that you can carry around. When iPod was introduced, its value proposition was "carry 1,000 songs you like in your pocket". This is very much like an extended version of Walkman's value proposition. But to realize this value proposition, the key is how to get the 1,000 songs you like into the device. Instead of starting from the user end, Steve Jobs started from the music producer end. At that time, the music companies were facing threat from music piracy through Internet. Apple offered a value proposition that would relieve record companies' pain. Apple signed agreement with some record companies to allow Apple to download their music titles from iTunes and in return, pay the record companies a percentage of the 99 cents that iPod would charge per title. Effectively, Apple would become the distribution channel for record companies through iPod and iTunes.

  Apple designed a website that enabled customers to easily search music titles and download songs to their iPod. The iPod had a friendly user interface for users to find the music title that he/she likes to hear. With a slick design and Steve Job's charisma, iPod was considered the coolest product by Job's fans when it was first released. With the arrangement with music companies and convenient download from iTunes, all those that bought iPod immediately found value and became engaged customers. Their word-of-mouth effect was very strong. Retention rate of engaged user was high because listening to music is part of daily activities. So, the net organic growth rate is positive, and iPod grew exponentially. This fast growth also attracted other music companies and audio content providers to partner with iPod. The cycle sped up the exponential growth.

The iPod is an MP3 player, considered by consumers within the digital music portable player category. The first digital music portable that held more than 1,000 songs was started in 1999. Sony released a digital audio player under the Walkman brand name in 1999. There were many digital music portable players entered the market from 1999 to 2001. The value proposition of "carry 1,000 songs in your pocket" was slowly accepted by consumers during this period. The iPod entered the market in 2001 when the market competition phase started. All other digital music portable players focused on product features competition, and their growth was linear. The iPod acted more like a platform that facilitated the network effects between users and audio content providers to build up a strong ecosystem to realize the value proposition.

- **Amazon.Com, Inc:** Amazon started to promote the vision of online retail by selling books online in 1994. It was the beginning of the Internet age, and Amazon was one of the early entries into the B2C e-Commerce business category. Its value proposition was gradually gaining market acceptance. In 1997, Amazon went public at the time of the Internet bubble even though they were still losing money. In 1998, Amazon started to build up its fulfillment centers in anticipation of its future growth. In 1998, Amazon expanded its product offering: music and video in 1998 and video games, consumer electronics, home-improvement items, software, games, toys, and other items thereafter. With more product offerings, it attracted more online buyers. Amazon developed its website to facilitate online ordering to improve buyers' online ordering experience. Behind the scenes, Amazon started building the cloud computing platform to support scaling of its online retail operation and the backend fulfillment centers ahead of growth to facilitate the cycles of network effects between items of product offering and online buyers. But this also incurred high fixed cost that made Amazon not profitable. In addition to B2C, it started to let anyone sell nearly anything through its platform charging a modest service fee for providing customer service, discount in express delivery through Amazon's relationship with UPS, and Amazon payment service. This would increase variety in product offering, including long tail products. This would attract more buyers and increase buyers' average purchase volume. Amazon also started the third-party seller affiliate program that let anyone post Amazon links and earn a commission on click-through sales. This not only enhanced the network effects between product sales and buyers' spending, but also incurred no fixed cost. Finally, Amazon became profitable in 2001.

- **Netflix**: Netflix was founded by Reed Hastings and Marc Randolph in 1997. Hasting has a computer science background with a MSCS degree from Stanford University. He founded Pure Software in 1991 which merged with Atria to form Pure Atria. Pure Atria was later acquired by Rational Software in 1997. Randolph had founded computer mail ordering companies and had run direct-to-marketing operation at Borland International before becoming the VP of marking for Pure Altria. They were inspired by Amazon's e-Commerce business and came up with the idea of online home video rental business. At that time the home video rental was dominated by Blockbuster and Hollywood Videos. They had large video rental chain stores with good coverage in most US cities and towns. All these stores carried extensive movie titles in the VHS tape recorder format, and in 1997, they started to carry movie titles in the DVD disc format. Their business model is rent-per title-per-day, with a fine for late return.

Even though most movie titles were in VHS tape recorder format, Hasting and Randolph decided not to carry the VHS movie titles because it was too expensive to stock and too delicate to ship. They tested the concept of the DVD rental by mail, by mailing a DVD disc to Hasting's house. After receiving the disc intact, they decided to start Netflix as the world's first online DVD-rental business with 925 titles - almost the entire catalogue of DVDs at the time. It was the rent-by-mail DVD service that used a pay-per-rental model. Users would browse and order the films they wanted on the Netflix website, put in an order, and Netflix would send them to renters' address. After renters had finished with the DVDs, they would simply send them back. Rentals cost around $4 each, plus a $2 postage charge. Users could keep the movie as long as they liked but they could only rent a new movie after they return the existing one. It launched the first DVD rental and sales site, Netflix.com, in 1998. In essence, Netflix offered the same value proposition that Blockbuster and other rental stores offered. The difference was that it gave people the convenience of selecting the movie titles at home and do not have to worry about a fine for late return. However, they require customers to own a DVD player.

At that time, most family owned a VHS format VCR, and most movie titles were in VHS format tape. DVD were first introduced to US in 1997, and few families owned a DVD player by 1998. Also, VHS had a lot more movie titles than DVD. Most consumers had already gotten used to going to large video rental store to rent movie. During the weekends, visiting large video stores was a family event. Therefore, Blockbuster and Hollywood Video did not see Netflix as a credible threat because they believed Netflix only appealed to a very small group of customers. Those who found Netflix appealing were people who (1) owned a DVD player, (2) not living close to a video store, (3) very often forgot or did not have time to return the rental video in time, and (4) tech savvy people. Netflix found it hard to penetrate the market and in 1998 it switched to a subscription business model where it charged a low flat-fee for unlimited rentals without due dates, late fees, shipping and handling fees, or per-title rental fees. They also offered a free trial as promotion campaign. This helped them to attract and retain customers. However, the growth was limited by the small DVD player installed base. In 2000, Netflix had 300,000 subscribers but were losing $57 million in the year. Netflix approached Blockbuster and offered to be acquired for $50 million. Blockbuster declined the offer as it considered Netflix was a niche player and the price tag was too high.

The picture quality of DVD is much better VHS but the difference can hardly be experienced in regular CRT TV. Flat screen TVs with larger screens, higher resolution displays and better viewing experience started to gain popularity over CRT curved TV in early 2000's. Families that owned a flat TV would be more likely to buy a DVD player because it can allow the family to have a better experience in watching DVD movies. Families that had bought DVD players would also be more likely to replace its CRT TV by a flat TV if they did not already have one. The growth of the flat TV in the early 2000s initiated a positive feedback dynamic that induced exponential growth in both the flat TV and DVD players. These dynamics also helped Netflix to achieve exponential growth in subscribers. Netflix reached 1 million subscribers in 2003, 2 million in 2004 and 4 million in 2005.

Netflix went IPO in 2002 while it had 600,000 subscribers. Netflix first became profitable in 2003. Netflix introduced their streaming service in 2007 that allowed customers to instantly watch TV shows and movies on their personal computer. In 2008, Netflix partnered with consumer electronic companies to allow streaming to Xbox 360, Blue-ray disc players and TV setup boxes. By the end of 2008, Netflix had 9.2 million subscribers. Through partnering with more electronic consumer companies to allowing streaming on PS3, Internet-connected TV and devices, Netflix expanded its subscription members to 12 million by the end of 2009.

Note that iPod and Netflix entered the market to promote a value proposition which was already accepted in the marketplace. They did not face the value proposition risk and immediately engaged in market competition phase. In the iPod case, there were many similar devices in the marketplace but there was no dominant player. In the Netflix case, it faced a tough competition with large video rental stores. Its challenge was how to survive and find a new way to win over the customers. While the existing players were having a product feature mindset, Apple and Netflix had a value proposition mind-set. Their focus was not on product features but on creating a cycle of network effects between the demand side and the supply side of a two-sided markets. The iPod started the cycle from the supply side by being a distributor for music titles. Netflix started the cycle from the demand side by building up a group of loyal subscribers. They further built infrastructure to facilitate the cycling of the network effects. It is interesting to note that Sony, as the inventor of Walkman and owner of many record companies, failed to invent Walkman in the Internet era. Instead, Apple invented iPod to become the Walkman in the Internet era.

Facebook and Amazon each initiated a new value proposition. After they had eliminated the value proposition risk, they expanded by taking a value proposition mind-set instead of a product features mind-set. Amazon invested in cloud computing and fulfillment centers ahead of growth to support exponential growth. Both concentrated on growth to build up customers before finding ways to monetize from these customers. Facebook started its cycle from the user side, from Harvard students to other universities to companies. Amazon started the cycle from the supply side, from books to music and video, and subsequently many other items.

## Managing Network Effects

Managing network effects includes discovering the proper economic agents that would play an important role in delivering the value proposition, assessing the impact of one side to the other side in the two-sided markets, providing structure to facilitate the cycle of network effects between the two sides, and balancing both sides to achieve growth and profit targets. This would be unique in specific industries and business environments. So, there is no KPIs commonly used in various product and service industries. Instead, one needs to define KPIs specific to the business to help product managers manage network effects between demand and supply sides.

The dynamic cycling of a two-sided market is like a chicken and egg problem. One needs to start the process by first building up the supply side or demand side. To increase the chance of solving the chicken and egg problem, one needs to concentrate their limited resources to build a foundation in a narrow entry segment in either side to start the process. Discovering the proper entry segment in either side is crucial to increase the chance of success. Apple found that the record company would be the appropriate entry point because they had a pain problem that iPod could help to solve. Facebook found that Harvard students would be proper entry point because Zuckerberg was a Harvard student himself and understood their needs. Netflix decided on consumer watching DVD movie because it was easy to handle and provided less problems with mail delivery. Amazon decided to start an online book business because people buy books based on its content and not on its touch and feel. Note that iPod and Amazon started on the supply side, while Netflix and Facebook started on the demand side. It is also important to build a foundation in the selected entry segment so that it is effective to trigger the dynamic cycling process. In the Netflix case, the entry segment is very small. To build a strong foundation, Netflix needed to build a small but loyal customer base as a leverage to start the process. Switching price-per-title to subscription pricing structure helped them build a small but loyal customer base.

The initial growth in Netflix was highly dependent on growth in the DVD player market. One can view this as the drive from the supply side, but this drive was exogenous, and Netflix had no influence on it. It was an external trend resulting from technology advancement in high resolution large flat TV and disc player. Netflix took advantage of this external trend to build up a strong demand side. Netflix further invested in streaming technology to leverage this. Then with the prominence of the internet, Netflix could establish a two sided market with consumer electronics on the supply side and movie watchers on the demand side.

In the process of building network effects between the two sides, it is useful to establish a metric that reflects whether you have found the right target groups on both sides of the two-sided markets. For the demand side, it would be the engagement level of the users. In many cases, the engagement level is based on dollars spent, frequency of visits, engagement history, etc. The right target group in the supply side would be those that could increase demand side's engagement level and/or increase the growth of new users. Identify the characteristics of the right groups on both sides and dedicate effort to find members with similar characteristics.

Amazon started with book sales and built up a group of customers. User's average amount of spending per month would be a measure of user engagement level. When Amazon added music and video as new product items for sales at a certain price, it could calculate the increase in engagement level of each customer. These new items would have a positive network effect on the demand side if the average engagement level of current user increases and the growth of new user increases. With specific product cost structure, one can calculate the net profit from these new items. If the net profit is positive, then Amazon could add more new products in similar categories to boost up the engagement of users and recruit new users. Even if the net profit is negative, Amazon may want to add new products to boost up the user volume which will enable them to negotiate a lower cost for future products. So, the increase in average engagement level and increase in new user growth would be good metrics to gauge the network effects of the supply side to the demand side. The network effects from the demand side to the supply side is reflected by the ability to negotiate a favorable price with the supplier because of high demand volume. The net profit would be a good metric to gauge profitability. Net profit is influenced by the price structure on both sides. Adjusting the price structure on both sides would find the right balance in growth of the two-sided market ecosystem and net profit. Dynamic pricing on both sides is important to shape the growth of the two-sided market ecosystem.

Agents on either side of a two-sided market platform can chose to (1) stay out of the platform, (2) participate in only one platform, or (3) participate in multiple platforms. Scenario (2) is referred as single-homing and scenario (3) is referred as multi-homing. Agents make their choices among three alternatives based on cost and benefits they perceive for each alternative. Consider two competing platforms Amazon and eBay. People can buy from Amazon or eBay. So, the buyer is multi homing in e-Commerce. Most people own either a Windows PC or a Mac, even though some own both. So the buyer is closer to single-homing in PC. Software developers are closer to multiple homing in PC and mobile phones because most of them develop software applications for more than one operating system. It can be proven mathematically that if either one side is close to single homing, one platform would dominate the market. The first one to build a strong ecosystem would be the winner, and a latecomer would find it hard to survive. If both sides are multi-homing, then multiple platforms would share the market. A latecomer can build a strong ecosystem to compete. Understanding the homing nature of the agents is very important in pricing strategy for both sides. If one side is very close to single homing, capturing market share as quickly as possible is critical. Therefore, early pricing strategy on both sides should be tilted more towards growing the ecosystem. Securing enough VC financing to support the early growth is also important. Consider monetization after you captured the major market share. If both sides are multi-homing, then rushing to build the market share is not as critical. Proper balance between growth and profit depending on whether the company has VC backing or not.

## Manage Scalability and Monetization

At the time when WeChat was introduced into the market, there were many similar products in the market, MiTalk (by Xiaomi), Momo and Talkbox. WeChat finally became the winner because it could scale up with support by Tencent's internal cloud infrastructure. All other similar services like MiTalk crashed after reaching 1 million active users. So, getting a product with good product-market fit is important but the ability to meet the exploding market demand is even more important in securing a strong competitive position. In the early phase where the focus is to eliminate value proposition risk, getting good product-market fit is the key metric. But in the market expansion phase where the focus is to eliminate market competition risk, getting market scalability is the key metric.

Can the value proposition of the product spread to the mass market cost effectively? Can the product be produced fast enough to keep up with surging demand? Can the product be delivered to the mass market in a timely manner and be cost effective? These are the important issued to be addressed to eliminate the scale up risk.

In the earlier phase of 0-1 product innovation, the product team needs to be flexible in the discovery of a product with good product-market fit to an initial market segment. The product team would rely on personal relation and world of mouth to spread the value proposition of the product, and leverage on existing distribution infrastructure to deliver the product. Also, the product team members have no specific functional role and therefore, need to do whatever it takes to get early adaptors. Product scalability is not important in the early phase because value proposition of the product does not yet have enough customer buying in. Getting product-market fit is the focus in this phase. If it is a software product, the product team needs to write code that expedites the delivery of certain functions to respond to customers' needs. However, the code may be so rigid that the team may need to change it later to support expansion into the mainstream market. In the software industry, it is referred as technical debt, and the process of changing the code structure to support scaling up the market is referred to as refactoring. If it is a hardware product, the product team needs to produce product on a small scale to test market acceptability and modify the product to get it closer to product-market fit. In the expansion phase, the product team may need to redesign the product so that it is scalable and can be produced and delivered to the mass mainstream market in a cost effective way. This may include decisions like whether the company should build its own production line with enough capacity and where to build it, or whether to outsource to OEM in difference regions or license to other manufactures. Whether it is a software or hardware product, the product team needs to switch from passive product improvement responding to customers' feedback in a niche market to active implementation of a product road map articulating how the future product improvements would fulfill the value proposition that is accepted by the mass market. The product road map needs to include activities that would make the product scalable and enhance the network effects between the demand and supply sides of the ecosystem. Communicating this plan to the supply side and the demand side of the two-sided markets would enable both sides to anticipate the network effects and act accordingly to induce exponential growth.

To prepare for exponential growth due to network effects, building capacity ahead of time to support the growth is very important. The company can raise funds to build capacity internally or make arrangement to get access from third parties. Very often, the company may need to leverage on external infrastructure to support its exponential growth. So, timing may play an important role in the elimination of scale up risk. Facebook raised financing to build up server capacity ahead of its growth. Apple arranged OEM from China to produce the iPod. Amazon raised financing through IPO to build cloud computing and fulfillment centers ahead of its growth. It later let anyone sell product through its platform without having the product pass through Amazon's fulfillment center. In doing so, Amazon leveraged on small merchants' warehouse capacity to further scale up its growth. Netflix went IPO to build up cash to support express delivery and invest in streaming technology to leverage the Internet infrastructure to further scale up its growth. The exponential growth of Amazon and Netflix leveraged on the Internet development, and Netflix's success also hinges on the proliferation of high resolution large flat TV. When the VHS format of VCR started to get into exponential growth, JVC licensed consumer electronic producers all over the world to produce the VHS format VCR with their own brand name. When Dell entered the PC market with a build-to-order business mode, its scalability is limited because the cost of acquiring new customers was too high compared to other PC manufacturers with more efficient distribution channel. This also resulted in higher production costs because of the lack of scale. The higher production cost and acquisition cost could not compensate for the saving in channel markup. When Internet came along, Dell leveraged on Internet online sales to drastically reduce sales cost which allowed Dell to scale up their sales quickly.

Making the product scalable and building capacity ahead of time in anticipation of growth are within the product leader's control to manage growth. The actual growth may depend on external infrastructure or external events. For example, the scale up of Facebook, Amazon and Dell depended on Internet and the scale up of Netflix depended on the growth of high resolution large flat TVs and the Internet. Facebook, Amazon, and Netflix would probably not exist if the Internet was not accepted by many users as a scalable communication infrastructure. Dell was formed before Internet. It built scalable product and production capacity, but its scalability came only after the Internet was introduced. Netflix built its business leveraging on the Internet, but its scalability came only after high resolution large fat TVs and DVDs were adapted by the mainstream consumers. So, the elimination of scale up risk does not only depend on the product team's decision, but it may also depend on timing. Therefore, the ability to assess the related industry trends and to factor these trends in managing scalability is very important.

The final but most important issue is monetization on the ecosystem members. The dynamic pricing in growing the ecosystem is used to balance between growth and profit. It is very likely that when the scale is up to a certain level, the net profit would become positive. But in an intense competitive situation like ride share, it is possible that the ecosystem keeps growing but still losing money in the operation. One monetization approach is to find something that is not related to the product but to the customers that the company can derive income from. In the iPod case, it is percentage of music title sales. In the Facebook case, it is advertisement. The lifetime value is not just from product sales to the customer but the net profit derived from the customers' engagement level. In the iPod case, it would be the profit from sales of iPods plus revenue from music title sales. In the Facebook case, it would be the average advertising income that can be derived from an engaged visitor. In the Netflix case, it would be monthly subscription of loyal customers. In the Amazon case, it would be the average monthly purchase per loyal customer.

# 0-1: Discover a New Product Idea and Turn it into a Good Product

I want to conclude his chapter by summarizing the journey of discovering a new product idea and turning it into a good product. For ease of reference, the 0-1 Journey diagram is given below. I want to repeatedly stress the point that the product is a means to deliver a value proposition. So, a better way to look for good product idea is to look for a new value proposition that would create value to the society. Value to the society does not change, but the way to realize this is different depending on the infrastructure status, technology level and local environment. Therefore, one can discover new value proposition ideas by turning an old idea into a new one, exploring human psychology, riding the wave, and from variations of the already accepted value proposition. To believe that a new value proposition would be accepted by people is a leap of faith. Before it is validated that there are people buying into the value, this remains a hypothesis. What is needed is a process to validate this hypothesis from facts. This is done through the design thinking process. This is an interactive process with potential users to understand their needs, challenge assumptions, validate hypotheses or redefine value propositions, and identify possible solutions to realize the value proposition.

As introduced previously, turning a possible solution into a product would face four levels of risk: market entry risk, value proposition risk, competitive market risk and scale-up risk. In dealing with each level risk, an iterative discovery and implementation process is needed. The lean startup approach is to apply this process when the company faces a new risk level. This is a holistic approach that combines new product-market fit discovery, business plan development, stage financing, a go-to market strategy, and market expansion to create a new business.

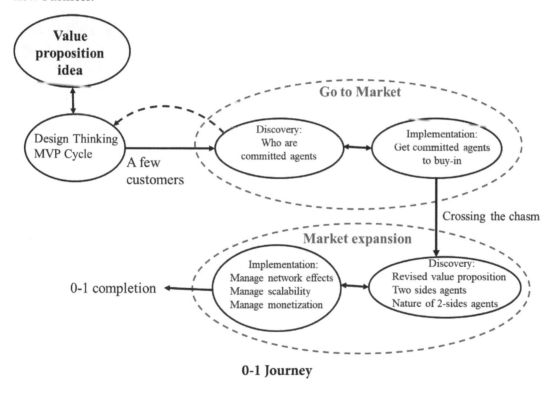

**0-1 Journey**

Minimum Viable Product (**MVP**) is an artifact that can collect the maximum amount of validated learning about the targeted customers with least amount of effort. This validated learning comes in the form of determining whether the targeted customers will find value in the value proposition that they are supposed to deliver, and if not, learn more about their preference. Iterate the **MVP** validation cycle and incorporate customer feedback in each cycle to develop a product that could be sold to a few customers in the targeted segment at a certain price. This would be a potential marketable product. The first level risk is eliminated once this is achieved and the product team is ready to go to market.

To turn the value proposition vision into reality, there are two big obstacles to overcome. One obstacle is that since the value proposition is new, the necessary infrastructure, complementary products/services that would enable the product to deliver the value proposition may be missing or incomplete. An example is the electric car lacking the recharging infrastructure. The other obstacle is that since the vision is just an ideal, pragmatic customers and economic agents would not buy-in unless it is proven real. So, one faces a chicken and egg situation.

There are two groups of customers and economic agents. One group is forward looking, emotional, and willing to try something new before seeing actual benefit. They are referred as the committed agents. The other group is pragmatic, rational, and only try something new when someone has derived benefit. They are referred as the opportunistic agents. To get started, focus on the first group within a targeted market segment. The targeted segment are people similar to the few buy-in customers captured in the **MVP** iterative cycle. Early marketing effort is to stir up excitement appealing to the emotion of committed agents to show how they would benefit from the value proposition. Some of them would be grabbed by the excitement and become committed agents. They have an interest to see many people accept the value proposition, so they would engage to help in refining the product to improve product-market fit. When they can derive value from the product, word of mouth effects will help recruit like-minded customers and economic agents to buy into the value proposition. This is a diffusion process originated from the early committed agents to get more people to buy-in the value proposition, thereby eliminating the second level risk. In this period, competitors entering the market promoting the same value proposition are helping to eliminate the value proposition risk. So, they are "partners" promoting the same cause. In this period, the business objective is to improve product-market fit and build ecosystem loyalty for the targeted segment. Use product KPIs as feedback data to support making informed decisions to improve product–market fit and eliminate the value proposition risk.

Once the value proposition risk is eliminated, the "partners" will turn into competitors and new competitors will enter the market. Some of these new competitors are established companies who believe the new value proposition may replace their current business. They may introduce a similar but stronger value proposition that is favorable to them. Because of these exogenous events, a new market structure emerges, and a chasm is created in the mind-set of the product team. To successfully cross the chasm, the product team needs to go through a discovery and implementation iterative process to revise the value proposition, discover new ecosystem members for this revised value proposition, and build a strong ecosystem to support the value proposition instead of focusing on getting better product features. The business model is represented by a two-sided markets model with cross network effects between the supply and demand sides. Define metrics of network effects specific to the business and use them as feedback to manage network effects between demand and supply sides to build a strong ecosystem. Proper management of network effects will lead to exponential growth and eliminate the competitive market risk. To anticipate the exponential growth, the product manager needs to manage scalability to eliminate the scale up risk. Finally, the product manager needs to emphasize monetization on the ecosystem members so the product can be self-sustainable and become a good product.

# Discussions:

1. Can you identify different ecosystems that play a role in supporting the smartphone value proposition? Can you specify the members within each ecosystem?
2. When the value proposition risk is eliminated and you are entering into the competitive risk phase, what kind of changes in the external environment would you expect? Give some examples from cases you are familiar with.
3. Can you give another example of a product that was very successful in the early stage but missed the boat when it went into the expansion phase? Can you explain why?
4. What is the difference between value proposition competition and product competition? Can you give some examples other than those discussed in this chapter? How would this impact on your expansion strategy decision?
5. Consider a product you like. From the framework of a two-sided market model, who are its supply-side agents? Who are the demand-side agents? How would you develop an expansion strategy?
6. Give some examples of products that are more single homing in either the supply side or the demand side. Given some examples of products that are multi-homing on both sides. When would we have a winner takes all situation?
7. Netflix's growth was highly dependent on growth in the DVD player market. What kind of risk Netflix is facing? Controllable or uncontrollable? How should Netflix reduce this risk?

# 7

# One to N
# Product Expansion

Cars were introduced with the value proposition "horseless carriage to provide transportation". To fulfill this value proposition, road infrastructure was required before cars could be a means to fulfill the value proposition. The steam car was the first to appear in the market, followed by electric cars, and finally gasoline cars. Eventually, gasoline cars dominated the market, not because gasoline cars were better than electric or stream cars, but because a strong holder structure was developed that supported gasoline cars as a means to deliver the greatest benefit in the value proposition. By 1920, when people talked about the car, they meant the gasoline car. The gasoline car became the de facto product category representing the car in delivering the value proposition "horseless carriage to provide transportation". Product is a term for something concrete that people can feel and experience, while value proposition is a term that is vague and only exists in our mind. With the supporting holder structure taken for granted, gradually, people replaced the end by the means. Further improvement on the product would be equivalent to increase the benefit of the value proposition. In 0-1, the ecosystem rather than the product plays a more important role in realizing the benefit of the value proposition. Therefore in 0-1, the competition is in building a stronger ecosystem to support the value proposition. In 1-N where the established holder structure is in place and is taken for granted, product category plays the key role in delivering value proposition. Therefore, in 1-N, the competition is among products in the same product category.

While car producers were the agents that played the central role in promoting the value proposition "horseless carriage to provide transportation", there were many other economic agents that played the role to provide holder support to the value proposition. All those products and services that played the supporting role to provide a strong holder structure of gasoline cars would become the new product/service categories. In addition to the gasoline car becoming a new category, gas stations, car dealers, garages, fast food chains and many others became new categories. In the 0-1 personal computer innovation, new product categories emerged such as PC, Operating System, CPU, office application software, PC peripherals, PC printers, etc. It is interesting to note that some of these categories have a dominant player, while others have many similar sized players. For example, in the PC case, there were many PC and PC peripherals players; while one dominant OS and CPU player. For these two types of product category, the 1-N product expansion strategy would be very different.

## Product Category and Product Attributes

Product category is defined as a type of product recognized by people as the means to deliver a specific value proposition. A cup is a product category. We recognize it as an open usually bowl-shape drinking vessel. The value proposition it delivers is quenching thirst. A personal computer is a product category. We recognize it as a multi-purpose computing machine whose size, capability and price made it feasible for individual use. The value proposition it delivers is "to help people process and manage personal information". A car is a product category. We recognize it as a four-wheel vehicle with an engine to drive the vehicle. The value proposition it delivers is "to provide convenient transportation". There is a hierarchical structure in product category. Computer as a product category is above personal computer in the hierarchical structure because a personal computer has function of a computer but delivers a different value proposition. Personal computers, servers, and mainframes are product categories under the computer category. Each of these categories deliver different value propositions. Gasoline cars and electric cars are not considered as under the car category but considered as variants of the car category because they deliver the same value proposition. Sedan, truck and SUV are considered under the same car category. When two product categories deliver the same valuation, then there is a possibility that one will replace the other and become the de facto standard for delivering that value proposition. In the car industry, looking at its history, the gasoline car category became the de facto standard for the car category around 1920. Now the electric car is coming back as a viable competing product category.

People buy value propositions, not products. So, people look for a product in a certain product category to fulfill their needs. Product features and product attributes are two different concepts. A product feature is a specific piece of functionality that has a corresponding benefit or set of benefits for the user. Users can derive benefits from using that functionality. So, a product feature is part of the product and represents what we can do with the product to derive benefit. Product attributes are characteristics that define a particular product and how they influence people's purchasing decision. Product attributes can be tangible or intangible; they can be part of product components or not part of the product components; and it can be descriptive or can have a set of specific numbers. An example of "not part of product components" is the number of engaged ecosystem members. So, product features can be part of product attributes. The hierarchical structure of product attributes is based on how they would influence people's decision with the product: whether to buy the product or have a business relationship with the product. A tree structure for a product in a particular category is illustrated below.

Attributes influence people's decision in engaging with the product

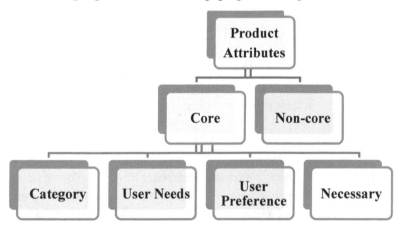

**Tree Structure for Product Attributes**

First, the attributes are broken into core and non-core attributes. Core attributes are those all products in that category must have. Non-core attributes are those that are not necessary to be included in all products in that category. For example, for a car, a sunroof is non-core. The core attributes are further decomposed into Category Attributes, User Needs Attributes, User Preference Attributes and Necessary Attributes. Each of these are further described below.

Category Attributes are those that reflect the product's effectiveness in delivering the value proposition in that product category. For example, Windows is an operating system category. Its effectiveness in delivering its value proposition is characterized by the types of software applications running under it, the number of engaged users, the protection from hacker attacks, and efficiency in managing hardware/software resources. These are its category attributes. For a personal computer, its category attributes are its operating system, CPU and engaged ecosystem members (users, software developers, peripherals producers, distributors, etc.). Note that the product ecosystem is a category attribute.

User Needs Attributes are those that reflect how the product is aligned with user needs and experiences. For example, how user-friendly it is, how easy to carry around, quality of the product, and aesthetic design of the product, etc. Depending on how the user would use the product to experience the value proposition, certain user needs attributes would facilitate in realizing the value. If you need to carry your personal computer around in performing your daily information management activities, you need a computer that is easy to carry around. You may want one with high reliability and at least water-resistant or better. In the example of a hand phone for construction work, user needs attributes are very loud ring tone, heavy vibration, and speaker volume. Depending on the value proposition that the product category supports, an attribute can be regarded as category or user needs attribute. For example, if VCR is regarded as a product category that supports "time shift", then tape length is regarded as a user needs attribute. On the other hand, if VCR is regarded as product category that supports "watch movie at home", then the 2-hour tape is regarded as a category attribute.

User Preference Attributes are those that reflect a user's preference on the look, feel, taste, and even smell of the product. Color is a typical preference attribute. Young people like cars with bright color. Established businessmen like cars with black or dark brown color. For certain products, surface texture is a user preference attribute. Some prefer a rough surface while others prefer a smooth surface. Some prefer a shiny surface while others prefer a dull surface. For food products, taste and textures are user preference attributes. Some like it hot, sweet, or sour, etc. Some like soft, crunchy, mushy, etc. For perfume and cologne products, smell is a user preference attribute.

Necessary Attributes are those that people take for granted for the product in the category and these attributes do not influence people's purchasing decisions because all products in the same category have these. For example, all personal computers come with a keyboard. People take for granted that all personal computers should have a keyboard and therefore in their purchasing decision, the keyboard plays no role. Necessary attributes are not important from a buyer's perspective but important from producer's perspective.

For an attribute that is part of a product, its attribute configuration is a specific characterization of that attribute that the company specifies. A product configuration is a specific characterization of product attributes that the company can specify. Some of these characterizations are descriptive. For example, a car with a red color. Some of them are a set of numbers. For example, a cardboard box size 12" x 12" x 6", or an iPhone with 5.5" screen size. Different product configurations of a specific product category would appeal to different people. For example, young people may prefer faster cars while older people may prefer safer cars.

In the 1-N product expansion, the product manager faces two important decisions. One is the product variety decision: what configurations and how many. The other one is product life cycle decision: when to introduce the next generation product. Understand how product attributes are viewed from different perspectives (buyers' perspective, producer's perspective, and potential partners' perspective) plays an important role in 1-N product expansion decisions.

## Product Attributes from Different Perspectives

From a buyers' perspective, the main reason they buy from a specific category is that they would want to enjoy the value proposition delivered by that category. The first consideration, therefore, is the category attributes. For most people, the ecosystem attribute is the one they would pay more attention to: how many people are using it and how many economic agents are supporting it. These attributes would reflect, indirectly, how others are deriving benefit from the value proposition. So, the product that emerged as the winner in the 0-1 competition would be more attractive. The more sophisticated buyers might take other category attributes that directly reflects the product's effectiveness in delivering the value proposition into consideration. After considering the category attributes, user needs attributes would be the next set of attributes to be considered. Buyers would consider how the product is to be used in their daily life and determine the importance of certain user needs attributes. Thereafter, non-core attributes would be considered. A non-core attribute can be packaged into the product or offered as an option. In some cases, buyers want to have the non-core attributes just to distinguish from the common product. In other cases, an option is included because it can deliver special additional value. Since these attributes influence buyers' perception on the value of using the product, these attributes determine the price they are willing to pay for the product.

The last set of attributes to be considered is the user preference attributes. Like buying a car, after you have selected a car model with all the options, you choose the color of the car. While you negotiate a price for a particular car model with options, you do not negotiate for its color. The price is the same for all available color. If the color you prefer is not available, you may choose a different color. User preference attributes do not influence the value of using the product, they just relate to personal like or dislike. In most cases, buyers would not want to pay extra for these attributes. A buyer can be rigid or flexible with regards to these attributes. For example, a buyer may insist a car with a red color or prefer a red color but would consider other color if red is not available. The former is rigid, and the latter is flexible.

From a producer's perspective, the product competitiveness is derived mainly from the category attributes. If the product emerged as a winner in the 0-1 competition, it has an initial competitive advantage in the 1-N expansion. To maintain this advantage, investments to improve attributes directly reflects the product's effectiveness in delivering the value proposition is the key driver.

User needs attributes play the role of attracting users in a different segment that uses the product differently to derive value proposition. These attributes customize the product to match the customer's needs and experiences. Through offering product variety with many different user needs configurations, the product would attract customers in many different segments and may be able to charge a higher price because of better product-user fit but would simultaneously incur higher unit cost. In an oligopolistic situation where all the major players are on par in category attributes, user needs attributes would be the source to derive differentiation.

Preference attributes play the role of attracting users with different tastes. Most people do not want to pay for preference attribute. So, a preference attribute with many configurations may attract more people with different tastes but can be costly.

Necessary attributes are treated as "necessary evil". We must have them, but no one would pay for them. So, try to make them available at the lowest possible cost.

Non-core attributes can be packaged into the product or offered as an option. Packaged into the product may or may not appeal to more customers, but it would increase cost. In many cases, this is used to elevate the status symbol of the customers. For example, many luxury cars come with sunroof as the standard. Huawei packaged the best zooming camera in its smartphone. Such non-core attributes not only elevate the product status, but also gives the company the possibility of charging a premium price. Non-core attributes may be offered as an option that requires the buyer to pay extra. Non-core attributes can also be a source of deriving differentiation.

From the potential partners' perspective, their main concern is whether they can derive business opportunity through the product. The product ecosystem is the one they would be mostly interested in. They are interested in whether they can offer products or services to further improve the product's user needs attributes and non-core attributes.

# 1 to N Product Expansion Decisions

In the 0-1 competition, the focus is on developing a strong ecosystem to support the value proposition. In the 1-N product expansion, the focus is on capturing more market segments and improving or maintaining competitive position. Comparatively, Apple's iPhone has less configurations than Samsung's Galaxy. Is more necessarily better? Some argue that a smaller product line is better because one can have economies of scale by having less configurations and it is also easier to manage production and distribution. Some argue that more is better because each configuration can better fit a market segment's user experiences. The answer may depend on the specific configurations and people's aspiration levels. When the car was first accepted in the US as a means to provide transportation, everyone desired a car with a low price. Ford's one model strategy won out because it could derive economies of scale and therefore Ford's car had a price advantage. As more people came to own a car, General Motor's multiple car lines for people with different social status won because configurations that matched people's aspiration became the determining factor.

Product variety does not focus on category attributes and necessary attributes, but on user needs attributes, user preference attributes and non-core attributes. Decisions on a specific configuration is based on a differentiation strategy and a cost and benefit analysis. Apply the design thinking process to design a differentiation strategy and to determine specific targeted segments. Use the customer's perspective to estimate the benefit of a particular configuration. The cost of a particular configuration depends not only on supply chain ecosystem, in-house or outsource production, and market locations, but it also depends on the scale and scope of configurations to be considered. More configurations would have a better match with different market segments' needs and thus may capture higher total market share but may incur higher operating and production cost because of the lack of scale in each configuration. Less variety would have economies of scale but may reduce market demand because some customers could not find a configuration that matches their needs. Given targeted market segments, one can perform a cost benefit analysis to obtain the optimal set of configurations based on cost-benefit trade-offs. Given a set of configurations, one can obtain the market segments best served by a specific set of configurations. Product variety decision is made through an iterative cost and benefit analysis (see diagram below for a straightforward illustration).

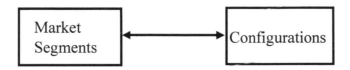

**Iterative cost and benefit analysis**

The concept of product life cycle is based on the life of a product in the market with respect to its sales and profit. It is the period that a product is introduced to when it is taken off the market. In general, a product life cycle is broken into four stages: introduction, growth, maturity, and decline. See diagram below.

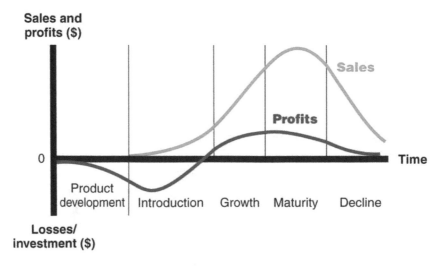

**Product Life Cycle Curve**

Product development is the phase where investments are made in developing a product that is ready to sell in the market, introduction is the phase where investments are made in marketing to let people know about the product. If the product is successful, it moves into the growth stage where market demand is increasing and investment on capacity to support the growth is required. In the mature stage, marketing cost and production cost are reducing, and this is the most profitable stage in the whole cycle. As more competitors enter the market, market share would be eroded, and price war would lead to decline in profit margin.

What is iPod's life cycle? The iPod had many "generations", and each generation has its product life cycle. Each generation has the revenue and profit curves as illustrated above. The concept of a product category life cycle can be defined as the life of a product category in the market with respect to its sales and profit. So, for a product category with many generations, the revenue and profit for the category at a particular time is the sum of sales and profit for all generations at that time. (See diagram below). A new generation product does not necessarily replace the old generation product. For example, when iPod 2.0 was introduced, iPod 1.0 was still selling in the market. Gillette had more than one razor brands selling in the market, and they are all in the same product category. Introducing new generations in a product category is a way to shape the revenue and profit curves for a product category, and thus a way to manage the product category life cycle. The introduction of product category life cycle is the 0-1 development, while 1-N expansion is the growth and the maturity stages. A product manager's main responsibility is to manage the 0-1 development to build a strong ecosystem, and leverage on the ecosystem to introduce new generations to prolong the maturity period in the product category life cycle.

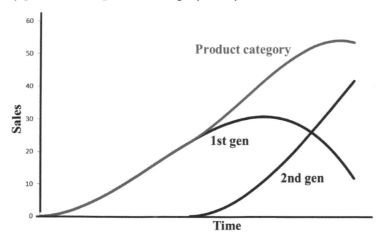

**Product Category Life Cycle Curve with Two Generations**

When the holder structure for the value proposition is in place and is taken for granted, people would replace the value proposition by its product category. Many consider 1-N competition to occur in the product features realm. The conventional practice is to go through customer surveys and ask customers to assign relative weights to the features. In new product generation decisions, these relative weights would be used to determine the portfolio of product variations that would maximize investment return. But this is just the fine-tuning of the product variations from the cost benefit perspective and would not lead to developing significant competitive advantages in the 1-N competition. Even though improvement of product features is important in 1-N competition, one should not forget that it is the value proposition that would drive people's demand not product features. In 1-N competence, the focus should be on improvement of product attributes, not just product features, to secure and maintain a strong market position

The purpose of a product variety design decision is to develop differentiation and reach out to more market segments in the market expansion. The focus is on user needs attributes, user preference attributes and non-core attributes. The product manager's goal in managing the product variety is to reach as many market segments as possible, cost effectively and within budget constraint. The purpose of the product category life cycle decision is aimed to maintain market leadership position throughout the category life cycle. The focus is on category attributes and non-core attributes. The product manager's goal in managing the product category life cycle is to make the proper product life cycle decision and product variety decision to improve profit and maintain market competitiveness. Depending on the market structure and the market position of the company, the decision focus to maintain market competitiveness is very different. One market structure is that there is a dominant player, another structure is that there are several large players with equal market share. Appropriate 1-N product expansion strategy under the two different market structure will be explored in the next two sessions.

## Dominant Leader Market Structure

If the company emerged as a dominant player in the 0-1 competition, then it must have built a much stronger holder structure as compared to other competitors. To maintain its leadership position, it would allocate majority of total investment to further improve key drivers in category attributes. The remaining investment would be used to broaden its market reach. It would develop an optimal portfolio of product variety to maximize profit from broadening market reach within their investment budget constraint. In doing so, it would strengthen the holder structure for the value proposition that enable the leader to respond to a frontal attack by its competitors offering better products with the same value proposition.

Introduction of a new generation is controlled by the desire to pace the improvement of key drivers in category attributes and to maintain the market leadership position. The improvement of key drivers in category attributes would run into diminishing returns, and people would aspire to the next level of hierarchical needs. If the key drivers for this next level needs are different from those for the lower-level needs, this could be an inflection point for the product. If the product leader can foresee this early and direct the team's attention to the improvement of those new key driver category attributes, the company could latch on to a new phase of growth. If the product manager fails to see this or the company does not have the skills and capabilities to latch onto this opportunity, a new competitor with the skill and capability to fulfill the next level needs might disrupt the company's market leadership position. Therefore, when the improvement in the key driver starts running into diminishing returns, the product leader should initiate a design thinking process to discover what would be the new key drivers in category attributes and make a decision to deal with this potential inflection point. Let us examine the history of Gillette's razor product line and see how it developed its strategy to maintain its market dominant position for more than 100 years.

King Camp Gillette came up with a new idea of safety razor in 1901 and founded American Safety Razor Company, which was later renamed Gillette Company. A safety razor is a shaving implement with protective devices to reduce the level of skill needed in injury-free shaving. A protective guard to a regular straight razor was commonly used at that time. Such safety razor required stropping before use and after time needed to be sharpened. Gillette invented a double-edge safety razor that used disposable blades with two sharpened edges. The invention was patented in 1901. Gillette also came up with a design that improved people's safety in shaving and ease for replacing blades. Gillette's invention gained acceptance in the US and Gillette quickly expanded its operations to markets outside the US. With a patent protection, Gillette adapted a premium pricing strategy that led to modest growth from 1908 to 1916. During and after the First World War, the U.S. Army issued Gillette shaving kits to its servicemen, making Gillette's safety razor the dominant player in the safety razor category.

Gillette's razor patent expired in November 1921. To maintain its dominant market position, it switched its pricing strategy of selling the razor at a very low price to capture market share and made money by the selling blades: now known as the razor-blade strategy. With the new pricing strategy, Gillette's growth was exponential. From 1917 to 1925, Gillette's unit sales increased by ten times. By the end of 1920s, Gillette's sales decreased in the US market because competitors had better blade manufacturing technology and Gillette ran into blade quality problems. To address the problem, Gillette introduced Blue Blade made from carbon steel in 1932. The carbon steel is harder and holds an edge longer. Blue Blade could give more shaves, thus reducing per shave cost. Gillette later introduced Thin Blade, also made from carbon steel, at a lower price and half the weight in 1938. Gillette invested heavily in advertising to regain its lost market position. Though Gillette was under heavy competition in the domestic market during this period, its overseas market was thriving. In 1935, half of its earnings came from overseas operation and in 1938 almost all of its earnings came from overseas operations. This enabled Gillette to expand into Latin America.

During World War II, Gillette dedicated its production to serve the US military. After the war, Gillette ramped up production by modernizing its manufacturing plants while Europe was rebuilding its industry. Gillette also introduced new products with more safety features. By 1950, it recaptured its dominant position in US. In 1960, Gillette introduced Super Blue Blade which was the first significant improvement in the razor blade since Blue Blade. The new blade was coated with silicon that can give a much more comfortable shave. Super Blue Blade was a big success and brought Gillette back to the dominant market position with over 70% market share by 1961.

In 1962, British Wilkinson Sword Company introduced the world's first razor blade made from stainless steel. In comparison, stainless steel blade is resistant to rust and stays sharp three times longer than carbon steel blade. Even though the cost of the stainless steel blade is higher than carbon steel blade, it can be used more times before replacement, which gave Wilkinson Sword the advantage to enter the world market. Two US competitors, Schick and American Safety Razor came out with their versions of stainless steel blade. The three companies came as a surprise to Gillette. At that time, Gillette had the stainless steel blade technology but it hesitated to come up with its stainless steel blade. Super Blue Blade had a very good profit margin, while the stainless steel blade had a low profit margin. The upper management was concerned that the introduction of stainless-steel blade would cannibalize its Super Blue Blade, thereby affecting profit. The frontal attack of stainless steel blades by the three companies brought down Gillette's dominant market position. In 1964, Gillette brought its own stainless steel blade to the market and regained some of its lost ground. From 1964 to 1971, Gillette introduced the improved stainless steel blade products and regained the market leader position.

Up until 1971, Gillette's razor was a one-blade system. The value proposition is "safe, easy to use, and comfortable shave at an affordable price". The first generation of the product focused mainly on safety. This was achieved by a unique double-edge safety razor design. The second generation was the Blue Blade made from carbon steel. In between there were improvements in handling, ease of use, ease of blade replacement and pricing strategy. The third generation, the Super Blue Blade, achieved by an advanced coating technology allowed the company to advance the value proposition to a higher hierarchy: from safety to comfort and close shaving. This success made Gillette complacent, and this gave small players opportunity to disrupt the market with the introduction of stainless-steel blades. Even though Gillette could respond, it failed to do so because it would hurt its short-term profit. As a result, Wilkinson Sword and Schick gained a position in the safety razor category. Gillette came up with its own stainless steel blade two years later to regain some of the lost ground.

Back in 1964, Gillette had been experimenting with a twin-blade razor system. The idea was that with tandem blades, a blade can pull whisker out of the hair follicle that enable the second blade to cut the whisker even shorter. The idea was turned into a razor with two blades set in a plastic cartridge with edges that faced each other. In the consumer testing, this twin-blade system outperformed the one blade system. In 1971, Gillette introduced the first twin-blade razor system Trac II that captured the premium market. This also set a new direction for Gillette's 1-N product expansion strategy. From 1971 to 1996, Gillette improved the twin-blade razor system in shaving efficiency, smoothness in shaving experience, and adjusting the design to contour. In 1974, Bic introduced the variant concept of disposable razor (instead of disposable blade).

Gillette responded and managed to secure a leadership position in the disposable razor market. However, disposable razors ate into the more profitable disposable blade market that Gillette was the dominant player in. Gillette cut its effort in disposable razors and concentrated on the twin-blade cartridge system. In 1980, Gillette introduced Atra, a twin-blade cartridge system with a pivoting head. In 1989, Gillette introduced the Sensor, a twin-blade system that could follow contour, and in 1993, introduced SensorExcel, a twin-blade cartridge system that gave a closer shave.

In 1996, it introduced Mach 3, a three-blade razor system that was an improvement over twin-blade system. Mach 3 had stronger blades that would last longer. It would reduce irritation and require fewer strokes. Market testing indicated that men much preferred Mach 3 over SensorExcel (2 to 1). Because of the high R&D investment on the three-blade system development, the replacement cartridge for Mach 3 was more than 35% above SensorExcel. Mach 3 was very successful, and it captured 15% market share in a period of six months after it was launched. From 2002 to 2005, Gillette introduced variations of Mach 3 with improvements in close shaving, reduced irritation, shaving efficiency and comfort.

In 2003, Schick introduced Quattro, a four-blade razor system to compete with Mach 3. Mach 3 and its variations were selling strong in the market from 2002 to 2005. Gillette was acquired by P&G in January 2005. At the time of acquisition, Gillette had more than 70% of the global market for razor and blades. Responding to Schick's four-blade razor system, Gillette introduced Fusion, a five-blade razor system on September 14, 2005. Fusion also included a trimmer blade for sideburns and shave under nose. Fusion was supposed to deliver less irritation and more comfort. The price of cartridge for Fusion was comparable with that for Mach 3. The company expected that Fusion would take over Mach 3 and became the flagship brand for Gillette. But after more than 10 years, Mach 3 still outsold Fusion. In 2019, Mach 3 sold 6.2 million units of cartridge in the US whereas Fusion sold 4.2 million units. In a number of customer feedback articles, Mach 3 was rated higher than Fusion in overall performance. Many users reported that Fusion gave a closer cut but created irritation because it had more blades.

Now that the timeline of Gillette's razor-blade historical development is described, let us analyze Gillette's expansion strategy and its responses to competitors. Shaving is one of the methods to remove hair in body grooming. However, shaving is only temporary hair removal since it cuts hair at the surface of the skin instead of removing hair from follicles. A razor blade system is a means to achieve the act of shaving. The demand for shaving is influenced by the social norms related to the presence or absence of body hair. The hierarchical needs for shaving start with safety as the lowest level. The next level is low cost per shave so that one can do this frequently. Then the next level is close shave. Following that is comfort, and then efficiency. Gillette's first razor blade system addressed safety and established a leadership position with support from the US military during and after World War I. From 1901 to 1971, Gillette had been improving the product to address the hierarchical needs using the one-blade system. The focus was on the material that the blades are made from, and coating on the blades to reduce irritation. As a leader, Gillette had developed a strong ecosystem that would enhance the improvements in key category attributes that support the aspiration of moving up the hierarchical needs. Even when competitors came and disrupted the market, it could respond effectively to regain market position. However, the improvements in its one-blade system ran into diminishing return. To overcome this stagnation, Gillette's product strategy moved from improving the blade to developing technology for multi-blades system.

Gillette introduced a two-blade system in 1971 which was very successful. This gave Gillette a boost in growth. See the graphs below. With the success in this new direction, Gillette invested heavily to develop a three-blade system. In 1996, Gillette introduced a three-blade system which was even more successful than the two-blade system. It gave a closer shave, improved shaving efficiency and provided less irritation. Competitor Schick came up with a four-blade system in 2003 and Gillette responded with their five-blade system in 2005. Multi-blades would give a closer shave and a higher efficiency, thus satisfying the aspiration of needs in the highest hierarchical level. More blades would give a higher efficiency in shaving but also inevitably lead to more irritation. The tradeoff implies that more blades may not be more desirable. Fifteen years after the five-blade system introduction, Gillette's three-blade system still outsold its five-blade system.

Gillette's product category life cycle strategy is to maintain the lead in key category attributes by introducing new generations that address a higher-level aspiration in the needs hierarchy. In between generations, it developed product varieties with configurations that matched with market segments, for example covering male and female segments. Pricing of razors and blades played an important role to balance between market share and profit. Pricing the razor low would increase market share but lower the profit. The loss in profit can be made up by a higher blade price. To find the proper balance, Gillette use market studies to find out consumers' price sensitivity to razor prices and tradeoffs with the lifetime value derived from blade sales. This linear expansion of the one-blade strategy would run into diminishing returns and the product category life cycle would start to decline. To extend the product category life cycle, Gillette changed its focus: from a single blade product to a multi-blade system.

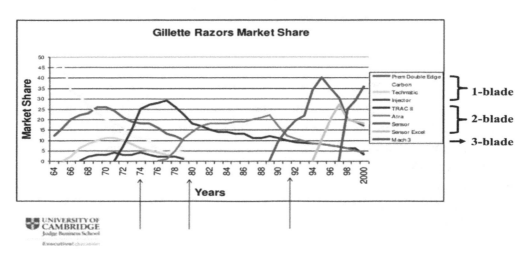

## Gillette and Wet Shaving (1964-2000)

From 2016, Gillette razor business had a sharp decline from 70% to 52% in 2019. Its main threat did not come from its long-time competitor Schick and Wilkinson Sword, but new-comers that focused on associated activities that consumers do other than just shaving and body grooming. Harry's, founded in 2012, manufactured and sold razor and men's personal care products via online and retail channels. It offered a subscription service where custom-ers receive hair glooming products by mail on a regular basis. Dollar Shave Club, founded in 2011, delivers razor blades on a monthly basis and sells related grooming products by direct home delivery. The rise of these two companies is the main reason for the fall in Gil-lette's market share. Would this be an inflection point for Gillette?

What should the smaller players do when competing with a dominant leader? The dominant leader must have developed a strong ecosystem that provides the highest value/cost ratio in key category attributes. The smaller players, on the other hand, must have a weaker ecosystem. They cannot compete head on directly with the leader. They can wait for the right opportu-nity when the leader runs into diminishing return in pushing the value/cost ratio or when consumers aspire to the next higher level needs to launch an attack to capture market share. Wilkinson Sword Company did this in 1962. Even though Gillette had successfully responded and gained back market share, Wilkinson gained a position in the market. Though the small players cannot keep up with leader's value/cost ratio in key category attributes, they can focus on user needs, noncore attributes and cost to fulfill a variation of the value proposition. Bic did this in 1974, Dollar Shave Club in 2011 and Harry's in 2012. Gillette successfully respond-ed to Bic but seems to have lost ground to Dollar Shave Club and Harry's.

# Oligopoly Market Structure

If more than one company emerged as strong players with comparable market share in the 0-1 competition, then all these players must have built equally strong holder structures. This is an oligopoly market structure where several players with more or less the same mar-ket share (i.e. there is no one dominant player) provide comparable value/cost ratio in key category attributes. For example, major personal computer companies (Lenovo 24%, HP 21%, and Dell 19%) all have Windows as their operating system and use the Intel chip as their CPU and have the same third-party application programs. So, their key category attri-butes are comparable. Another example is in the smartphone market. Aside from Apple, all major smartphone manufacturing use Android as their operating system and use comparable chips. Since they cannot develop competitive advantage through category attributes, they should instead turn their attention to establish a differentiated market position within the category (can be viewed as a product sub-category) by designing a portfolio of product varieties with appropriate user needs and non-core attributes, operation efficiency and effectiveness. The product manager could lead the team to go through a design thinking process to discover a market position that the company can establish with its skill and capabilities and make optimal product variety decisions to achieve the market position. By having regular new products launch with consistent messaging, companies would strengthen their market position and establish a brand name in the product sub-category. The product manager can then also introduce a product with a cool and exciting feature that delights the customers through a non-core attribute.

Let us examine the historical case studies of the hand phone market to illustrate and support this argument. A mobile system has two basic infrastructures: the cellular system with location of base stations and switches, and the mobile terminals like handsets or car mounted devices. Telecom services in most countries, including the US, were under government regulations prior to 1990. Private industries engaged in the mobile communication business were in the business of manufacturing equipment for cellular systems, installing cellular systems, manufacturing mobile terminals, and distributing mobile terminals. In 1977, the FCC in the US approved AT&T to operate a cellular network. In 1983, the first analog based cellular system AMPS (Advanced Mobile Phone System), along with Motorola's hand phone Dyna-TAC, was launched in Chicago, and later in Washington D. C. and Baltimore. AMPS was also referred to as the 1G mobile system. At around the same time, there were many analog based 1G mobile systems in different parts of the world.

After the first introduction of the AMPS in 1983, Motorola took the lead to continue improving the cost efficiency of AMPS and established it as the major 1G mobile standard in the US, with about 200 major US cities adopting the AMPS network. Many mobile device manufacturers like Motorola, NEC, Oki, Nokia, Panasonic, and Ericsson deployed advanced semiconductor technology to reduce the weight and size of mobile device. This marked the beginning of mobile phone to the consumer market, and the number of subscribers started to grow quickly. Motorola, as a company strong in semiconductor technology, took the lead to bring out the smallest and lightest hand phones. Towards the end of 80's, Motorola became the leader in the hand phone, and continued its leadership in the 90's.

In the mid-80s, each country in Europe started with a different analog based 1G mobile system. The countries in Europe are close to each other and the mobility of European citizens across countries in Europe is much higher. With each country having its dominant 1G standard, roaming emerged as an important issue for Europeans who traveled frequently to other countries that had different mobile standards. Therefore, the European countries had a very strong desire to work together to develop a mobile system standard that would greatly increase the value of mobile communications from the roaming perspective. Thus, while different players in the US were improving their 1G analog mobile systems, Europe was taking steps to develop its standard digital cellular network called GSM (Global Systems for Mobile communications).

In 1991, GSM took off very quickly. GSM could do both voice and data communications and thus could enable mobile service operators to offer more services to the subscribers. SMS (short messages system) had been a runaway success for many mobile operators in Europe and Asia. GSM system is also more cost effective than the analog mobile system, so for developing countries in Asia who had looked at mobile communications infrastructure as a way to improve their existing telecom infrastructure, GSM was a natural choice. GSM first swept over Europe and then over Asia-Pacifica, Australia, and Africa. Ericsson and Nokia were the two major GSM system vendors for these countries.

Both Ericsson and Nokia not only supplied telecom equipment to telecom operators, they also manufactured and marketed hand phones that were the "terminal devices" for the communication system. However, they looked at hand phones very differently. Ericsson looked at the hand phone as a necessary extension supporting the communication system. Ericsson put large amounts of R&D in further improving and developing new technologies for the communication systems. In early 90s, Ericsson was the market leader in telecom equipment supply, and played a more influential role leading to the success of GSM. While Ericsson was focusing a lot more on driving the digital cellular technology, Nokia paid more attention to the mobile terminal: the hand phone.

The telephone set had traditionally been a practical "terminal device" for communications. A fixed line phone was attached to a home, or to an office. People paid less attention to its design if it worked. Functionality and price were the main attributes for a purchasing decision. A firm focusing in driving the cellular system would compete in the hand phone market via a low-cost strategy especially when everyone could produce phones with similar functionalities. Setting up manufacturing plants in those parts of the world with low-cost labor would be their strategic moves. This was Ericsson's hand phone strategy.

However, when mobile communications began to proliferate, the lower-level hierarchical needs were more or less satisfied, and aspiration for the higher-level needs emerged. As the hand phone was getting smaller and easy to carry, it became a personal item that an individual would always carry. A latent need emerged that was not noticed by most telecom suppliers: a phone that can represent the owner. In early 90's, Nokia started to focus on a strategy called "humanized technology": exploit technology to design reliable hand phones to fit personal taste and living styles. Nokia believed that once the cellular mobile infrastructure was built and regular mobile communication services were offered, the hand phone would be the key to drive up the number of subscribers. When all phones have similar functionalities, then phone design would play the key role in influencing buyer's decision, and Nokia's position as the "fashion hand phone" in the mobile phone market enabled it to charge a premium on their phone products.

To further drive the fashion statement, Nokia moved to have regular new product launches every 35 days by 1998. The new models had the same inner phone device, but the outlook would have replaceable face plates designed to fit different lifestyle in different countries. There were different Nokia phone models for the sporty individuals, for executives, for yuppies, for heavy users, for teenagers, for ladies, etc. This modular design enabled Nokia to achieve economies of scale and scope. With this strategy, Nokia overtook Motorola towards the end of 90's and became the leader in the hand phone industry during the 2000s. Ericsson, on the other hand, lost its competitiveness in the hand phone market and merged its hand phone business with Sony in 2002.

In 2003, Motorola launched a frontal attack on Nokia's "fashion design" space by releasing Motorola Razr with a unique clamshell design and a thin profile. Its objective was to regain its top position lost to Nokia. As opposed to a normal hand phone design with interface components exposed, the clamshell design keeps the interface components such as key and display inside the closed clamshell. This can protect the interface components from damage and unintentional use, and made the hand phone shorter and narrower so that it is easier to carry around. The disadvantage, however, is that the connecting hinge is prone to fatigue or failure. Its slick design grabbed a lot of attention and gained back some lost ground. Motorola's division was profitable again in 2006. In four years, 130 million units were sold, becoming the bestselling clamshell hand phone in the world. It continued to roll out new generations of Razr with better design but the thin profile clamshell design lost its appeal to feature-rich touchscreen design and lost market share in the late 2000's.

Samsung entered the semiconductor industry by acquiring Korea Semiconductor in 1974. It then entered the mobile device business by acquiring Korea Telecommunication in 1982. At that time, Motorola was the leader in Korea's market. To compete with incumbent Motorola, the marketing team suggested a handset with unique features specific to Korea situation. The design team decided to focus on improving the phone connectivity due to specific mountain topography of Korea. Samsung invested heavily in designing a premium handset that would have good connection in the mountainous areas. In 1993, Samsung succeeded in developing such a handset and introduced it into the market, branding it as AnyCall. Samsung marketed this unique feature with a slogan: 'Strong for Korean geographical features'. In two years, Samsung overtook Motorola and became the number one handset company in the Korean market.

In the early 1990s, GSM became a digital standard adopted in Europe and many Asian countries. While it was making its way to expand into the US market, Qualcomm introduced a new digital standard based on CDMA (Code Division Multiple Access) called IS-95 that was backward compatible with existing US analog cellular systems in 1995. In 1996, Samsung launched CDMA service in Korea and designed the phone for CDMA system. In one year, it captured more than 50% of the CDMA market in Korea. It also exported its CDMA phone to countries with CMDA service, including US, Latin America and Hong Kong. In 1999, it captured more than 50% of worldwide CDMA phone market. However, the major world wireless market was GSM based that accounted for 70%. To further its growth, Samsung had to penetrate the GSM phone market. With Motorola, Nokia and Ericsson as the major incumbents, Samsung needed to choose a market segment to enter and design a unique product for that segment. Samsung chose Europe as its entry point. They found that Europeans preferred products with geometry, balance and simple design. With this finding, Samsung adopted "simple" as the design concept, and designed a sophisticated hand phone with unique functionality that suited the tastes of Europeans. Successful entry into the GSM market enabled Samsung to further grow its hand phone business by selling to countries with GSM, including Asia, India, and North America. With strong support from its electronic and semiconductor manufacturing businesses, it developed economies of scope in supplying phones in 6 major configurations to fit different markets. This gave Samsung the advantage in selling phones in different countries with different tastes. In 2007, Samsung surpassed Motorola and became the world's second largest hand phone company. In the process, Samsung developed strong relationships with telecoms in many countries and economies of scope capability that allowed it to sell many hand phone models in various markets.

When the hand phone was first introduced, key drivers of category attributes that reflected the effectiveness in delivering hand phone value propositions were compatibility with the telecom base stations, operating system for hand phones, and mobile processors. Making telephone calls was the basic needs and a simple operating system was enough. Therefore, compatibility with the base station and a mobile processor were the key driving attributes. Motorola, as a semiconductor company with good connections to AT&T, had the advantage and quickly became the leader in the mobile phone industry as the 1G analog wireless system was growing in the US. As many semiconductor companies rushed in to provide mobile processors, Motorola's advantage as a semiconductor producer was neutralized. Compatibility with the base station emerged as the key driver. Ericsson and Nokia developed the GSM digital wireless system in Europe. When they built up GSM based stations throughout Europe, they had the advantage to supply hand phone in Europe. Samsung got into the market as a semiconductor producer and set up a CDMA digital base station in Korea. As telecom wanted to have as many hand phone suppliers as possible, they would open up their base stations' standard and welcome all hand phone vendors to participate. This would level the playing field for all hand phone producers in the market.

As the base station technology and mobile chip technology were improved, all hand phone producers would release new models based on the new improved technology. Therefore, they could not develop a competitive advantage through category attributes, and instead they derived differentiation by focusing on user needs attributes and non-core attributes to establish a certain market position within the product category. Nokia developed a portfolio of fashion design phones to establish the "fashion hand phone for different individuals" position. Samsung leveraged its economies of scope capability to develop the "phone to fit different market" positions. Ericsson failed to develop a position and became marginalized. Motorola had the first mover advantage but could not maintain this position because it failed to establish a position. After Nokia took over the Motorola, Motorola launched a frontal attack with a unique clamshell fashion designed phone that delighted the customers. Even though it helped to regain some position, one design did not help to establish a market position. Samsung leveraged strong support from its electronic and semiconductor manufacturing businesses to achieve economies of scope and scale. This gave Samsung the advantage in selling phones in different countries with different tastes.

From 1990 to 2005, Motorola, Ericsson, Nokia, and Samsung were the major hand phone producers. They were all on par in category attributes. Their main differentiation came from user needs attributes (fitting specific needs in different regions) and non-core attributes (clamshell design, replaceable face plate design).

As technology advancement made communication faster and cheaper, people moved up the hierarchical needs. They aspired more functions in the hand phone other than just voice communication: SMS, and Internet connection. Thus the operating system capability became a new key driver. Ericsson, Motorola and Nokia saw this coming and since they did not have competence in software, they formed a joint venture with Psion Software in 1998 to develop Symbian as an operating system for hand phone. Symbian OS was used by all major hand phone producers, and they all continued to play the same differentiation game through user needs and/or non-core attributes. With a sophisticated mobile OS, the hand phone can do more than just communication, it can be a handheld mini personal computer, and the hand phone category evolved into smartphone category. This was an inflection for Motorola, Nokia, Ericsson, and Samsung. Motorola, Nokia, Ericsson, and Samsung did not have the core competence to respond to this effectively and this gave Apple a golden opportunity. Steve Jobs took the approach of shrinking the iMac into a smartphone. This gave rise to the iPhone with a more powerful OS (iOS) as compared to Symbian. Apple also introduced an exciting non-core attribute: touch screen user interface. Working exclusively with AT&T, Apple neutralized the compatibility attribute. With a stronger grabber (touch screen UI) and a strong holder (iOS), iPhone quickly established a strong position in the smartphone category and disrupted the smartphone market.

Let us analyze the oligopoly competition in the history of hand phone market. In the early hand phone market, the key category attributes are getting access to base station technology through telecom, mobile processors, and hand phone OS. Motorola, Ericsson, Nokia and Samsung were all on par in providing these attributes. Ericsson and Nokia were in the base station and hand phone business, but this only gave them a slight advantage as telecom opened its base station connection to all hand-phone producers. Motorola and Samsung were in the semiconductor business, but this also only gave them slight advantage as there were many semiconductor companies that could provide mobile chips. In the beginning, hand phones only performed simple functions so its operating system was very simple and all hand phone producers could develop its own. Competition among these players was mainly based on establishing differentiated market positions within the category by designing a portfolio of product varieties with appropriate user needs attributes and non-core attributes.

As the base station and mobile chip technology improved, more data could be communicated more effectively, and people aspired more applications besides voice communication. They aspired a new product category: the smartphone. Sophisticated mobile OS emerged as a key driver for the smartphone category attribute, which the hand phone companies could not respond effectively to. Apple took this opportunity to introduce the iPhone that disrupted the old market. It is interesting to note that Samsung was the only one among the four that could pivot to develop a new growth path. This will be discussed in more details in the next chapter.

# Summary in 1-N Product Expansion

In the market structure with a dominant player, the dominant player would mainly use new product generation to control the improvement of key drivers in category attributes to maintain the market leadership position. Consideration of product varieties is secondary, and its main objective is to reach different segments. In between generations, product portfolio configurations are determined by using a cost benefit analysis to maximize investment returns. Smaller players in the market would focus on user needs, non-core attributes, and cost to gain a niche position in the market.

In the oligopoly market structure, the oligopoly players would use new product generations to keep on par with all players in improving key drivers in category attributes and focus their competition by deriving differentiation from user needs attributes and non-core attributes.

In both market structure situations, the major players need to keep track when the people aspire to have their next-level needs met. This would be a situation where the major players are facing an inflection point. Such an inflection also presents new opportunities for a new entrant with appropriate core skills and competence to enter and possibly disrupt the market.

# Discussions:

1. Consider a product category not discussed in this chapter. What is its product category attributes, user needs attributes, user preference attributes and non-core attributes? How do different companies competing in the category leverage their advantage to develop differentiation?

2. In what ways is targeting user segments easier or harder when selling a hardware product versus a purely software product? How can companies measure alignment of segments to the attributes of their different product configurations?

3. Consider the following companies: Microsoft, Ford and Google. What core value propositions do they provide? How did they extend the lifecycle of their products? How did each consider their customer segment when they designed and sold their products?

4. From the Gillette and wet shaving (1964-2000) graph, if you were a product manager, what conclusion/hypothesis will you make?

5. What is the ecosystem under which Gillette's product lie? What other products do consumers associate with shaving (adjacent product)? How do new players like Dollar Shave Club take advantage of the adjacent product category?

6. If your product lost out in the 0-1 winner take all situation, what should you do? Can you give an example?

7. Can you identify different inflection points that the car industry faced in the car history? What happened? Can you anticipate what the inflection points for this industry would be in the future?

# 8

# Good to Great

In 1-N product expansion, the focus is on improving the product category attributes that will provide a higher satisfaction of the value proposition. This will strengthen the eco-system supporting people to derive more value out of the value proposition. The leading players will pace the improvement of key drivers in category attributes to maintain their market leading positions. Each will strengthen its ecosystem to support the value proposition. They will collectively build a market barrier that any new player will find it hard to penetrate. Their growth will be linear in the sense that growth is proportional to the amount spent to foster growth. This will lead to diminishing returns while customers will aspire a higher-level need for the value proposition. If the key drivers for the higher-level needs are different from those for the current level needs, all the leading players will face an inflection point. This is also an opportunity for a new player to enter by addressing the higher-level needs and disrupt the market.

In the last chapter, we discussed how Gillette, as a dominant player, did its 1-N product expansion and how it managed through the different inflection points. We also discuss how major hand phone companies competed during their 1-N expansion and how they managed through inflection points in the hand phone industry. In 1-N product expansion, companies maintain their competitive advantage positions through the development of new product generations to strengthen their ecosystems to support their value proposition. From the surface, they are competing in product attributes, but in looking deeper, they are competing in the strength of their ecosystem and their ability to survive and prosper from the inflection point caused by people's aspiration for a higher need.

There is another approach in doing 1-N product expansion. Instead of focusing on improving the product's value proposition, one can focus on using the product ecosystem as a pivot, to actively help others succeed in providing new value propositions based on the product and expand the product value proposition. Leveraging on other's effort, the product can achieve an exponential instead of a linear growth. This is a **great product**.

## What Makes a Product or Service Great?

Steve Jobs coined the term "insanely great product" referring to a product that is "so cool, so innovative, so ahead of its time, it is insanely great". He used this term to describe Macintosh and iPhone before they were first introduced into the market. The definition of a great man/woman is based on his/her achievement on contributing value to the society. So, for a young man/woman just starting out, regardless of how cool, smart, creative and ahead of its time he/she is, we would not say that he/she is a great person. This should be the same when we refer to product. I would not refer to a product that is "cool, innovative and ahead of its time" a great product, let alone an insanely great product because the value it could contribute to the society is not known yet. I would refer it as an "insanely cool product". An insanely cool product might or might not evolve into a great product. Even if it does, it may take a long journey with many unexpected twists and turns. It would need a leader with the right mind-set to guide the product evolution in this long journey.

A **great product** is one that is taken for granted by others to create 0-1 product innovations based on it. This would result a new business and a new market. So it is a source of innovation and a foundation in creating new marketplaces. A good product contributes to the company's growth. A great product not only contributes to its company's growth, but also contributes to the growth of the economy.

What would trigger an entrepreneur to initiate 0-1 product innovation to realize a new value proposition? The starting point of 0-1 product innovation is to create a new value proposition to the society. There are two main drivers that would trigger 0-1 product innovation. One driver is the improvement and proliferation of infrastructure that would provide a new possibility to deliver a new value proposition that has not been experienced before. When most people take this improved infrastructure for granted, then creative entrepreneurs would initiate 0-1 product innovation to deliver a new value proposition based on such infrastructure. Consider the following example. The road network and vehicles can be considered as transportation infrastructure that would expedite traveling from point A to point B. As the government expands the highway network and most people begin to own a car, new rural developments along the highway would spring up that would provide new businesses opportunities for entrepreneurs. The shopping mall is the 0-1 product innovation triggered by the highway infrastructure improvement and most US families own more than one car. Another example is the bullet train in China. A bullet train connecting Shanghai and Beijing is a good product that provides more convenient transportation between the two large cities. When China built the bullet train network that connects many cities and towns throughout the country, with small towns in remote area, it upgraded the transportation infrastructure in China. This triggered many entrepreneurs to develop many 0-1 business innovations like tourism, cost effective supply chains, and community development that dramatically influenced the urban and economic development in China. The bullet train network in China evolved from a good product to a great product.

The other driver is the 1- N upstream technology improvement that would trigger 0-1 product innovation in downstream products. An example is the 1-N linear improvement in semiconductor technology that led to 0-1 personal computer innovation. Moore's law triggered many 0-1 product innovation in the downstream IT product industry. Improvement of Internet technology also provided a new infrastructure to wireless communication which has since triggered a lot of 0-1 product innovations.

So, a downstream end-use good product would evolve from a good product to a great product when its market proliferation would upgrade its existing hard/software infrastructure. An upstream technology component product that is critical in many end user products can also evolve from a good product to a great product. Consider critical technology component products like semiconductors, displays, batteries etc. By investing to push the technology front of these technology component products and make them openly available would encourage many entrepreneurs to engage in 0-1 product innovation based on these products. Another direction is to invest to drastically reduce cost which would then encourage others to engage in 0-1 product innovation based on these products.

Not all products can evolve from good to great. For example, Gillette's razorblade can become an excellent product but cannot evolve from good to great because its value proposition is an end in itself.

In the following sections, a few case studies on how a leader leads the team in a long journey to evolve a product from good to great are presented. The first case is the twisted journey of Macintosh, evolving from cool to good, then from good to great. The journey was not smooth. During a period, the Macintosh almost disappeared in the market. The second case is the journey that the leader of Tencent took to turn QQ from cool to good and evolve QQ to WeChat that became a great end-use product. Third case is how TSMC evolved from a good OEM service provider to a great semiconductor foundry. The first two cases are end-use products that evolve from good to great. The third case is an upstream critical technology components that evolve from good to great. It is important to note the mind-set that the leader had in each of these cases that successfully turned a good product to a great product.

## iPhone and Android

When the personal computer was gaining acceptance as a new product category in the early 80s, the key drivers for category attributes were computation speed and number of available application software. Ease of use was considered as "nice to have" and is a non-core attribute. Apple's Macintosh lost out to the IBM PC because the IBM PC had a lot of office application software and its processing speed was faster. Even though the Macintosh had an exciting GUI, it was not the main concern in people's buying decision. The IBM PC became the dominant player in the PC market. As more people were using the personal computer daily, the ease of use emerged as one of the key drivers for the PC category attribute, as people were aspiring to next level needs. The PC with Windows OS and Intel CPU had GUI which was comparable to the Macintosh. The Windows OS is running under DOS and Microsoft trained DOS software developers to develop applications under Windows. So more third-party software vendors developed application programs running under Windows than Macintosh. The PC with Windows and Intel outpaced IBM PC and Macintosh in capturing the PC market. Since the PC users are mostly single homing, the first that captured a good size of the market would become the dominant player. By early 90s, the PC with Windows and Intel chip took over the market dominant position from the IBM PC.

The Macintosh could not compete in the category attributes and focused its attention on developing a niche market position by focusing on user needs attributes and non-core attributes. In 1985 John Scully bundled Macintosh with Apple's laser printer, Mac-specific software that facilitated users to design, preview, and print page layouts complete with text and graphics to create a sub-category: desktop publishing. Apple also focused on Macintosh's outlook design, multimedia software technology and "plug and play" feature. One analyst noted: "The majority of IBM and compatible users 'put up' with their machines, but Apple's customers 'love' their Mac". This allowed the Macintosh to be sold at a higher price. To keep up with the premium image, Apple had to invest a lot more on R&D as compared to other PC companies. By 1990, The Macintosh captured around 8% of worldwide market share. Because of the high-cost structure, Apple could not follow suit when other PC companies dropped their prices. Apple started to lose market share as the PC price competition intensified. From 1990 to 1997, Apple tried various ways to move Macintosh to the mainstream market. Apple tried but failed to introduce a low-end product. Apple worked with IBM jointly to develop PowerPC chip to compete with Intel chip, but this led nowhere. Apple experimented with licensing a handful of companies to make the Mac clones, but this was stopped when Steve Jobs returned to Apple in 1997. At the time Steve Jobs came back, Apple incurred a loss of $1 billion, and the Macintosh worldwide market share dropped to around 3% with continued downward trend.

The first thing that Steve Jobs did when he returned was to improve Apple's financial performance and regain Apple's image. He launched the iMac with unique outlook design with translucent case came with multiple colors. It supported peripherals not necessary built for the Mac platform. He restructured the supply, production, and distribution chain to reduce production cost and expanded its market reach. Jobs focused on refining the iMac to offer a cutting-edge, tightly integrated user experience. Jobs also decided to switch to Intel chips and made iMac compatible with Windows. In 2001, Apple introduced a new OS X that offered a more stable environment. The OS X was upgraded every 12 to 18 months which allowed Apple to generate extra revenue and gain loyalty. Unlike other PC companies that relied mostly on third party software developers to provide software applications, Apple developed various software programs internally for media creation, organization, editing and publishing (including iTunes, iMovie, iPhoto, etc.).

Steve Jobs managed to bring Apple back to profitability, thereby enabling the company to invest in R&D to maintain its technology edge. However, its worldwide market share was still declining, though at a much slower pace. The iMac worldwide market share was around 2.4% in 2001. While the Macintosh lost out in the mainstream PC market, Apple developed unique skills in industrial design, graphical OS development, multimedia software, advanced user interface technology and also developed a loyal group of Mac fans.

Apple's entry into the digital audio device market was a coincidence rather than a planned strategy. In 1999, Steve Jobs discovered that an Apple-invented technology, FireWire, can transfer data much faster than the standard technology used at that time. Apple planned to use the technology to support the "digital hub" strategy where the Mac played the role as the nucleus of digital media universe. Portable MP3 had been in the market since mid-1990s. The first MP3 that could hold 1,000 songs appeared in the market in 1999. There were also many portable digital audio devices in the market. However, most of these devices had a user interface that did not scale well when searching for thousands of songs. Moreover, since these are standalone devices, they need to transfer music from CD through a computer; and the speed of transferring thousands of songs from CD to the device would take hours. By late 1999, digital music had become big news because of the dispute between the music industry and illegal file sharing sites like Napster.

With all these events happening, Jobs suddenly realized that digital music could be an entry point for Apple's digital hub strategy. With its core competence in software and hardware integration, user interface technology, industry design, and internal FireWire technology, Apple developed a sleek MP3 device with the size of a pack of cards that can download music from CD through Mac in minutes. It had a scroll wheel interface design that can scale well in finding songs in the music library. Apple also included the digital rights management technology that enabled it to be a distributer for major record labels through downloading from iTunes. So, it had provided a complete solution to realize the value proposition "carry your favorite songs in your pocket that you can listen to anywhere at any time". Apple branded the MP3 device iPod as an entry point for its digital hub strategy. Apple released the iPod in November 2001. In 2002 it had made several improvements and made it Windows compactable. Sales started to ramp up quickly in 2003. This marked the new growth phase for Apple on a path to become a full-fledged digital convergence company.

In 2004, Steve Jobs decided to develop a hand phone that has no buttons but a touch screen. It would combine iPod and the functions of a personal computer. It is a device that people can make calls, listen to music, play games, get access to email, and manage information. The concept of integrating a hand phone with a personal computer and with a touch screen user interface was first conceived, patented and prototyped by an IBM engineer Frank Canova, Jr. in 1992. The technology status and the communication infrastructure were not advanced enough to realize the value proposition until more than 15 years later. To develop the smart phone Steve had in mind, he saw that there were two approaches. One approach would be to expand from iPod. Starting in 2005, Apple had the new iPod device able to play movies, TV shows, and music video. So, the upward path is to expand its operating system to manage data (including voice) exchange and computation. The other approach would be to scale down the iMac to produce a product that is more phone-like (voice and data exchange) and add iPod capabilities. He gave the iPod team and Mac team the mission to develop the smart phone he had in mind.

Apple had been interested in multi-touch technology and had been working with Finger-works that had developed various multi-touch technologies, including Touchstream key-boards and the iGesture Pad. In 2005, Apple acquired Fingerworks and its multi-touch technology. The Mac team successfully developed iOS, incorporating the multi-touch tech-nology to create the first iPhone that was released in June 2007. With a unique touch screen and a sleek design, iPhone grabbed a lot of attention when it was first released. Since its OS (later rename iOS) was derived from the Mac OS X, it would be effective in managing e-mail capability, Web access, text messaging, an address book, a calendar, a camera, and many personal digital assistant functions. Apple also worked exclusively with AT&T for a period. This motivated AT&T to promote the iPhone that helped Apple quickly establish a beach head in the crowded hand phone market in the US. A year later, Apple released the iPhone 3G that was faster and able to install third-party applications. Originally, Steve Jobs did not intend to let third-party developers build native apps for the iOS. However, com-plaints from developers prompted Jobs to revert the decision. Apple released a software de-velopment kit (SDK) on March 6, 2008, that was a free download for Mac users. Developers subscribing to the Apple Developer Program could get technical support, test applications and distributions of mobile apps through the App Store. Apple would have to approve each application before it went on sales and Apple would keep 30% of the retail price. Apple released a software package, iPhone 2.0, which enabled iPhone and iPod users to install mobile apps through Apple's App Store. The large install base of iPod users attracted mobile app developers to develop games and other applications running on the iOS platform.

In 2008, many smart phone producers rushed into the market with their version of touch screen devices to compete with iPhone. Most of these devices ran on Nokia's Symbian OS or Microsoft Mobile OS. Window Mobile OS was licensed to smartphone producers since 2003. It had been gaining market share steadily and peaked in 2007 with 42%. Up to 2008, smartphones were competing on their designs and applications that came with the phone. Both Symbian OS and Windows OS were closed systems to third party developers. Apple's move to enable users to install mobile apps through App Store triggered Nokia and Microsoft to follow suit. However, Symbian's SDK was difficult and expansive, and thereby prevented small developers from using it easily. Microsoft released SDK free with support and opened its Windows Market Place for Mobile in 2009, but Window Mobile OS was losing its customers to Android starting 2008 and had lost the market momentum to build up enough mobile apps. The key attribute drivers for the smartphone category in 2008 would be the number of mobile apps and power of operating system, not the touch screen. Leveraging on the iPod and Mac ecosystems, the iPhone had much stronger key attributes as compared to other smartphones that ran on either Symbian or Windows Mobile.

Android was founded in 2003 with the vision of developing an advanced operating system for digital cameras. Later they switched their attention to provide an OS for the hand phone that would compete with Symbian OS and Windows Mobile OS. Android ran into financial difficulty and in 2005, was acquired by Google. Google's vision was that when everyone would own a smartphone, it would be the next platform for its advertising business. An early prototype of Android had a physical QWERTY keyboard, but the success of iPhone caused Google to shift Android's focus to touchscreen. Android is free and open-source software; its source code is known as Android Open Source Project (AOSP), which is primarily licensed under a permissive free software license that allows users to use the software for any purpose - to distribute it, to modify it, and to distribute modified versions of the software under the terms of the license, without royalties. Google offered smartphone makers Android that support touch screen and Google Mobile Services (GMS) for free. GMS includes core apps such as Google Chrome, and since September 2008, the digital distribution platform Google Play. Google provided Android SDK for third parties to develop mobile apps that can be downloaded from the Google Play. Since the Symbian OS was difficult for third parties to develop mobile apps and because the Windows Mobile OS cost $25 per copy while the Android was free, many smartphone makers using Symbian or Windows Mobile switched to Android when they released the new model. Starting from 2008, the Windows Mobile had a sharp decline and by 2011, it was down to 3% and was replaced by Windows Phone that was discontinued in 2017. The Symbian OS market share was 52% in 2008 and dropped to 0.1% in 2015. As the Android captured more and more smartphone makers, its Google Play became an attractive platform for mobile app developers to distribute their products. By 2020, Android and iOS were the two major mobile OS players with the Android accounting for 72% or market share and the iOS accounting for 27%. Apple is the only smartphone maker using iOS whereas Android is used by many other smartphone makers.

Nokia struggled by trying to improve the Symbian and switched to the Windows Phone but failed to regain market position. In 2013, it sold its mobile and device division to Microsoft. Motorola shifted to Android, replacing Symbian and Windows Mobile as its operating system in 2008. Motorola was split into two companies, Motorola Solution and Motorola Mobile, in January 2011. Motorola Solution was the successor of the original Motorola and Motorola Mobile was the spin-off of its handset business. In August 2011, Motorola Mobile was sold to Google. In 2007, before the iPhone 3G was introduced, the worldwide mobile phone market was dominated by Nokia (37.8%), Motorola (14.3%) and Samsung (13.4%). The emergence of the iPhone 3G and Android created a new smartphone category that completely disrupted the mobile phone market. Nokia and Motorola could not adapt to this change and sold off their handset business. Samsung was the only major handset maker that successfully adapted to this inflection point to become the largest smartphone maker in the world.

Samsung had been using multiple OS: Symbian, Windows Phone, and its own proprietary OS. By 2013, Samsung dropped all of them and focused primarily on Android. In 2013, it introduced the Galaxy Series as a line of high-end Android smartphones that could compete with the iPhone. In terms of key category attributes, Android was comparable with iOS. So, Galaxy was competing with iPhone in user needs attributes and touch screen. Samsung Electronics manufactured semiconductors, batteries, camera modules, image sensors, and LTD displays and sold these to its competitors like Apple, Sony, and Nokia. So, Apple's success in iPhone also benefited Samsung. While Nokia and Motorola were defending iPhone's attack and struggled financially, Samsung Electronics could benefit from iPhone's success financially and could invest to adapt to the new competitive environment. Samsung was very skillful in managing many product lines matching to specific customer segments and differentiated itself by offering many product lines as compared to the iPhone that had only a few product lines. The Galaxy was also priced a bit lower than the iPhone and was more popular than the iPhone outside US. China emerged as the second largest economy in 2010 and many smartphone makers in China using Android emerged as major players in the smartphone market.

As more and more people carry smartphones as a personal device wherever they go, smartphones became part of the communication infrastructure that supports our daily activities. New 0-1 product ideas that leverage on this new communication infrastructure started to emerge in late 2000s. This included the sharing economy (e.g. Uber, Airbnb, bike sharing, etc.) and online services (DoorDash, Intracart, etc). US telecoms upgraded 3G to 4G in the early 2010s also helped to accelerate such development. This development created new ecosystems that are not part of the smartphone ecosystem but have positive network effects with the smartphone ecosystem. These new ecosystems promote new value propositions that would rely on the smartphone as part of their communication infrastructure.

Tencent launched its QQ free service in early 1999 and in nine months, reached 1 million users. It was anticipated that the growth would be exponential, and the major concern was how to monetize. At that stage of China's economic development, medium and small firms would not want to pay a lot for banner ads. Also, it was the time of the Internet bubble burst, and large firms shrunk their budget for online advertisement. Consequently, QQ's banner ads income was unable to generate enough cash to sustain user growth. Tencent introduced membership subscription model with QQ users paid an annual fee of $12-20 to receive premium value-added services such as customized QQ icons and ad-free conversation boxes. This model failed since the value-added services did not entice enough users to sign up. Tencent also lacked an online payment system at the time to allow users to transfer funds conveniently, and many users simply did not bother to sign up for the value-added services.

In November 2000, China Mobile, the largest wireless carrier in China, introduced its data application service platform - Monternet. It served as a bridge between the mobile device and the internet to allow mobile phone users to make the most out of the content that the internet offered. On Monternet, users can purchase services from service providers like Tencent and pay the service fee as part of their phone bill. Then, China Mobile will give 70% of this service fee to the service provider. Monternet not only changed users' mobile phone into a powerful, integrated information terminal instead of an ordinary communication tool, but it also brought many internet companies like Tencent and Sina back from the edge of a cliff. Monternet provided Tencent the opportunity to expand its instant messaging service by serving as a reliable payment channel. Through China Mobile's payment system, Tencent's wireless value-added services resulted in $1.5 million net profit by the end of 2001. This helped Tencent to invest and promote its QQ service.

In March 2002, as QQ's registered user accounts surpassed 100 million, the majority of Tencent's revenue still came from wireless value-added services. Yet, China Mobile began to reduce its revenue-sharing percentage to service providers and this prompted the Tencent management team to find a way to be less dependent on China Mobile. To gain complete independence in terms of revenue collection and to make the payment process easier, safer and faster, Tencent introduced its virtual currency system, Q coins, in May 2002. Despite being a virtual currency, the exchange rate between Q coins and Renminbi was fixed at 1 to 1. Users can purchase Q coins by charging their mobile phone bills, through the online banking payment system, and through gift cards sold at convenience stores. With Q coins, users can purchase QQ related products and services directly online. Due to QQ's popularity, Q coins became broadly accepted by online stores and gaming sites. It even acted as a medium of exchange for real world goods as people could spend Q coins at an online gaming site and receive gifts in the real world.

The Q coin payment system had fundamentally shaped Tencent's business model of selling virtual goods and became the foundation for Tencent's expansion. With the establishment of the Q coin system, all Tencent needed to do was to integrate Q coins into each of its services and products. To fully leverage its massive user base, Tencent decided to focus on growing microtransactions since "small numbers multiplied by big numbers equal big numbers". QQ Avatar Show was such an example.

QQ Avatar Show was an avatar designing system on the top of QQ. Initially each QQ user was given an avatar that was a cartoon human figure wearing only underwear. Users can then use Q coins to purchase virtual clothing, accessories, and even background settings from the QQ Show Shop to decorate their avatar figures that appeared on IM's conversation box, chatroom, as well as QQ bulletin boards. Surprisingly, QQ Avatar Show took off among QQ's massive user base that mostly consisted of students and young professionals, who naturally possessed strong senses of self-awareness. Indeed, no one would like to present their virtual figure as someone stripped down to underwear. The Avatar Show quickly evolved into a virtual lifestyle as fashion-prone users were keen on trying out different virtual goods on their avatar figures. The prices of such virtual goods varied between 50 cents to a dollar (Renminbi) and would cost users a few dollars to prepare a full set of clothes for the avatar. Micro-transactions like these small amount purchases provided Tencent with a sustainable stream of revenue on a consistent basis. Currently, micro-transactions on virtual goods and games comprise more than 70% of Tencent's total revenue.

A series of entertainment services were then developed. Among them were QQ Pets, QQ Dating, Qzone, and QQ Games. Tencent's goal behind these developments was to bring as many real-life elements as possible into the virtual social world they created for the users. By 2010, QQ has 650 million monthly active users, Tencent had $2 billion revenue, and a market capitalization of $32 billion.

With 650 million monthly active QQ users, Tencent started to adapt a strategy of leveraging its zero user acquisition cost advantage to copy any successful internet related business and crush any internet startup company. Starting in 2010, Tencent's public image began to deteriorate. It was conceived by many as anti-innovation and a public enemy. As Tencent grew, it had many groups, each responsible for a specific business. Internal politics within the company made it sluggish in responding to external changes. In late 2010, Tencent was concerned about its future as the trend was moving to mobile and its QQ migration into mobile was not that successful. Tencent was facing an inflection point.

Tencent's top management started to diagnose the problem that Tencent faced with the goal to find a new path for its future. This internal activity later extended to include many top brains in the industry. Through a series of intensive brainstorming and constant iteration through the discovery process, they reached the conclusion that what they need is to have a change in mind set. Instead of copying others' success, Tencent should encourage internal entrepreneurship, nurture its ecosystem, suppress internal politics, and encourage internal cooperation. Finally, the company should take more calculated risk. This change in mind set impacted the decision on QQ's migration to mobile that transformed the company.

Allen Zhang was a renowned computer coder and product manager in China. He created Foxmail, which is a freeware email client that had 32.92% market share in China by 2001. Foxmail was acquired by Tencent in 2005 and Allen was appointed the head of Tencent's research and development center in Guangzhou. In late 2010, Allen organized a team of 10 developers to work on a smartphone messaging app. He was inspired by Kik messenger, which he worried might eventually threaten QQ instant messenger. Tencent had a Mobile Internet Group working on a mobile version of QQ. In Tencent's tradition, no other groups in Tencent could work on this as this "belongs" to the Mobile Internet Group. Even though other groups came up with similar prototypes, the one developed by the Mobile Internet Group would be selected.

As a result of the executive meetings on transformation, Pony Ma, the CEO of Tencent, decided to open this to all groups within Tencent with "Mobile QQ" prototype to compete. There were three prototypes competing within Tencent and Ma would make the final decision. Allen's prototype was one of the three. Ma who had a product manager background and called himself "Chief Experience Office" would make the decision based on the intuitiveness of the product. He designed a "half sleep test" where he put himself in a half sleep mode and the prototype that he can navigate through in this mode would pass his test. Among the three, Allen's prototype passed the test. Ma finally selected Allen's version and named it Weixin (WeChat). Ma agreed that choosing Allen's version incurred some risk as Allen was in the R&D Center, not the front line person in product development. Ma trusted his own judgement and felt WeChat's intuitiveness could enable it to capture users of all age groups.

Ma was correct. WeChat very quickly captured more than 10 million users, ranging from young kids to the elderly. At that time there were many similar products in the market, MiTalk (by Xiaomi), Momo, and Talkbox. Tencent had the internal cloud infrastructure advantage that enabled them to scale up the WeChat services, while others like MiTalk crashed after reaching 1 million active users. Growth in WeChat was organic. It started by migrating QQ users to WeChat, then began to spread to all people in all ages due to WeChat's intuitiveness. It started off as a simple text messaging service, and gradually added more features to create an amalgam of various two-sided markets social networking paradigms: part Facebook, part Instagram, and even part walkie-talkie. Besides sending short mobile phone messages and pictures, users can hold down a button that records a voice message. Within two years, it had nearly 300 million daily active users.

WeChat has what every Internet company executive dreams about: stickiness. Average daily usage of WeChat is 90 min, compared to that of Facebook's 38 min. With growing active users, WeChat launched new services that transformed it into one of the world's largest standalone mobile app platforms. Tencent partnered with banks to launch WeChat Pay in 2013 that enable its users to pay bills, buy groceries, and do pretty much anything using their phones. Also, WeChat extended its feature to allow users to register as an official account (公众号; also called "public account" in English), which enables them to push feeds to subscribers, interact with subscribers, and provide them with services. By the end of 2014, the number of official WeChat accounts had reached 8 million. Official accounts can be used as a platform for services such as hospital preregistrations, visa renewals, or credit card services. With this, WeChat evolved into a service platform. It also introduced free mobile games — with virtual items available for purchase — to provide a profitable business with little or no advertising.

In 2014, on Chinese New Year, the WeChat introduced a feature for distributing virtual red envelopes, modeled after the Chinese tradition of exchanging packets of money among friends and family members during holidays. The feature allows users to send money to contacts and groups as gifts. When sent to groups, the money is distributed equally, or in random shares ("Lucky Money"). The feature was launched through a TV promotion during New Year where viewers were instructed to shake their phones during the broadcast for a chance to win sponsored cash prizes from red envelopes. The red envelope feature significantly increased the adoption of WeChat Pay. According to the Wall Street Journal, 16 million red envelopes were sent in the first 24 hours of this new feature's launch. A month after its launch, WeChat Pay's user base expanded from 30 million to 100 million users, and 20 million red envelopes were distributed during the New Year holiday. In 2016, 3.2 billion red envelopes were sent over the holiday period, and 409,000 were sent at midnight on Chinese New Year. This made WeChat Pay the major player in the mobile payment industry.

Enterprise WeChat was launched in 2016. The app was meant to help employees separate their work from their private lives. In addition to the usual chat features, the program let companies and their employees keep track of annual leave days and expenses that need to be reimbursed, while also allowing employees to ask for time off or clock in to show that they were at work. In 2017, WeChat launched a feature called "Mini Programs" (小程序). A mini program is an app within an app. Business owners can create mini apps in the WcChat system. With a large active user base, this attracted many 0-1 mobile internet companies to join the "WeChat Internet" ecosystems. This includes e-Commerce (JD 京东, PinDuoDuo 拼多多, Yunji 云集, Weee (Online Chinese grocery in US)), search (Sogo 搜狗), News/ Novel (Qutoutiao 趣头条 , China Literature 阅文), Ads (Weimeng 微盟), Mobility (Didi, Mobi), Fintech (WeBank), and many more. Many of these are unicorn companies and some of them are financially backed by Tencent.

WeChat had evolved from QQ and became part of the communication and payment infrastructure. This attracted more and more entrepreneurs to develop 0-1 businesses based on WeChat. In January 2018, WeChat announced a record of 580,000 mini programs and became one of the world's largest standalone business development platforms. Each of these businesses created an ecosystem that is not part of the WeChat ecosystem but have positive network effects with the WeChat ecosystem. These new ecosystems promote new value propositions that would rely on the WeChat as part of their communication and payment infrastructure in China.

# Taiwan Semiconductor Manufacturing Company (TSMC)

In the 1980s, the semiconductor industry was vertically integrated. Semiconductor companies, referred as integrated device manufactures (IDMs), owned, and operated their silicon wafer fabrication facilities. Many large computer and electronics companies are IDMs that developed their own process technology to manufacture their own chips and IC devices. These firms also did assembly and testing of their chips and IC devices. Since silicon-wafer fabrication is highly capital intensive, the semiconductor manufacturing process presents high market barrier to small companies and startups. IDM built production capacity to meet peak demand and thus would have excess capacity in low demand period. Managing excess capacity to increase ROI for the facility investment became an important consideration for IDMs. They found that they could "sell" excess capacities to small electronics companies that had no fabrication facility by offering manufacturing and packaging services to them. Occasionally, IDMs may "cross sell" excess capacity to each other to optimize excess capacity management. This is an early sharing economy model.

The semiconductor industry was growing rapidly in the late 70s and the beginning of the 80s. This also brought about the growth of IDMs and its excess capacity. A fabless manufacturing industry started to emerge, leveraging on the abundance of excess capacity. Many senior engineers left their companies and formed fabless semiconductor companies. They would focus on design and have the device manufactured by one of the IDMs. There were some issues in this business model. The IDMs sold excess capacity to fabless customers as a secondary business. Service to the customers were secondary with little guarantee on time delivery and customer support. The IDMs dictated the design, development flow, and available techniques to customers. It would also run into IP protection issues. However, this was the only solution for new electronic company startups that did not want to invest heavily in silicon-wafer fabrication facilities. These companies had to tolerate the drawbacks even though they complained about the service.

Morris Chang had spent 25 years at Texas Instrument, an IDM, working in advanced semiconductor design and manufacturing processes. While at Texas Instrument, he had worked on a transistor project where manufacturing was done by IBM. In the early 80s, he had interactions with many top engineers who left their firms to form their own fabless semiconductor companies. So, he was well-aware of the limited service that IDMs could deliver and the pain point of fabless semiconductor companies. In 1985, he was recruited by the Taiwanese government to become the Chairman and President of a government-sponsored research organization, Industrial Technology Research Institute (ITRI). The institute was formed to promote industrial and technological development in Taiwan. To get Taiwan into the semiconductor industry, Chang developed a semiconductor wafer fabrication plant on the ITRI campus. This later became the first semiconductor wafer fabrication plant of the Taiwan Semiconductor Manufacturing Company (TSMC) that he founded in 1987. TSMC was founded with financing from the Taiwanese government, a Dutch tech giant Philips, and some other investors. Morris Chang was the Chairman and CEO of TSMC. Chang's vision was to develop a pure-play foundry business model: concentrate only on providing manufacturing, testing, and packaging services to fabless semiconductor companies.

The first TSMC fabrication plant was two process nodes behind the IDM at that time. By addressing the pain point of fabless semiconductor companies and lower service charges, TSMC managed to attract customers even though it was behind the technology curve. In the 80s, there were many Chinese engineers working in semiconductor companies in Silicon Valley. Many of them were born in Taiwan and came to US for advanced degrees and became US citizens. They had been in the high technology circle in Silicon Valley and had built up relationships with technology companies in the area. With TSMC providing dedicated manufacturing services and low labor cost in Taiwan, many of them saw the opportunity of returning to Taiwan to form fabless semiconductor companies to design electronic devices to ride the wave of the IT industry in Silicon Valley. Other senior Chinese engineers from IDMs in the US wanted to return to Taiwan and decided to join TSMC to further their career path. This reverse brain drain helped TSMC to establish its early position although it was behind the technology curve.

In four to five years, TSMC caught up and was only one process node behind and the orders started to take off. Besides pushing on the technology front and expanding capacity, TSMC also integrated new features and offered new services that helped customers reduce the design cycle and shorten their time to market. For example, the availability of many IP blocks (a reusable unit of logic, cell, or chip layout design) would help the customers to reduce their design cycle. These IP blocks were developed by third parties known as IP vendors. This is very much like third-party software developers for PC and smartphones. TSMC incentivized third-party IP vendors to commit to TCMC process node roadmap and developed IP blocks even before the process node was available. As TSMC advanced in the process node, it became a preferred choice for new designs.

In 10 years, TSMC caught up with IDMs process node and the cross-network effects between TSMC and fabless semiconductor companies disrupted the semiconductor design and manufacturing industry. New pure-play foundries entered the market, but TSMC maintained as the leader in the foundry market with more than 50% market share. Some less efficient IDMs would not expand, and many moved their production to TSMC. TSMC continued to make investments to push the technology front, expand production capacity, and develop a large portfolio of process libraries, IP blocks, design and reference flows that help customers reduce design cycle.

By 2014, TSMC was on the forefront of the foundry industry for high performance and low power applications. In April 2018, TSMC was the first to mass produce its 7-nanometer node in the semiconductor industry. Samsung had 7 nanometer nodes one year later and

Intel planned to have it by 2021. As the semiconductor process node technology is one of the key drivers for smartphone category attributes, TSMC's leadership position in the process node technology drew major players into the smartphone industry like Apple and Qualcomm to place orders with TSMC to manufacture their chips to maintain their market leadership position.

## Journey from Cool to Great Product

The journey starts with 0-1 turning a cool product that grabs people's excitement into a good product by developing a strong ecosystem that supports the value proposition and all members within the ecosystem derive net benefit. Continue to strengthen the product ecosystem through 1-N linear expansion is necessary to sustain the good product position so that it can wait and grab the right opportunity to break out from good to great. A great product is one that offers opportunity for others to have 0-1 innovation and develop new ecosystems on top of the product. The new ecosystem is not part of the product ecosystem system but have positive network effects with the product ecosystem. While providing opportunities to others to develop new ecosystems may not provide direct benefit to the product, the cross network effects between the new ecosystems and the product ecosystem would prolong the life cycle of the product category and drive sustainable growth in the product category. (See the Good to Great Journey below) Hence, to turn a good product to a great product, the product leader must have the mind-set of letting others benefit from the company's product success, instead of keeping all the benefits to the company. Let us examine the journeys of the three cases above and see how the mind-set played the key role in turning a good product into a great product.

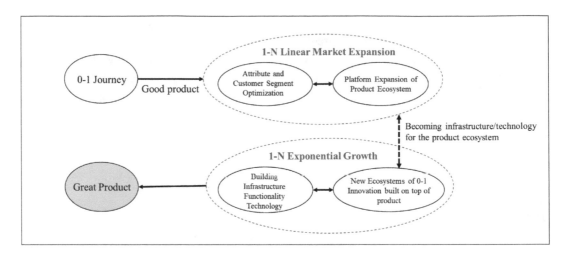

**Good to Great Journey**

From the surface, one would argue that the iPhone is a different product from the Macintosh. The iPhone is in the smartphone category and the iMac is in the personal computer category. But if we examine the product history, one could conclude that the iPhone is a 1-N expansion of the Macintosh, except it is not the 1-N linear expansion discussed in the last chapter. The journey that Apple took that turned Macintosh from a good product to a great product had gone through twists and turns.

When the Macintosh lost to the IBM PC and later to the Windows-Intel-PC, Apple was forced to step back to build core competence in design and software hardware integration, multi-media software, and user interface technology to secure a strong defensible position in a niche premium market. As the hand phone category evolved into smartphone category, the hand phone became a handheld mini personal computer. Thus, the OS became one of the key attributes for the smartphone category. Jobs saw the opportunity and leveraged Apple's competency in design, user interface technology, OS, and hardware software integration to successfully launch iPhone that quickly established a strong position in the smartphone category. The decision to allow third party apps to run on the iPhone was the pivotal decision that turned it into a great product. Steve Jobs had a strong inclination towards a closed system. He might have learned the lesson in Macintosh's failure and experienced strong push back from third party mobile app developers, which influenced him to finally decide to make the iPhone semi-open and to provide support helping third parties develop mobile apps for iOS. Apple also distributes mobile apps through its App Store. Other smartphone makers were not software companies and could not respond effectively as they were not strong in the OS development. Microsoft and Google are both software companies that offer OS for smartphone markers. Microsoft lost out to Google because Google offered all smartphone makers free Android while Windows Mobile OS was licensed at $25 per copy fee. The reason being that Google looked at Android as a way to advance its advertising business and thus decided to offer it for free, whereas Microsoft looked at Windows Mobile OS as a product to generate revenue.

With Google offering Android free to all smartphone makers, this helped the penetration of the smartphone category to people all around the world. When large populations in a region have a smartphone, communication infrastructure in that region is upgraded to a new level. Many entrepreneurs would develop 0-1 innovation based on the new communication infrastructure, leveraging on the smartphone penetration in the region. They would do a "cross time" creative imitation and turn an old value proposition to a new value position. The smartphone became a **great product**.

The journey that Tencent took that turned QQ from a good product to a great product followed a different path. Different from the Macintosh, QQ was successful in dominating the instant messaging market in China. Tencent developed a mind-set of building a "Tencent QQ Empire": leverage on QQ's huge user base to copy and crush any successful internet startups. Tencent was considered public enemy number one and began losing its way when the PC that acted as the end-point device for the communication network was slowly replaced by smartphone. Tencent faced an inflection point. The management went through a soul-searching exercise and changed their mind set. Tencent decided to switch from "Winner takes all and dominate the market" to "nurture the ecosystem members to get a win-win". The selection of WeChat was not based on product feature and development team experiences but instead, based on the intuitiveness and user experience of people of all ages. The inclusion of mobile payment services and the proliferation of WeChat to all people in China, from kids to elderly, upgraded the communication and payment infrastructure in China. This gave opportunities to Chinese entrepreneurs to have 0-1 innovation creating different kinds of mobile commerce businesses in China. WeChat became a **great product**.

OEM (Original Equipment Manufacturing) had been a growth model for many industries in developing countries, including Taiwan. A product company would outsource its manufacturing to an OEM company in a developing country to leverage its lower labor cost to reduce production cost. TSMC started off pretty much like an OEM model with two process nodes behind the IDM. What this means is that from the beginning, its mind-set was to help, passively, the fabless semiconductor companies succeed. It struggled to compete and gain a position in the IDM's excess capacity market by offering services that help customers reduce design cycle and shorten time to market, not the most advanced technology. When its process nodes technology caught up with IDM, TSMC's pure-play foundry business model would completely replace IDM's excess capacity model and become a platform of choice for many fabless manufacturing companies. As TSMC took over IDM's excess capacity business, some IDMs would run into financial difficulty. Therefore, not only did TSMC replace IDMs excess capacity business, but many IDMs did not expand and instead, became TSMC clients. This created positive feedback that furthered TSMC's revenue growth and expansion of its ecosystem.

TSMC ploughed back its profit into investing to advance its process nodes technology. By 2014, TSMC was in the forefront of the foundry industry for high performance and low power applications. TSMC provided the most advanced technology to all major smartphone makers to develop its latest model to maintain their market leadership position. If TSMC could maintain its technology leadership and dedicated open foundry position, many advanced 0-1 technology product developers would count on TSMC to provide the latest technology to manufacture its advanced products, like advanced AI chips and smart IOT devices. TSMC turned from passively helping fabless semiconductor to reducing cost in critical component production to actively triggering fabless semiconductor companies to succeed in 0-1 downstream product innovation. TSMC's foundry evolved from being a good service to becoming a **great service**.

# Discussion:

1. iPhone disrupted the smartphone industry by focusing on expanding and building its product ecosystem rather than just competing on product attributes. What structural factors (related to the product) allowed it to achieve a thriving ecosystem? In what ways did Samsung attempt the same shift? Did it work? Why or why not?

2. Of the four major hand phone producers, only Samsung successfully managed the inflection point. Can you give reasons for why this is so? Did Samsung do anything different from what it did before the inflection point?

3. What is the difference between companies developing games to be sold through iPhone and Google Play and Uber developing a business on top of iPhone and Google Play? Would anyone develop a regional business on top of the smartphone if the smartphone's penetration in a region is 10%? What are the key drivers for the emergence of the sharing economy?

4. In your opinion, what key decisions were most influential in building up Tencent's product ecosystem? In what ways did Facebook fail to achieve this with its own product? What are the general takeaways companies can have about how to build an ecosystem and user stickiness through digital product offerings (think like League of Legends)?

5. What are the key drivers for WeChat to become a great product? Does market domination imply greatness?

6. How is the business model for TSMC in the early days different from TSMC in the present date?

7. What are other examples of companies focusing on the win-win in their product ecosystems? In today's zeitgeist, Tesla is taking the EV market by storm, but it retains a lot of technology and infrastructure to itself (think autopilot, supercharging station tech, battery tech, etc.). Do you think it can dominate with this strategy? Why or why not? What do you suggest Tesla should do?

# 9

# Never Too Late!

I have a good friend, a Professor of Economics at the University of Texas at Austin, who once told me an interesting story while we were having dinner one evening. One day, he was browsing the university bookstore to find a new book and ran into a freshman student who was attending his economics class. He forgot the student's name but had a good impression of the student's performance in class. He asked the student how he was adjusting to campus life. The student replied that he was doing very well, but that he decided he wanted to quit college next year. My friend was shocked to hear this and asked whether he was unhappy with the university. The student told him that he liked the university and loved campus life, and his decision to quit college was after careful consideration. He said that during the year, he received many orders from college students asking him to assemble a personal computer for them. In the beginning, he was just doing it to help some friends and make some pocket money. When the orders kept coming in, he felt that he needed to grab this business opportunity quickly. After careful consideration, he decided to quit college even though he liked the university and the campus life. After hearing how the student made his decision, my friend felt that the student was too impulsive and was concerned that the student might make a mistake that would influence his future. As a professor, he felt obliged to give the student advice on his academic and career development. He told the student that the personal computer industry was very crowded with many big players like IBM, Compaq, Apple, and

HP. Even though he got some orders from college friends, to quit college and plunge into the personal computer market would be very risky. My friend tried to persuade the student to change his mind and continue the college program. The student thanked my friend for his kind advice but decided to follow his passion to start his own PC business without finishing the undergraduate program. Later, my friend found out that the student he talked to is Michael Dell, the founder of Dell Computer.

Xerox monopolized the copier market for a long period of time because of its patent protection. When the Justice Department forced it to give up its patent protection, both IBM and Kodak entered the copier market with a similar product and used a similar marketing approach. Though their products were considered by many to be better than Xerox's product, they only took a very small market share away from Xerox despite their great marketing efforts. Later, a small Japanese company entered the copier market by introducing a drastically different product and a totally different marketing approach. It managed to capture a large market share in the copier market in a relatively short period of time.

Prior to 1978, the US airline industry was regulated with a few international airlines that could provide air routes that covered the world and many intrastate airlines that could provide air routes only within a particular state. After the deregulation, all the airlines were free to compete without regional restriction. American and United were international airlines before deregulation and had already built up the infrastructure to provide strong support in offering full services and extensive air routes that covered most of US cities. This gave them the advantage which had allowed them to quickly become the strong incumbents that dominated the US airline industry. All the intrastate airlines that extended their service to provide air routes that covered cities outside of their states would have to build new infrastructure to support such services. They were like latecomers in the US airline industries that serve the US market. Most of the intrastate airlines that expand their service nationally failed except for Southwest Airlines who evolved into a profitable major airline in the US airline industry.

A successful product indicates that many people have accepted its value proposition. A latecomer entering the market would have no value proposition risk. The major risk it is facing is market competition risk. If the latecomer can manage this risk properly, then it is never too late to enter a market. The conventional wisdom is that an incumbent has the first mover advantage, and to overcome this advantage a latecomer must be financially strong and deploy advanced technology to enter a market. However, the above cases are examples of a latecomer that captured a strong market position in a crowded market with many strong players without being in a strong financial position or using advanced technology. So where can a latecomer derive its advantage?

To identify a latecomer's opportunity in a market with strong incumbents, one needs to first understand where the incumbents derive their strength. In a market with a single dominant market leader, it must have built an ecosystem that enabled it to improve key drivers in category attributes more effectively than its competitors. This is the real strength of the dominant incumbent. In an oligopoly market where there are several big players, these players must provide comparable value/cost ratio in key category attributes and derived differentiation from user needs attributes and non-core attributes to establish a certain market position within the product category. Each of the oligopoly players must have developed its unique ecosystem that would enable it to maintain its position in the sub-product category. This is the real strength of incumbents in an oligopoly market.

If the latecomer enters the market trying to compete head on with a strong incumbent, it will need to build up an ecosystem comparable with the incumbent. Since the incumbent would continue to improve and strengthen its ecosystem, the latecomer would find it hard to win in this catchup game. For an established incumbent, its supporting ecosystem can be easily identified and hard to change. The stronger the incumbent's ecosystem, the less likely the incumbent can respond effectively when the latecomer launches a product with a supporting ecosystem that goes against the incumbent's ecosystem. This is where the latecomer can find its advantage. For the latecomer to successfully enter a crowded market, it should leverage financial and technological tools to exploit this advantage.

## Variations of Value Proposition: Revise Thinking

To develop an ecosystem that goes against or conflicts with the incumbents, the latecomer can use the reverse thinking process to develop a variation of the incumbent's value proposition. Instead of following the 'normal, logical' direction of the incumbents, turn it around and look for opposite ideas. This approach is very appropriate to apply when the latecomer enters the crowded market where the incumbents are engaging in 1-N product expansion by improving its ecosystem to maintain its first mover advantage. The following few cases illustrate how this reverse thinking process can be applied.

## The Copier Market

In 1960, Xerox introduced its first "dry" paper copier machine, the Xerox 914. It was a bulky machine that weighed about 648 pounds with a price tag of $29,500. At that time, there were "wet" paper copier machines which cost about $400. These machines were sold in conventional distribution channels for office equipment. The Xerox 914 was clearly a much better product than the "wet" paper copiers, but the price was also much higher. Xerox decided to target large corporations that produce and reproduce large volumes of paper documents. Instead of selling the machine, Xerox leased the machine and charged customers on a per page basis. Xerox built a dedicated direct sales force to sell the product and a team of repair engineers to maintain the machine. For this group of customers, the desire for a "dry" paper copier machine outweighed the more expensive price per page. The big customers also appreciated the services provided by the direct sales force and the maintenance program. Because of the needs of large corporations for large volume document production, Xerox continued to improve the speed and performance of its copier even though it led to more complex and unreliable machines. To support leasing these machines to large corporations, Xerox further expanded its customer support and services. Within a short period of a few years, Xerox dominated the volume production "dry" copier market and because it owned the patent, it held a monopoly position in the "dry" paper copier market.

In 1972, the Federal Trade Commission filed an antitrust lawsuit accusing Xerox of illegally monopolizing the paper copier market. After more than two years of antitrust battle, Xerox finally agreed in 1975 to settle by releasing its patent rights. This gave other companies the opportunity to enter the copier market. The two most prominent ones were IBM and Kodak. They produced and leased a similar product as Xerox. Like Xerox, they used the direct sales approach to target the same customer group that Xerox was selling to. They tried to be better, but despite a greater marketing effort and a better product, neither of them gained significant market share.

Xerox was later disrupted by Ricoh, a small Japanese company. Using a different technology (not better than Xerox's technology), Ricoh produced a copier that was much smaller and simpler than the big, complex Xerox copier. Savin/Ricoh (Savin was a US company that distributed copiers manufactured by Ricoh) also turned Xerox's offer strategy around. Instead of direct sales, Savin/Ricoh distributed its copier through office equipment dealers. Instead of pitching the service, Savin/Ricoh built a smaller copier that was more reliable. Instead of leasing, Savin/Ricoh sold its copier. Savin/Ricoh was more appealing to the group of medium-sized businesses more concerned with reliability and cost per page and less concerned about speed, performance and services. The Savin/Ricoh offering was an instant success. This attracted other Japanese companies to enter the market playing a similar game.

However, the success of these Japanese companies had very little impact on Xerox's financial performance. Moreover, Xerox viewed these companies as attacking the low-end market that had a low profit margin, and therefore the upper management largely ignored the Japanese competition. This gave these companies the opportunity to build up assets that would eventually allow them to attack the high-end market later after they dominated the low-end market. To survive in a low-margin business, these Japanese companies developed competence in efficient engineering design and low production costs. These skills gave them cost advantages when they later attacked the high-end copier. Xerox lost its market share quickly when the Japanese companies assaulted the high-end market: 65% in 1977, 54% in 1978, 49% in 1979 and 46% in 1980.

## Southwest Airlines in US Airline Industry

In the 60's, the airline industry was dominated by American Airlines and United Airlines. They offered full services and had extensive air routes that covered most US cities. The Air Southwest Company, the original name of Southwest Airlines, was founded in 1966 as a commuter airline serving three cities in Texas: Dallas, Houston, and San Antonio. In 1971, it entered the established commercial airline business by offering bare-bone transportation for a rock bottom price. It further segmented the business travel market by focusing on the customers in the business commuter market traveling between the three major cities in Texas. It provided no onboard meal service, no baggage transfer handling service, and no reservation service. Instead, it offered low prices, no-frill, and convenient commuter schedules between the three cities. Southwest created a new strategy based on the observation that there was a group of travelers who preferred low cost rather than full airline service. Throughout the 1970s and 1980s, Southwest expanded to other geographic market segments within the United States. It first expanded its service to include other cities within Texas, and then it branched out to cities in Louisiana, Oklahoma, Arizona, New Mexico and finally to cities in California and the Midwest. Instead of the hub-and-spoke network system that all other airlines developed to support offering national full-service coverage, Southwest developed a point-to-point network system to support its national no-frill coverage. In 1990, Southwest Airlines became a major airline with a fleet of 94 planes serving 27 cities. Southwest's strategy was copied by other major airlines in the middle of the 1990s. For example, United Airlines introduced its Shuttle by United in 1994 with service between cities on the west coast. But Southwest Airlines still maintained its leadership position in the no-frill, low-fare market segment because its point-to-point network system structure was more cost effective in supporting the no-frill service as compared to United Airlines' hub-and-spoke network.

## Xiaomi in Smartphone market

When Xiaomi entered China's smartphone market in 2010, there were many large players in the China market, including Apple, Samsung, and Huawei. But in short 3 years, it captured 5% of China's smartphone market and quickly overtook Apple in China. Xiaomi took a very different approach from all other smartphone producers. First, it focused on building a group of super loyal fans that are enthusiastic about smartphone technology. These users tended to be extremely vocal about their smartphone functionality and usability. Xiaomi built loyalty by constantly tweaking its version of the Android based on user suggestions and offering weekly updates. When users gave Xiaomi suggestions, Xiaomi would notify the users when it adopted their suggested tweaks. This would give the users a long-lasting sense of achievement and a strong sense of ownership. They would tell their classmates, friends, roommates, and everyone about Xiaomi. As a result, word-of-mouth had become a very strong marketing channel for Xiaomi. So, it's the sense of participation that makes their users loyal fans of Xiaomi. Through a survey study, it was noted that Xiaomi users were about twice as engaged as other iPhone/Android users.

Second, different from all other smartphone producers, it only sold its products through its own online websites where it encouraged its fans to interact, exchange ideas and provide suggestions. Through its website, Xiaomi also offered services such as mobile applications and games via its software, and also an array of accessories from multicolored batteries and casings to hats, and even dolls of the company's rabbit mascot.

Third, while other smartphone producers tried to make money from selling their smartphone, Xiaomi sold its high-spec smartphones almost at cost to capture loyal fans and then derived its profit from selling games, services, and array of products to loyal fans through its websites. In 2013, Xiaomi sold 20 million smartphones mainly in the China market and its revenue reached $5.2 billion. With users downloading more than 1 billion apps, it enabled the company to generate substantial revenue streams from paid apps, games, advertising, and other fee-based services. Xiaomi's focus was to develop an ecosystem that could support the scale of loyal customers with high engagement activities. In 2014 Xiaomi started to expand its market outside China. In the second quarter of 2021, Xiaomi surpassed Apple to become the second largest seller of the smartphone worldwide, with a 17% market share.

## Dell Computer in PC market

In 1984, IBM PC clone was a very big market with many big players including IBM, HP, and Compaq. They all sold the product through electronic retail store channels with specific product configurations. Since retail space was limited, the key driver for a PC company was the retail space to display their products. IBM, HP, and Compaq occupied most of the retail space and for a new entry with no sales record, most retail stores would not give it retail space. Dell entered the market using the reverse thinking strategy. Why not without retail space? Instead of displaying product configurations on retail space that the customers could select from, Dell let the customers specify their preferred configuration and made to order, then Dell would ship the products directly to the customers. IBM, HP, and Compaq adapted a "**build to stock**" business model, while Dell adapted a "**build to order**" business model. These two models require very different ecosystems and core competence to support efficient operations. From the production perspective, a build to stock model needs efficient planned production, while a build to order model requires an efficient flexible production capability. A build to stock model would source its components worldwide and use value/cost ratio as the metric for selection. A build to order model would source its components from nearby suppliers with flexible turn-around time as the metric for selection. A build to stock model would sell the products through retail channels and a build to order model would sell through one-to-one direct sales. The marketing and distribution cost for these models are very different. For the build to stock model, the major cost is the channel mark up, while for the build to order model, the major cost is the direct customer acquisition. The fax machine was gaining market momentum in the late 1970's and by 1984, all companies and many individuals owned a fax machine. This became the main direct sales channel for Dell. This was a passive direct sale channel in the sense that it could only take orders from customers that knew about Dell. This meant that it did not enable Dell to contact new customers easily. Thus, the cost of acquiring new customers was very high and it was hard for Dell to scale up its direct sales. This resulted in a higher production cost because of the lack of scale. The higher production cost and acquisition cost could not compensate for the saving in channel markup. Therefore, in the 80's, Dell was less competitive, cost wise, as compared to the incumbents that adapted a build to stock model. At one time, because direct sale was not scaling quickly, Dell tried to sell its products through a retail channel. But very quickly, Dell found out that this was not compatible to the build to order model and stopped the retail channel. When the Internet came along, Dell was one of the first to launch a direct sales website in 1996. The Internet online sales provided an active direct sales channel that not only reduced the direct sales cost, but also allowed Dell to scale up the sales quickly. In the late 90s, Dell had the cost advantage over the incumbents with the build to stock model. The incumbents could not respond, and Dell disrupted the PC market. Now, Dell is the third largest personal computer producer in the world.

## Synthesizing from Case Examples

Note how the latecomer in the above cases uses reverse thinking to create a sub-product category that the incumbent found it hard to respond. In the copier case, Savin/Ricoh applied reverse thinking in product design, business model, and pricing. In the Southwest Airline case, Southwest Airline applied reverse thinking in service offering and backend supporting system structure. In the Xiaomi case, Xiaomi applied reverse thinking in the smartphone ownership experience and business model. In the Dell case, Dell applied reverse thinking in customer purchasing experience and backend supply chain structure. The important point is that the reverse thinking process can allow the latecomer to find a sub-product category that would require an ecosystem that is against or in conflict with the incumbent's ecosystem. Because of this, the incumbent would find it hard to respond quickly and this would give the latecomer time to establish a position in the sub-category.

Since the reverse thinking to create a sub-category is going against the incumbents which dominate the mainstream market, the market that the latecomer could successfully capture would be a niche market. The challenge would be how to leverage its entry success to expand into the mainstream market. If the market environment remains stationary, then the incumbents' ecosystem would give them the competitive advantage in the mainstream market. If the latecomer is impatient and tries to expand to the mainstream quickly, it would encounter failure. It is important that the latecomer takes advantage of entry success to build up a strong ecosystem to maintain its first mover advantage in its sub-category market position and looks for opportunity for expansion as the market changes dynamically. One common mistake that a latecomer makes is that it is too eager to expand after the initial success and fails to build a strong ecosystem to solidify its sub-category. The result is that it loses its first mover advantage in the sub-category and fails to establish a position in the mainstream.

In 1981, People Express played Southwest's strategy by offering no-frill low-cost service between major cities in the northeastern part of the United States. People Express achieved financial success only 7 months after its inception by earning $500,000 on revenue of $8 million and continued its growth in the early 1980s. In 1986, the company announced its intention to convert from a no-frills to a full-service airline to attract the big corporate business travelers. People Express acquired some struggling full-service airline companies that had a hub-and-spoke network structure to support offering full services. People Express could not build a strong hub-and-spoke network structure in time to support its new intended service. Moreover, People Express could not match the major airlines in providing full airline service. In 1988, People Express was completely dissolved.

TMC committed the same mistake. TMC applied reverse thinking coming up with a jewelry hand phone and successfully captured 6% of China hand phone market within 2 short years. Then the Board set a target for TMC to replace Ericson to become the 3rd largest supplier of hand phone in China within a few years. To achieve that, TMC had to enter China's first tier city markets where the buyers were more sophisticated and desired hand phones with more advanced functions provided by the latest technology. Finally, TMC lost its hand phone market position in China. Fortunately, TMC leveraged jewelry phone's success to buy out Alcatel, a French mobile phone company, and entered the worldwide market.

Ricoh/Savin continued its business model to build its ecosystem to strengthen its position in the medium and small enterprise. They never tried to compete directly with Xerox and maintained as a strong niche player. Their expansion came from applying the same technology to develop a fax machine that sold to companies and individuals.

Dell had once tried to use channel sales to scale up its growth. Dell was quick to discover that this would drag the company into competing with incumbents on their own ground. Dell withdrew from it and concentrated on building its build to order model. The arrival of the Internet enabled Dell to scale up through online purchasing.

## Leverage on Inflection Points

If the external market environment remains the same, an incumbent would practice the strategy that has proven successful to secure its market leadership position. One reason being that practicing a particular strategy would allow the incumbent build up assets, organization structure, and competence that would increase efficiency in implementing that strategy. Also, in a stable market environment, a proven successful strategy would be less risky and more likely to be successful in the future and would strengthen the company's position in the market. This would be the incumbents' mind set.

Continuous improvement of the key drivers in category attributes would run into diminishing returns. Also, according to Maslow's theory, people would aspire to the next level of hierarchical needs when their current needs are satisfied. The key drivers for this next level needs may be different from those for the lower-level needs, and this could present an inflection point for incumbents competing in the same product category. Incumbents that could adapt the change and be able to make improvements of those new key driver category attributes could latch on to a new phase of growth. And those who failed to see this or do not have the skill and capability to latch onto this opportunity would become not competitive and decline. This can be illustrated in the following diagram.

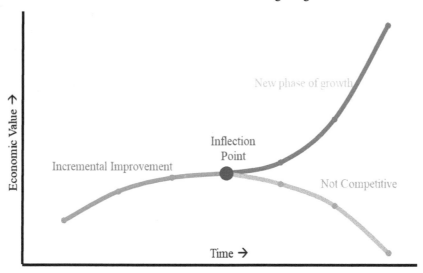

This is referred as a natural inflection point as it would come naturally when the 1-N product expansion ran into diminishing returns and people aspired to the next level needs. Natural inflection points would appear many times in the 1-N expansion of a product category as the key driver product attributes run into diminishing returns and people move up in hierarchical needs.

Besides natural inflection points, there are other inflection points induced by exogenous events: technology advancement, changes in demographic, changes in infrastructure, changes in other industries, government policy, and macro-trend induced by disruption at a global level: e.g. green initiative, pandemic, and geopolitics, etc. These external events would create a trend that dramatically change the progress of a company, an industry, or even the worldwide economy. These events may change people's preference or provide new possibilities to have a 10X increase in value. These are referred as exogenous inflection points since they are induced by external events.

An inflection point, whether it is natural or exogenous, presents a new situation that all companies have not faced before, and this neutralizes the incumbents' first mover advantage. There are three possible outcomes in an inflection point. The first is that the incumbent could adapt itself and successfully manage through the inflection point to create a new opportunity of growth and maintain its market leadership position. The second is a re-shuffling in the existing players' positions. The third is an outsider enters and establishes a strong market position (or even dominates the market). Hence, all inflection points, whether natural or exogenous, would present a good opportunity for the latecomer or existing small player with appropriate core competence and assets to disrupt the market.

The following industry cases describe how the incumbent responded to the inflection points and how latecomers exploited the inflection points to enter the market successfully. Some latecomers even overtook the incumbent and disrupted the pecking order.

## Razor-Blade System Industry

Early generation of Gillette's razor system was a one-blade system and the early strategy was improvement on safety shave, ease of use, and ease of replacement to fulfill the value proposition. As the improvement of the one blade safety system ran into diminishing returns and consumers aspired to have a more efficient shave, blade quality became the key driver to fulfill the new level of needs. Gillette's response was carbon steel blade. Wilkinson Sword Company entered the market as a latecomer with the world's first razor blade made from stainless steel. In comparison, the stainless-steel blade is resistant to rust and stays sharp three times longer than carbon steel blade. This gave Wilkinson the competitive advantage as compared to Gillette's carbon steel blade. Even though Gillette responded with its steel blade after two years and slowly regained its lost position, Wilkinson exploited this opportunity to establish itself as a credible player in the market.

When blade quality improvements went into diminishing return and consumers aspired to have a smooth and closer shave, the key driver would move to the multi-blade system. Gillette invented the twin-blade system to fulfill these higher-level needs. Even Bic entered the market as a latecomer with a disposable two-blade system and established a position in the market, Gillette quickly responded and established a leadership position in the disposable razor blade system.

When the multi-blade system ran into diminishing returns and consumers aspired to have shaving as part of personal care, packaging shaving products with other personal care products and convenience became the key drivers. Harry's and Dollar Shave Club entered as latecomers in early 2010 to provide razor blades and related grooming products and delivered the packaged products on a regular basis by direct home deliver. These two entrants had caused Gillette's market dominant position to sharply decline from 2016 to 2019 from 70% to 52%. Gillette has not yet come up with a credible response.

## Hand Phone Industry

The hand phone fulfilled people's need in voice communication anywhere and anytime. To realize the value proposition, a mobile system with two basic infrastructures is needed: the cellular system with location of base stations and switches, and the mobile terminals like handsets that could be carried around daily.

The first major 1G analog mobile standard was deployed in the US in 1983, with many mobile device manufacturers applying semiconductor technology to reduce the weight and size of the mobile device. Motorola, as a semiconductor company, took the lead to bring out the smallest and lightest hand phones and quickly became the leader in the hand phone industry in 1990s.

In the mid-80s, each European country started with a different analog based 1G mobile system, and roaming emerged as an important issue for Europeans who traveled frequently across many European countries. This prompted the development of a digital cellular network called GSM (Global Systems for Mobile communications). GSM could do both voice and data communication, and this could enable mobile service operators to offer more services to the subscriber. This introduced an inflection point to the carrier service and hand phone industry. GSM became the latecomer in mobile service that swept over Europe and then over Asia-Pacifica, Australia, and Africa. GSM overtook the analog 1G system. Ericsson and Nokia were the two major GSM system vendors, and they were latecomers in the hand phone industry. In the 2000s, Nokia overtook Motorola as the leader in the hand phone industry.

Qualcomm introduced a new digital standard based on CDMA that was backward compatible with existing US analog cellular systems in 1995. This was an inflection point for the digital mobile system and hand phone industry. In 1996, Samsung launched the CDMA service in Korea and designed the phone for CDMA system. CDMA was also deployed in the US, Latin America, and Hong Kong. Samsung leveraged on this inflection point to become a latecomer and one of the major players in the hand phone industry.

By the late 90s, email became the popular media for communications. Especially for businesses, people wanted to get access to their email anywhere and anytime. The solution would be to have the hand phone getting access to email. This was an inflection point that Blackberry entered the market as a latecomer.

As people's communication needs were satisfied, people aspired to use the hand phone as a handheld mini personal computer that can manage their daily activities. Thus, the hand phone category evolved into smartphone category. To achieve this, the key driver would be a more powerful operating system. This gave rise to the iPhone with a more powerful OS (iOS) that disrupted the smartphone market.

## US Car Industry

In early 1900, cars in US were 50% steam, 35% electric and 15% gasoline. The first inflection point occurred when oil fields were discovered all over the world. This led to oil companies building gasoline stations in towns and along roadsides between towns that ultimately established a gasoline refilling infrastructure. The gasoline car became the latecomer that dominated the US car market.

Ford created the production line concept and developed a workflow that could achieve economies of scale. Ford grew to become the largest car company in the US in the late 1910s. William Durant bought up many car companies to form General Motors (GM). GM could not consolidate the different production lines to achieve economies of scale. By 1920, General Motors nearly collapsed. As the car was viewed as an asset that would represent one's social status, people aspired a higher-level value proposition- "different cars for different economic and social classes". GM, with multiple car production lines was perfect to meet a higher-level value proposition. Alfred Sloan, the new Chairman and CEO of GM, advanced a strategy of promoting different car brands that helped customers to derive an identity from the car brand they drove. By the late 1920s, GM surpassed Ford and became the largest car company in the U.S. car market.

The US car industry exploded after the Second World War. With the development of the highway system and a boom in the economy, most families would own a car. Urban planning and development assumed that all families had a car. The streets, the roads, and the highways were wider and better paved as compared to those in Europe and Japan. Also, the US is mostly open terrain and so the roads and highways are mostly straight and flat. Europe and Japan have many mountainous terrains and the roads tend to be winding with ups and downs. Also, the gasoline price in US was much lower than that in Europe and Japan. As a result, most car owners in the US in the 50s - 60s period preferred a big car with large horsepower and a soft ride. Gas economy and car handling were less important. In the 70s, most US made cars were big, gas guzzling, soft suspension, comfortable, but not good in handling. In comparison, European cars were more compact, better gas economy, solid suspension, and good in handling. Japanese cars were small, very good gas economy, good in handling and reliable.

A major exogenous event happened in 1973 that created an inflection point in the US car industry. The first oil crisis began in October 1973 when the members of the OPEC proclaimed an oil embargo. This resulted in a sharp increase in the gas price and a long line in every gas station. Suddenly, the gas economy became the key driver in car purchasing. This was when foreign import cars from Europe and Japan started to make their way into the US car market in the 70s. Consumers started to experience how good car handling and reliability would improve their experience of owning a car. By 1980, Europe and Japanese cars captured a large market share in the US car market.

Environmental concern in the 70s resulted in the enactment of the Clean Air Act of 1970 (1970 CAA). This legislation authorized the development of comprehensive federal and state regulations to limit emissions from both stationary (industrial) sources and mobile sources. This was an inflection point for the car industry. To meet the regulatory standard, all car producers invested in R&D to develop a catalytic converter device that converts toxic gases and pollutions in exhaust gas from an internal combustion engine into less-toxic pollutants by catalyzing a redox reaction. This research would take time for the car companies to meet the standard, and the industry predicted it would meet the requirement by 1978. In 1973, Honda first announced its CVCC engine that allowed for more efficient combustion and did not require a catalytic converter or unleaded fuel to meet the 1975 Environmental Protection Agency emissions standards for hydrocarbons and carbon monoxide. The oil crisis and emissions standard requirement helped Honda, as a latecomer in the car market, to gain a strong position in the US with the CVCC engine.

Recently, the green initiative would create an inflection point in the car industry all over the world.

The key idea of applying the reverse thinking in the stationary market environment is to create an ecosystem that goes against the incumbents' ecosystem. The opportunity of an inflection point is that some strong outside forces are disrupting the incumbents' ecosystem. Any player that can leverage these outside forces would come out as a winner. If you see a trend in technology advancement that may present an inflection point to the product soon, you can use reserve thinking to capture a proper position in the market that can exploit the technology trend and wait for the inflection point to come. Netflix saw that technology trend in digital recording and digital TV. It used reserve thinking to establish a niche position in the movie rental market that could exploit the technology trend. When digital TV started to replace CRT TV, it presented an inflection point in the movie rental market and Netflix disrupted the market. Dell also used this combined approach to disrupt the PC market.

## Leverage Your Advantage

An incumbent may not be strong in all market segments. Some segments, the incumbent neglects because they do not provide adequate return. These are the segments that the latecomer can apply reverse thinking to establish a niche position. Some segments the incumbent is not doing well because it lacks the understanding of the business environment in those segments. If a latecomer has a better understanding of the business environment in one of these segments, it can enter and establish a strong position in that segment.

Amazon was founded in 1994 and eBay was founded in 1995 and both became successful B2C online retail players. In 2003, eBay entered the China market through acquisition of EachNet, China's most prominent auction player. In 2004, Amazon entered the China market through the acquisition of Joyo, one of the large online retailers in China. Both eBay and Amazon used the same business model as in US, with slight localization adjustment.

JD started as an electronic retailer with a shop in Beijing in 1998. Alibaba started as B2B in 1999 helping companies in US to source suppliers in China through an online platform. When SARS broke out in China in 2003, both JD and Alibaba faced an inflection point.

They pivoted and adapted to the situation by building a B2C online platform selling basic daily needs products. Both JD and Alibaba understood the culture and business environment in China much better than executives and managers in eBay and Amazon. Both leveraged their advantage, and each built a strong (but different) ecosystem that supported their B2C online retail business. JD built its own delivery chain while Amazon built its online payment infrastructure. Alibaba and JD became the largest B2C online retailers in China while both eBay and Amazon left the China market.

Microsoft Windows was an OS dominated the PC market. In seeking market expansion, the logical move was to penetrate the smartphone market. Windows Mobile was released in 2003 targeting the emerging smartphone device. The smartphone evolved from hand phone. The hand phone was used mainly for voice communication and therefore required a simple operating system. All hand phone producers developed their own OS. As people aspired more applications besides voice communication, people aspired to have a handheld device that would manage voice communication and many other applications. The smartphone evolved from the hand phone as a new product category. A smartphone would require a more sophisticated OS. All smartphone producers were hand phone producers before, and they got used to the idea of developing their own OS as opposed to licensing an OS from a third party. As the hand phone companies did not have competence in software, the major hand phone companies - Nokia, Motorola and Ericsson - formed a joint venture with Psion Software in 1998 to develop Symbian as an operating system for hand phone. The vision was that Symbian would be used by all smartphone producers. When Microsoft started to market Windows Mobile to the smartphone companies, it used the same business model as Windows marketing to PC. However, unlike PC producers, the smartphone producers got used to the idea of developing their own OS. Therefore, Windows Mobile faced stiff competition from Symbian and its expansion in the smartphone market was slow.

Apple was a personal computer company that owned its OS. It leveraged its OS advantage and entered the smartphone market as a latecomer by producing its own smartphone. Google leveraged its advertising business advantage and entered the OS smartphone market as a latecomer by offering the Android for free to all smartphone producers. Android is an open system and smartphone producers can refine Android which made them feel they have their own OS. Very quickly, Android overtook Windows Mobile and became the OS platform for all smartphone companies except Apple. Windows Mobile was later replaced by the Windows Phone that was discontinued in 2017.

# First-Mover vs Latecomer

In the marketing literature, first-mover advantage of a product is defined as the competitive advantage gained by first capturing a significant market segment. First mover advantage enables the product to establish strong brand recognition, customer loyalty, and strong ecosystem that would build a barrier for latecomers to enter the market segment. Some people confuse first product with first mover in a product category. Altair 8800 was the first personal computer but was not first mover in the personal computer category. Apple II was the first mover in PC category. But Apple II did not win in the PC category, it was latecomers like Lenovo, HP and Dell that dominated the PC world market. Historically, there were more cases where latecomers succeed in a product category. The table below summarizes a few cases in technology area. A follower is one that enters the market while the first mover has gained momentum in establishing its market position, and a latecomer is one that enters the market after the first mover has established a strong market position.

**First-mover or Follower/Latecomer Advantage?**

| Product | First mover | Follow/Latecomer | Winner |
|---------|-------------|------------------|--------|
| Web Search Engine | Yahoo! | Google | Google |
| Social networking | My Space | Facebook | Facebook |
| Graphical OS | Apple | Microsoft | Microsoft |
| Ride Sharing | Uber | Lyft | Uber leading |
| Discount Store | Kmart | Wal-Mart | Wal-Mart |
| E-Commerce | Amazon | Alibaba | Amazon, Alibaba in China |
| Smart phone | Apple | Samsung, Huawei, Xiaomi | Samsung Xiaomi Apple |

It is noted that first-mover does not necessarily have the advantage as claimed in the marketing literature. Hence, rushing to introduce the first product in a new category is not a prudent decision. For any new product category, there is only one first mover but many latecomers. Hence, it is important for product managers to have the right mind-set and the competence and skill in managing latecomer products. Remember, it is never too late to enter a product category market, but have to know how!

## Discussions:

1. How did Google emerge as a latecomer in the online advertising platform?
2. What is the risk of applying reverse thinking to enter as a latecomer in an established market? How do you minimize this risk?
3. For an incumbent, do natural or exogenous inflection points presents more risk than opportunity? How should an incumbent prepare for such events?
4. Windows, Apple iOS, and Android are the major incumbents in the operating system category. Windows dominated the PC segment, and Apple iOS and Android dominated the smartphone segment. Would there be another operating system emerging in a different segment? What segment? Who would be a credible latecomer in this new segment?
5. What would be the proper mind-set for the PM to be successful in managing a latecomer product? What competence and skill should the PM develop to successfully manage latecomer products?
6. Choose an established market that you like. If you had a choice of entering that market, how would you try to win as a latecomer?

# References

The cases examples in this book are based on content information from books, articles in business and management journals, cases studies prepared for course discussions in business and management classes taught in various Universities, Wikipedia, website links related to the cases, and personal interactions with people in the cases. Books, articles and case studies are listed below.

1. Steve Blank, "What Drones and Crop Dusters Can Teach About Minimum Viable Product", Harvard Business Review, February 2014,
2. Steve Blank, "Why the Lean Start-up Changes Everything", Harvard Business Review, May 2013
3. Paul Carol, Big Blues: The Unmaking of IBM, Three Rivers Press, September 1994
4. Alexander Chernev, "Gillette Fusion: Building a $1Billion Brand" Kellogg School of Management, Northwestern University, Case Study, November 2009
5. Thomas R. Eisenmann, Michael Pao, and Lauren Barley, "Dropbox: "It Just Works"", Harvard Business School, Case Study, 9-811-065, October 2014
6. Walter Isaacson, Steve Jobs, Simon & Schuster; 1st edition, October 24, 2011
7. Haim Mendelson, "Airbnb: The First Five Years", Stanford Graduate School of Business, Case Study, October 2018

8. Brian Merchant, <u>The One Device: The Secret History of the iPhone</u>, Back Bay paperback edition, May 2018

9. Yongkyun Na and Edison Tse, "The Case Study of Samsung Electronics", Department of Management Science & Engineering, Stanford University, Case Study, October 2009

10. Matt Saucedo, Reema Shah, Howie Rosen, and Steve Ciesinski, "Aerobotics", Stanford Graduate School of Business, Case Study, November 2018

11. Herbert Simon, "The Science of Design: Creating the Artificial", Design Issues, Vol 4, Numbers 1 & 2, Special Issue: Designing the Immaterial Society, 1988

12. Edison Tse, "Grabber-Holder Dynamics: A Framework for Creating and Shaping Innovation", Atlanta Competitive Advantage Conference, Atlanta, GA, June14-16, 2007

13. Edison Tse, "Historical Development in Mobile Communication Service" Department of Management Science & Engineering, Stanford University, Case Study, September 2003

14. Edison Tse, "IBM: Ups and Downs", Department of Management Science & Engineering, Stanford University, Case Study, March 2021

15. Edison Tse, "Latecomer Advantage", Department of Management Science & Engineering, Stanford University, Case Study, March 2008

16. Edison Tse and Jonathan Qui, "Tencent: From Instant Messaging to One of the most Valuable Technology Company", Department of Management Science & Engineering, Stanford University, Case Study, June 2020

17. Thomas Watson, Jr. and Peter Petre, <u>Father, Son & Co.,: My life at IBM and Beyond</u>, Banton, February 2000

18. David B. Yoffie and Michael Slind, "Apple Inc. 2008", Harvard Business School, Case Study, 9-708-480, September 2008

CPSIA information can be obtained
at www.ICGtesting.com
Printed in the USA
JSHW080749181122
33321JS00003BA/9